Rethinking International Development series

Series editors
Andy Sumner
King's College London
UK

Ray Kiely
Queen Mary University of London
London, UK

Rethinking International Development series is dedicated to publishing cutting-edge titles that focus on the broad area of 'development'. The core aims of the series are to present critical work that is cross disciplinary, challenges orthodoxies, reconciles theoretical depth with empirical research, explores the frontiers of development studies in terms of 'development' in both North and South and global inter-connectedness, and reflects on claims to knowledge and intervening in other people's lives.

More information about this series at
http://www.palgrave.com/gp/series/14501

Bridget Kenny

Retail Worker Politics, Race and Consumption in South Africa

Shelved in the Service Economy

Bridget Kenny
Department of Sociology
University of the Witwatersrand
Johannesburg, South Africa

Rethinking International Development series
ISBN 978-3-030-09895-7   ISBN 978-3-319-69551-8 (eBook)
https://doi.org/10.1007/978-3-319-69551-8

© The Editor(s) (if applicable) and The Author(s) 2018
Softcover re-print of the Hardcover 1st edition 2018
This work is subject to copyright. All rights are solely and exclusively licensed by the Publisher, whether the whole or part of the material is concerned, specifically the rights of translation, reprinting, reuse of illustrations, recitation, broadcasting, reproduction on microfilms or in any other physical way, and transmission or information storage and retrieval, electronic adaptation, computer software, or by similar or dissimilar methodology now known or hereafter developed.
The use of general descriptive names, registered names, trademarks, service marks, etc. in this publication does not imply, even in the absence of a specific statement, that such names are exempt from the relevant protective laws and regulations and therefore free for general use.
The publisher, the authors and the editors are safe to assume that the advice and information in this book are believed to be true and accurate at the date of publication. Neither the publisher nor the authors or the editors give a warranty, express or implied, with respect to the material contained herein or for any errors or omissions that may have been made. The publisher remains neutral with regard to jurisdictional claims in published maps and institutional affiliations.

Cover credit: Simon Gush

Printed on acid-free paper

This Palgrave Macmillan imprint is published by the registered company Springer International Publishing AG part of Springer Nature.
The registered company address is: Gewerbestrasse 11, 6330 Cham, Switzerland

To Stephen.
And to Alexandra, with her feet on the ground
and her eyes looking to the sky.

Preface and Acknowledgements

Alberto Giacometti is quoted as saying, "[I]f I make life-sized figures that become very thin, there must be a motive: one reason is that, for them to be true, they have to be light enough for me to take them with one hand and put them in a taxi beside me" ("Alberto Giacometti, a conversation with David Sylvester," *The Guardian*, June 21, 2003). This has been a heavy project for me. I have joked with my friends that its working title "Shelved" was a double entendre signifying how often I put it aside. When Giacometti talks about making very thin sculptures, he compares his work to the real person. He observes that his sculptures are pared down. They deviate from the person who has weight and comportment and yet lifts with little effort. They are his attempt at the lightness of form. For his own reasons, they need to be able to come with him, to fit next to him companionably in a taxi. This is a book about South African retail worker politics over many decades based on my observations and interpretation of the extensive and generous time and words that many people have given me. As a white academic lecturing in a South African university for 20 years, I take seriously critiques about knowledge production. I offer this story as a product of my engagement in the world. Like Giacometti's figures, it is real enough. I don't need it to sit next to me on its journeys from here, though.

That I have made this thing is a result of many people's support. First and foremost, I thank the women and men who work or worked in retailing who have patiently explained their experiences to me. I thank SACCAWU for facilitating much of this research and for always being open to discussion and debate. Particularly, I thank Comrades Bones

Skulu, Mduduzi Mbongwe, Patricia Appolis, Darlington Ndlovu, Mike Tau, Lisema Lekhoana, Maxwell Cindi, Mike Abrahams, and Mike Sikani. I also thank Alke Boessiger, Keith Jacobs, Michael Bride, Ian Campbell, Bastian Schultz, and Bethuel Maserumule for assistance and discussions around the Wal-Mart research.

I give special thanks to Eddie Webster and SWOP and to Gay Seidman for encouragement over many years to finish this project. To those who read chapters, I am particularly indebted: Peter Alexander, Shireen Ally, Franco Barchiesi, Heinrich Böhmke, Jeremy Daphne, Stephen Greenberg, Gillian Hart, Mark Hunter, Jonathan Hyslop, Ulrike Kistner, Thembi Luckett, Alan Mabin, Bethuel Maserumule, Prishani Naidoo, Alf Nilsen, Srila Roy, Melanie Samson, Ben Scully, Gay Seidman, and Ahmed Veriava. The usual disclaimers apply.

To other colleagues and friends for support, I thank Glenn Adler, Maurizio Atzeni, Carolina Bank Muñoz, Asanda Benya, Andries Bezuidenhout, Sithembiso Bhengu, Andreas Bieler, Philip Bonner, Katherine Bowie, Michael Burawoy, Iain Campbell, Claire Ceruti, Crispen Chinguno, Ingrid Chunilall, Marlea Clarke, Jacklyn Cock, Jane L. Collins, Marcelle Dawson, Irma du Plessis, Zimitri Erasmus, Kally Forrest, Leonard Gentle, Don Glass, Sarah Godsell, Pamila Gupta, Simon Gush, Shireen Hassim, Mondli Hlatshwayo, Isabel Hofmeyr, Mehita Iqani, Eli Kodisang, Jack Kugelmass, Andrea Lasker, Maria Lepowsky, Kezia Lewins, Alex Lichtenstein, John Logan, Johannes Machinya, Ntsiki Mackay-Anderson, Sangeetha Madhavan, Matlhako Mahapa, Sedzani Malada, Cambridge Manzini, Miranda Martinez, Josephine Mashaba, Darlene Miller, Miller Moela, Norman Mokoena, Tshepo Moloi, Dunbar Moodie, Sarah Mosoetsa, Danai Mupotsa, Nathaniel Ndala, Vivienne Ndatshe, Mbuyiseni Ndlozi, Noor Nieftagodien, Lorena Nunez, Cedric Nunn, Caroline O'Reilly, Jamie Peck, Mosa Phadi, Beth Pointer, Nicolas Pons-Vignon, Deborah Posel, Rob Rees, Phineas Riba, Greg Ruiters, Rachel Sherman, Ari Sitas, David Szanton, Bukiwe Tambulu, Kaiser Thibedi, Malehoko Tshoaedi, Nicole Ulrich, Natasha Vally, Salim Vally, Lucien van der Walt, Cobus van Staden, Karl von Holdt, Antina von Schnitzler, Shannon Walsh, Hylton White, Michelle Williams, Eric Worby, Bongani Xezwi, and Nkosinathi Zuma. I thank the Sociology Department at Wits University for its community. Thanks also to the Tribe of Moles. A special thanks to Srila Roy and Alf Nilsen for getting this moving again.

Thanks to Michele Pickover and Gabriele Mohale at Wits Historical Papers. I thank Diane Stuart for early editing on the manuscript. Thanks to Jenny de Wet for creating the first draft of the index. A great debt of gratitude I save for Caroline Jeannerat for her editing and detailed and careful comments and for her patience.

My lovely family, thanks for listening for so very long: Louis Greenberg, Bronwyn Harris, Anne Kenny, Mary Kenny, Tom Stapp, David Kenny, Ginger Crumpler Kenny, and my parents, John Kenny and Barbara Kenny.

This book could not have been finished if not for the comrade/friendship of Shireen Ally, brilliant, funny, and intractable that she is, who sat with me not once but each time this object appeared again on my horizon.

To Alexandra Greenberg, this book has literally spanned your lifetime. Thank you for your empathy and for your humour. To Stephen Greenberg, for too much to list, except to say thanks for your steadfastness and grounding.

* * *

The cover photo is by Simon Gush, who braved a mall late at night to get me the shot. I thank him for permission to use it. He also took two of the images used in Chap. 8 and assisted me in editing and scanning my photographs. I thank him for permission to use his images. William Matlala has graciously provided me with the third image in Chap. 8, and I thank him for giving me permission to use it. I thank Kally Forrest for permission to use the photograph from her personal collection in Chap. 3. I thank Paul Weinberg and Africa Media Online for permission to use his photograph in Chap. 3. I thank Kenneth Hlongwane and Mary Boyeasse for assistance with finding the photograph in Chap. 2, and Museum Africa for permission to use it. Cartographer Wendy Phillips drew the map in Chap. 1, and I thank her for giving me permission to use it.

I acknowledge the Faculty of the Humanities, University of the Witwatersrand for an ad hoc grant in support of this project. I thank Anne Campbell for her stellar administration of this funding. I also acknowledge funding from a Carnegie Mellon Social Justice Grant, administered by the University of the Witwatersrand, for time off to draft the first version of this book. I thank Hugo Canham for his support. I acknowledge a National Research Foundation grant from the Competitive Programme for Rated Researchers (CPRR), 2012–2014 (Grant Number: 78778), and an Incentive Funding for Rated Researchers (IFRR) grant, 2011–2016, for support for research for this project. Finally, I acknowledge UNI

Global Union for funding for research in 2013. I thank Alke Boessiger and Keith Jacobs for support toward that research. This work reflects my own interpretations and not those of the funders.

Chapter 2 is derived, in part, from an article published in *African Studies* in 2008, available online: http://www.tandfonline.com/doi/abs/10.1080/00020180802505012, used with permission of the publisher.

Chapter 4 is derived, in part, from an article published in *International Labor and Working-Class History* in 2016, used with permission of the publisher (licence number 4057840499763). And, in part, from an article published in *Law & Policy* in 2009, used with permission of the publisher (licence number 4057841439556).

Chapters 5 and 6 partially draw on an article published in *Qualitative Sociology* in 2007, used with permission of the publisher (licence number 4057841112280). And Chap. 5 draws, in part, from a chapter published as "The 'Market Hegemonic' Workplace Order in Food Retailing" in *Beyond the Apartheid Workplace: Studies in Transition*, edited by Eddie Webster and Karl von Holdt, 217–42 (Durban: University of KwaZulu-Natal Press, 2004), used with permission of the publisher.

Chapter 8 is derived, in part, from an article published in New South African Review 4, edited by Gilbert M. Khadiagala, Devan Pillay, Prishani Naidoo, and Roger Southall, 56–74 (Johannesburg: Wits University Press, 2014), used with permission of the publisher.

Johannesburg, South Africa   Bridget Kenny

Contents

1 Introduction: Precarity in Store — 1

2 Servicing a Nation: White Women Shop Assistants and the Fantasy of Belonging — 27

3 Rupturing Relations: Abasebenzi as Collective Political Subject — 61

4 Regulating Retail: The Category "Employee" and Its Divisions — 91

5 Signifying Belonging: Restructuring and Workplace Relations — 119

6 "Tools Down, Everybody Out to the Canteen!": Wildcats and Go-Slows, Political Subjects Reconfigured — 153

7 "To Sit at Home and Do Nothing": Gender and the Constitutive Meaning of Work — 185

8 Consuming Politics: Wal-Mart, the New Terrain
   of Belonging and the Endurance of Abasebenzi   209

References   237

Index   271

LIST OF ABBREVIATIONS

ACDWU	African Commercial and Distributive Workers Union
ANC	African National Congress
CCAWUSA	Commercial Catering and Allied Workers Union of South Africa
CCMA	Commission for Conciliation, Mediation and Arbitration
CCTV	Closed circuit television
CEO	Chief executive officer
COSATU	Congress of South African Trade Unions
CUSA	Council of Unions of South Africa
FAWU	Food and Allied Workers Union
FOSATU	Federation of South African Trade Unions
GDP	Gross domestic product
JSE	Johannesburg Stock Exchange
NEDLAC	National Economic Development and Labour Council
NUCAW	National Union of Commercial and Allied Workers
NUCCAW	National Union of Commercial, Catering and Allied Workers
NUDAW	National Union of Distributive and Allied Workers
NUDW	National Union of Distributive Workers
NUM	National Union of Mineworkers
NUMSA	National Union of Metalworkers of South Africa
SACCAWU	South African Commercial, Catering and Allied Workers Union
SAHA	South African History Archive

List of Figures

Fig. 1.1	Map of Gauteng and the greater Johannesburg region	20
Photo 2.1	OK Bazaars in downtown Johannesburg, 1956	33
Fig. 2.1	Employment in retail trade by race and gender, 1946/47–1977	48
Fig. 2.2	Shop assistants in retail trade by race and gender, 1946/47–1977	49
Photo 3.1	Women workers meeting during Edgars strike, 1985	81
Photo 3.2	OK Bazaars strike, 1986/87	82
Photo 5.1	Warnings against "Shrinkage," c. 2000	136
Photo 5.2	Worker checking stock in warehouse, c. 2000	141
Photo 6.1	Contract merchandisers playing cards, c. 2000	164
Photo 6.2	"Nobody is born to be a casual for life," c. 2000	171
Fig. 6.1	Selected occupational categories in wholesale and retail trade by gender and race, 2000	173
Photo 7.1	Street scene in Daveyton, c. 2000	194
Photo 8.1	In the aisles of a Wal-Mart subsidiary in Johannesburg, 2017	213
Photo 8.2	A Game store in Johannesburg with a mural of the South African flag, 2017	216
Photo 8.3	A Cambridge Food store in a busy street, 2017	217

CHAPTER 1

Introduction: Precarity in Store

In 2005, Ruth Ngobeni and a determined group of contract cashiers and bag packers gathered together after their Sunday shift in the alcove of the ATM outside a Hyperama supermarket where they worked. They were employed by a temporary employment agency, not the retailer, but most had worked in the shop for many years, and many had previously worked directly for the retailer. Leaving packages with household purchases against the wall, they filed into the alcove, sat on the floor on pieces of cardboard or leaned against the windows. Around their shoulders, the afternoon sun peered into the nook. A security guard wandered in wanting to know what the meeting was about. Balancing her hips on a narrow window ledge, one woman looked over to him, paused, stood up firmly and laughed, saying that the *workers* (*abasebenzi* in isiZulu) were meeting and that he should not disturb them. About 25 black workers, mostly women in their 30s from surrounding townships, met to decide on a course of action to contest erratic variances in their payday schedules.[1] Labour legislation regulated these, and workers had requested that a Department of Labour inspector come to the shop to assist them. The inspector had visited, but had spoken only to permanent workers who were employed directly by the retailer, and not to the contract workers themselves. On that sunny afternoon in greater Johannesburg, Ruth and her colleagues redoubled their determination to seek an audience with the inspectorate.[2]

© The Author(s) 2018
B. Kenny, *Retail Worker Politics, Race and Consumption in South Africa*, Rethinking International Development series,
https://doi.org/10.1007/978-3-319-69551-8_1

Nearly a decade later, in 2013, another contract cashier at a subsidiary of Massmart, a South African company acquired by the international retailer Wal-Mart in 2011, described how her manager required a group of workers to stay at work until midnight because the tills were not balancing. Ninah Ndlovu had been at work since 7 a.m. and her shift ended at 4 p.m. The company used a new till point technology that was often incorrect, according to workers, but that could only be reconciled after a few days. Regardless, managers kept workers late that night. Ninah remembered: "I left a child [at home]. I even had to sleep at the police station because I couldn't get home."[3] She said that the company offered them R8 for transport as compensation, barely enough for commuters to get anywhere, let alone home across Johannesburg, late at night with only limited and dubious transport options. Worse still, they were not paid an overtime rate or a night allowance, as South African labour law would legislate. Going as a group after this event, the affected contract workers demanded that the retail management listen to their complaints. These women service workers said, "the situation at [the store] makes us angry every day." A shop steward said, "[Y]ou need to stand up for yourself and speak out if you are wronged. If they [managers] do not listen, mobilize your fellow workers, the workers [abasebenzi], and take up the issue."[4]

The image of precarious wage work is a familiar one in South Africa. Around the world, as well, retail jobs are often described as low wage with precarious working conditions; so, too, are they often filled by women (Coulter 2014; Luce 2013; Grugulis and Bozkurt 2011; Lichtenstein 2006; Chan 2011). We meet Ninah at the tills in a South African store now owned by Wal-Mart, but it was not Wal-Mart's recent entry into South Africa that introduced the sector to practices of poor wages and insecure conditions. From the late 1990s until the present, working conditions in South African retail have remained bleak. Workers' grievances around pay schedules, underpayment of wages, and working time highlight their roles as household providers and earners. Yet these South African retail workers continue to make collective demands at the site where their precariousness is most acutely inscribed.

Both Ruth and Ninah narrate resolute and collective responses to such persistent grievances in stores, invoking the emotive sign "workers" – abasebenzi. Examining one of today's most prevalent and ubiquitous categories of precarious employment – retail work – I explore why it is that a primarily black, female, low-wage, and low-skill service workforce has, in fact, returned over and over to the workplace as a crucial site of politics. In order to explain why and how retail worker politics carries on, this book tracks the changes in social relations and semiotic meanings that configured the collective political subject "workers" in retail since the 1930s.

South African retail workers' ongoing labour politics are constituted out of a longer history in which the collective political subject abasebenzi came to signify contestation over forms of political relation. Retail worker politics endured (in changing form) because of three interrelated dynamics: retail spaces are sites of nation and belonging; labour law revised and redrew boundaries reinscribing the subject "employee" in relation to forms of employment in the sector; and workers reformed the gendered, raced, classed political subject of abasebenzi within these "social sites" (Hall 1985, 99). Precisely because labour and blackness are bound so tightly into one another ideologically and materially in South Africa, precarious wage labour and worker politics became such a tense site of affective return, an enduring place of antagonism, at different moments. This book tracks a history of nearly a century of the reproduction of and changes to South African retail worker politics, to argue for the continued salience of labour politics today.

I briefly consider how precarious worker politics is often explained through presentist accounts of economic interest, strategic leverage, or trade union strength. Instead, I insist on a conjunctural analysis (Hart 2016, 3) in which the histories of relations and meanings bear on the reproduction of concrete "subjects-in-struggle" (Hall 1985, 112) discussed in the remaining sections.

"Two for the Price of One": The Inadequacies of Instrumentalism

In the context of economic insecurities and the continuing devaluation of labour under late capitalism, arguments from different quarters suggest that Ruth and Ninah's workplace politics is anachronistic. First, economic restructuring and changes to work have led to an overall decline in reliability of the steady job (Standing 2011). Worldwide, various forms of part-time, casual, and contract employment have increased. Generally speaking, many forms of "non-standard" employment relegate workers to precarious labour market positions, with low wages, insecurity, minimal benefits, and reduced collective voice creating real difficulties for mobilizing in these sites (Stanford and Vosko 2004; Standing 1999; Kalleberg 2013; Vosko et al. 2009; Felstead and Jewson 1999).

So, too, for South Africa, as working conditions have declined for many workers, including what has been prominently documented as fragmentation through casualization and externalization of employment (Standing et al. 1996; Kenny and Webster 1998; Clarke 2004; Theron 2005; Webster et al. 2008; Barchiesi 2011).[5] Combined with increasing unemployment and household precariousness, a "crisis" of survival has come to characterize work for many under neoliberalism in South Africa (Fakier and Cock 2009; Bezuidenhout and Fakier 2006; Mosoetsa 2011; Benya 2015).

Furthermore, in the global South, wage labour itself provides income to fewer people (Breman and van der Linden 2014; Breman 2010; Lindell 2010). Precariousness runs deep; it is a symptom of the inability of economies to absorb labour at all, of the growing surplus population relegated to a "wageless life" (Denning 2010; see also McIntyre and Nast 2011). It is widely recognized that most South African households rely on multiple sources of income coming from a diverse (and shifting) membership (Mosoetsa 2011; Scully 2016). In the post-apartheid context, less secure access to the labour market has meant that household poverty is particularly tied to the composition of income sources. And, wages are a declining source of income for many households (International Labour Office 2015a; Ferguson 2015; Scully 2016): the official rate of unemployment increased from 22% in 1994 to 25% in 2015 and jumped again to 27.7% in the first quarter of 2017, much higher if we include discouraged work seekers (International Labour Office 2015b; Statistics South Africa 2015, 2017).[6] In the poorest South African households, wage income accounts for a relatively small proportion of overall income, between 15% and 25%, with most of these households relying predominantly on state grants (Finn 2015, 3; see also Ferguson 2015).[7]

Thus, worker politics relates to a shrinking category of labouring people and to conditions that make it more difficult to sustain. In this context, debates have pointed to the greater relevance of other sites and social movements outside of work and wage labour (Ferguson 2015; see also Standing 2014). They offer a critical corrective to a stale tradition which asserts the preeminent subject position of worker as vanguard or norm (see important critiques by Naidoo and Veriava 2005; Desai 2002). In this context, then, Ninah and her companions' retail worker politics seem ever more out of place.

Retail workers' efforts seem misdirected for a second reason: contemporary South African retail workers appear to have little bargaining power. They have little structural power – power from their position in the workplace or labour market – due to a context of high unemployment and low skills. They have weak associational power – power from their collective organization (see Silver 2003, 13–16; Wright 2000, 962) – due to the fact that their trade union has lost force, the South African labour movement itself has fractured, and the ruling African National Congress (ANC) has embraced neoliberal policies (Buhlungu 2010; Satgar and Southall 2015; Nieftagodien 2017; Bramble and Barchiesi 2003; Marais 1998). And, while Ruth and Ninah's workplace politics could potentially invoke symbolic power – the power to define discursive publics (Chun 2009, 13) – in fact, retail workers have had little success wielding moral leverage for their struggles in a broader arena. Precarious workers across the global South, indeed, can and do utilize different forms of power to contest their exploitation (see Agarwala 2013; Selwyn 2012; Zhang 2015; Chun 2009). Yet, while lack of strategic leverage may help to explain the limited successes of South African retail workers, it does not explain why they continue to act collectively in sites of apparent little power and to dedicate their energies to contesting labour relations as an enduring site of political subjectivity. In short, economic interest and instrumental reason cannot so easily explain worker politics. In such approaches, the South African "worker" is often naturalized as a figure of presumptive resistance (Webster et al. 2008) but in fact requires a deeper conjunctural explanation.

Finally, those who study retail worker organizing emphasize the role of trade unions in the sector. Where retail unions have institutional power, they have organized workers and won important gains (Coulter 2014; Mrozowicki et al. 2013; Bailey et al. 2015). Where unions are weak or compromised, they help to explain worker fragmentation or demobilization (Tilly and Galván 2006; Ikeler 2016a). In South Africa, historically the key retail sector union, the South African Commercial Catering and Allied Workers Union (SACCAWU), has been critical to retail worker mobilization in certain periods. It has lost capacity and strength, which also has been an important factor in explaining why conditions in the sector have stagnated. But, despite its distance from many shop floors, retail workers continue to act collectively. This book expands analysis beyond trade union power and institutional leverage to explain retail worker politics.

Unlike those who dismiss worker politics as obsolete and those who argue, often prescriptively, for sourcing new forms of bargaining power, and distinct from those who focus on trade unions politics, I start from these precarious workers' actions to understand their political imaginaries, forms of collective organization, processes of subjectification, and assertions of political subjectivity. This book asks a different set of questions: not, who is the "new" subject of contestation or what is the best strategy, but rather, why have South African retail worker politics endured, how has it changed and to what effect?

To answer these questions, I return to the constitution of the sector under white women's employment in the 1930s and trace three intersecting contours to the present: retail as a site of nation and belonging; the law and its role in structuring political subjects; and articulations of race, class, and gender in the constitution of abasebenzi. The political subject has endured but under dynamic conditions which have altered its deployment and effects.

SERVICING SOUTH AFRICA: RETAIL SPACES AS NATION

What, then, can retail as a site add to our understanding of labour politics? First, retail work has globally become one of the key sites of employment growth and economic expansion. It even is, "in many ways *the* new generic form of mass employment in the post-industrial socio-economic landscape" (Bozkurt and Grugulis 2011, 2; see also Coulter 2014). It remains, however, understudied. Second, service labour is affective (Hochschild 1983; Hardt 1999): it operates through emotion, language, and interrelation. As such, it offers access to the symbolic mapping of systems of relationality and, in particular, inequality (Sherman 2007; Hanser 2008; Otis 2012). Third, as this book will show, retail arenas evoke "the nation." They mark the nexus of consumption and labour, of distribution and production, of gender and race, and of public and private. Retail arenas are political "publics" (Kenny 2015) in which capital, workers, consumers, and the state converge to model ideas of the market and of the polity.

C. Wright Mills (1956) understood the significance of retail spaces in the constitution of the nation. The "fabulous salesroom" was a symbol of national economic prowess and societal self-confidence in the United States. The grand store became a new "Universal Provider," offering up virtually all that the institution of the family gave before: "from womb to grave, it watches over you" (Mills 1956, 166–167). As he put it, "What factory is geared so deep and direct with what people want and what they are becoming." He continued, the store "*is* the world – dedicated to commodities, run by committees and paced by floor walkers" (Mills 1956, 167, italics in original). Indeed, as Walter Benjamin (2002) and Georg

Simmel (2004) understood, retail arenas are particularly emotive spaces of the intersection of modern belonging and capitalism.

Not only did the commodity fetish reify social relations and upturn social worlds through the distribution of value in objects projecting longing and marking status, but the shop itself came to signify a version of the polity. For example, in the United States, consumer culture became ingrained into national identity, projecting a "land of desire," which tied together retailers, modern business systems, marketing techniques, moral worlds, state policy, and the symbolism of vast plenty securing the idea of America (Leach 1993; see also Cohen 2003). In Nazi Germany department stores not only signified luxury and abundance but also posed a danger to the idea of nation when Jewish ownership was linked to cosmopolitan consumer culture in antithesis to national identity (Lerner 2015). In Argentina, the idea that workers could participate in the economy as consumers drove a Peronist nationalist agenda and provoked debates over inclusivity in spaces of consumption (Milanesio 2013). Even in the Soviet Union of the 1930s, retailing represented not capitalist abundance, but modern socialist efficiency and egalitarian participation (Randall 2008). Australian supermarkets epitomized access to markets and consumer products, changing gender relations within the country, and ultimately the relative modernity of Australia in the world (Humphrey 1998). In postcolonial contexts, retail has lent itself to claims of comparison to metropolitan progress. Thus, across contexts, retail stores represent not merely spaces where consumer culture happens, but more evocatively the nation as symbol of modernity, success, inclusion, and worldliness.

Not only as discursive symbol but also as concrete sites of the service relation tying together labour and consumption, retail arenas became terrains of contested belonging. For Mills, the shop workers were key to constituting the nation in the market (see also Kocka 1980). "Salesgirls" made possible the appeal of the great salesroom to the public: "her personality … must become the alert yet obsequious instrument by which goods are distributed" (Mills 1956, 184). In the process, "the salesgirl becomes self-alienated" (Mills 1956, 184). Arlie Hochschild (1983) coined the term "emotional labour" to capture the affective relationship at the centre of service work, so important to decades of research.[8] Retail management used class and gender to sell new desires while controlling female workforces, even as women workers asserted their own relations within service work (Benson 1986; Johnson 2007; Frank 2001).

Retail shops offered customers spaces of engagement with and in the public (Zola [1883] 1991; Abelson 1989; Friedberg 1993), as middle-class women became shoppers, venturing out into streets and stores. Retail arenas animate a contender for citizen – the consumer, representing the promise of equal participation in the market.[9] Indeed, in South Africa, the consumer has always provided a counterpoint to the worker (Magubane 2004; Comaroff 1996; Burke 1996; McClintock 1995; and see Weeks 2011). Deborah Posel argues that consumption contributed to "the making of the racial order [in South Africa] … [as] a way of regulating people's aspirations, interests and powers as consumers" (Posel 2010, 160). Thus, in the post-apartheid period, access to the market has proffered a post-racial future (Nuttall 2008; Mbembe 2008; cf Kenny 2015). This is particularly true under South Africa's post-apartheid neoliberal discourse which "takes the market as its model, to which it can articulate freedom, democracy, and flexibility as opposed to apartheid state repression and rigidity" (Hart 2008, 689; see also Veriava 2013, 212–284).

This book tracks four moments of retail spaces as nation, where retail workers serviced South Africa, constituting symbolic spaces and concrete places (see Massey 1994) in which the polity and the economy converged, and which contribute to explaining retail worker politics over time. In Johannesburg's chain and department stores in the 1930s to the 1960s, the first moment, white female shop assistants sold modernity to an imagined white nation through service in shops. This generation of women retail workers made spaces of consumption "familiar" (du Plessis 2011) and eased the tensions between Johannesburg's everyday racial order and the thrill of shopping (Chap. 2). In the 1970s and 1980s, the second moment, hypermarkets, modern, shiny, and huge retailing spaces located off highways, opened with new formats, fixtures, and technologies. Self-service came together with shopping as entertainment for a new model white housewife-consumer, precisely as black service workers entered the labour market. These shops projected South Africa into a future, beyond fractious racial engagement and onto a terrain of world-class retailing (Chap. 5). In the third moment, the 1990s and early 2000s, these retail stores became neoliberal realms of casualized and contracted black labour serving a flagging ideal of white consumer, even as the market was changing under the cynical sign of shareholder value (Chaps. 5 and 6). The fourth moment is the present day epitomized by Wal-Mart's acquisition of a South African retailer, in which the retail store becomes more narrowly the distribution channel for commodities, now to working-class black consumers through state encouragement, and where service itself is given little attention by managers but where market access and consumption come to define nation (Chap. 8).

Retail is a key site of job growth and economic expansion in South Africa. Consumer spending (and debt) bolsters national economies (James 2015), and retailing operations have restructured global capital flows (Lichtenstein 2009). Retailers drive supply chain dynamics as a catalyst to development; they offer the world's commodities to a democratic citizenry as a sign of "making it." In each of these conjunctures of national belonging and concrete relations, retail workers' disposition and politics changed. This imbrication of retail space and nation describes one dimension shaping workers' struggles and their ongoing attachment to the workplace as a site of contestation.

Law and the Category of "Employee"

Labour law is the second contour tracing changes within the concrete articulations shaping retail worker politics. Ching Kwan Lee (2007) demonstrates the importance of labour law in producing contradictions that both offered openings and presented limitations to workers' struggles in firms in China depending on competing discourses and practices at national and local state levels. In the case of South African retail workers, the critical contradictions were and continue to be reproduced internal to the law itself, which must be understood as definitive of South Africa's colonial/post-colonial context (cf Burawoy 1985). Law was central to state making in South Africa, and labour law was foundational (Chanock 2004a). This book traces how labour law constituted the category "employee" and its corollaries in retailing, in turn materializing conditions against and through which retail workers struggled. By "establishing factitious categories for work relations" (Tomlins 1993, xi), in our case narrowly observed through changes to labour legislation, law named the subject of labour rights as well as constituted the character of relations within the labour market and the workplace. Lived labour law in retail workplaces produced multiple signifiers: the liberal subject; formal "equality" at a site of unequal relations; the necessity for state mediation and the idea of state protection; boundaries of collective identity; the measure of popular participation in the polity; and the terrain of the market (Tomlins 1993).

Unlike "human rights," which interpellate a universal subject of recognition and have driven discursive claims in post-apartheid South Africa and globally in late liberalism (Klug 2005; and see Povinelli 2011),[10] formally speaking, labour law mediates a relationship of (conflicting) interest. The subject of labour rights enters a contract, in which "rights" reflect the established parameters of expectations and duties of parties to the contract. In the abstract, the relationship between employee and employer establishes the conditions for a market exchange to happen, in which parties are "equal" (the labour right mediates this relationship to balance power); each party brings to the deal something the other wants – labour power for the wage (Kennedy 1985, 956). In mediating this relationship, then, in practice labour law sets into motion a complex of categories and relations that define political subjects. Yet labour law is constituted within specific social relations in time and place (Tomlins 1993). As with retail spaces, four moments of conjuncture are highlighted in which labour law interpellated the political subject within retailing.

Between the 1930s and the 1960s, white workers were hired as service workers and defined as "employees" in industrial relations law. This designation proffered them rights to belong to a state-recognized trade union, which allowed them access to state-protected fair procedure and the right to bargain with employers. Thus in South African industrial relations, the white worker was designated the liberal subject of law (Chap. 4). Yet, law-making in retail defined the category "employee" with several internal variations: white women had a secondary status compared to white men; the use of "casual" as distinct from "permanent" employment prioritized the indefinite employment contract as the core site of relationality; and the difference between part-time and full-time employment defined the contract in terms of working time. These variations relied in practice on differentiation by age and gender. Furthermore, in retailing the legal mechanisms establishing bargaining between unions and employers operated in variance to the norm, with the state intervening directly to set conditions. Even for white workers in the sector, then, the ideal form of liberal subject was attenuated by the deviations, thereby constituting "employee" in more complex relational terms (Chaps. 2 and 4).

Second, "employee" was split externally through the excision of African workers from the category. They were defined alternatively as servant/native/labourer in a chain of significations that spoke not only to their exclusion from the employee category but also to the ambivalences attached to the subject of labour rights. Thus, while black workers "chose" to enter work, they did so under the coercive control of the state

(Chanock 2004a), and they entered not a relation of presumptive equality but one defining them as a bulk labour supply (Chaps. 2, 3, and 4).

When black workers were hired into service jobs in the 1970s and 1980s, the second moment, they organized collectively to contest labour relations that defined them outside the category of employee. They consciously challenged the boundary between mass labour and individuated, feminized service workers, redefining the labour process in shops through a firm race-class subject, abasebenzi. For African workers who were not "employees" under law to reject existing categories opened up new possibilities through demands to be related to as full subjects in the employment relation. Labour law reform in the 1980s responded to the increasing militancy of black workers in these endeavours and for the first time unified the category employee in terms of race in order to incorporate black workers into the industrial relations system (Chaps. 3 and 4). This shift in the notion of employee ensured that it remained definitive of an affectively potent relationship.

Post-apartheid labour law reforms in the mid-1990s marks the third moment of conjuncture. In retailing, following the deracination of the employment contract, employers increased their use of casual labour in non-standard shifts. Thus the norm of the full-time permanent worker came to be contrasted with the casual worker. While democratic labour law between 1995 and 1998 sought to unify the contract of employment further by expanding the definition of employee and by levelling basic conditions across sectors, legislation covering retail enabled the employment of casual workers, as historically defined in the sector, until 2003 when it was finally reformed in line with national law. In turn, this revision contributed to the growing use of labour broking, already increasing from the mid-1990s, and further complicated the category of employee. The democratic subject of labour rights – central to the political order (Mamdani 1996) – was, in fact, re-divided again (Chaps. 4, 5, and 6).

Finally, in 2015, the last moment highlighted (and which points to the future), another reform of labour law introduced regulatory changes governing the use of temporary employment services in order to limit labour broking. It offers potentially important protections, but also redirects the crux of the employment contract back to the normative nexus of employer and employee as site of relationality and subject of law. In retail, this safeguard then has paradoxically recreated the division between full-status employees and partial part-timers as employers rehire people as "general workers" (Chap. 8).

In each of these moments, because of how divisions were reproduced, the normative subject of labour law became defined in terms of standard conditions; most critically, in retailing this happened around working time, the standard shift. Retail worker politics were shaped by these imbrications. In this way the contradictions that are contained in the category of employee over time explain the enduring emotive power of the labour relation as political terrain.

The importance of labour law in shaping the terrain of retail worker politics is twofold. First, it suggests that the governmental liberal subject as represented within work and wage labour (Barchiesi 2016a, b) is not as singular and cohesive (and perhaps overriding) as presented. Furthermore, the very ambivalences of its form, as will be shown in retail, reproduced its affective power for workers. The foundational division of (white) "employee" from (black) bulk labour supply, that dominated the colonial and apartheid periods, has been reinscribed into law in different forms, as in labour broking and its ongoing association with unskilled, manual labour, or indeed, in the most recent iteration of general worker. Thus the way in which the subject of labour law has been split, unified, and split again over time has reconstituted a racialized labour relation through the Other, "black labourer," to employee *and* reenergized this site as political terrain for workers.

The second importance of this argument is that these articulations constituted "workers" in relations in these sites and not as identities. Abasebenzi could be said to be struggling for a relationship of "equality" with employers, as an "adult" subject able to participate and make decisions, in contrast to being a mass supply of labour. Because these workplaces continued to be defined around such relationships, retail worker politics has endured. But, they carry further contradictions as politics reproduced further divisions. Thus, retail worker politics itself has functioned, on one hand, to reinscribe forms of domination constitutive of wage labour in South Africa. And, in reproducing in new forms the foundational contradiction in South African law between the "free" worker whose labour power is her property to wield and the mass labour supply that embodies property as input (owned by whoever pays for it), retail worker politics exposes the shaky ground of labour relations in South Africa's post-colony and points toward questions about the future of the political subject abasebenzi. This book shows that the esteemed category "employee" in retail operated through its difference with others, and with its splitting (in different conjunctural moments). This relationship itself helped to constitute the political subject.

"Subjects-in-Struggle": The Political Subjectivity of Retail Workers

Finally, a third contour describes the articulations of race, class, and gender constituting abasebenzi in different moments. Political subjectivity has been framed by a dominant literature as a matter of "recognition," as an end point to be worked toward, an ethical achievement of an (evolving) autonomous subject who participates in mature deliberative politics (Taylor 1994; Habermas 1994; Honneth 1996; and see Fraser and Honneth 2003). Yet for critics, a "politics of recognition" based on claims from an a priori identity or on the ego-psychology of achieving "identity" can be viewed rather as "the pursuit of sovereignty" (Markell 2003, 14; see McIvor 2015),[11] which can reinforce hierarchy (Kalyvas 1999) and depoliticize action by returning to the state or law as arbiter (Brown 1995). In late liberalism, especially in the settler colonial context where different "projects and worlds" exist within it (Povinelli 2011, 76; and see 2002), recognition offers a main form of inclusion. In so doing, it becomes a "mode of governance" (77), however, subjecting people to being affirmed within acceptable categories. Elizabeth Povinelli (2011) argues, though, that many live not quite connected into the vocabulary and regulatory schema, variously catching and slipping through it. She suggests asking a different question than how political subjects are produced through recognition. Instead, she queries the "conditions of life" of those not quite able to enter such politics (77). They are, she argues, living, "enduring" the "abandonment" of economies and of political orders. For me, the idea of enduring leads to the issue of method and suggests seeking a "conjunctural analysis" (Hart 2016; see also Hall 1985, 2003, 105) in order to understand political subjectivity. "Enduring," as I use it, is another way of saying "reproducing," which must then be shown – the precise conjuncture between discourses of domination and lived experience. There are no "guarantees" (Hall 1986) that explain that moment a priori. Why and how do retail worker politics persist?

To many, South African workers' ongoing claims around work seem to offer at best a view of a "melancholic" labour politics (Barchiesi 2011), an attachment to past signifiers that have lost their grounding but cannot be let go, or at worst demands of a self-interested labour elite, out of touch with the realities of South Africa's economy, but acting from their structural position as wage earners (Seekings and Nattrass 2005, 2015). Compellingly, Franco Barchiesi (2011) describes the history of how wage labour became the route to incorporation into colonial and apartheid orders of control and post-apartheid citizenship. The governmental technologies of white administrators and ANC policymakers alike produced a nexus of citizenship and wage labour, which subjectified black workers. His subsequent conclusion is that work is reproduced as a site of "anti-blackness" (Barchiesi 2016a, b), which can only ever affirm the objectification of black people. This book confirms that the labour relation was and continues to be constituted through racial subjugation. Yet articulations of race and labour are over-determined (Hall 1980, 1985).

Political subjectivities are constituted as historical articulations of discursive practices and lived relations, which are indeed over-determined – that is, have multiple, intersecting vectors shaping them – yet "concretely" so (Hall 1985). As Stuart Hall explains in his discussion of Althusser's concept of interpellation, there is a gap between the discursive naming of the subject and the turn to the hail, by which the "relation to the rule" is constituted (Hall 1985, 102; 2000, 26; see Althusser 1971). If subjectification describes the process by which subjects are produced, Hall outlines the problematic thus (in relation to Foucault): "it is not enough for the law to summon, discipline, produce and regulate, but there must also be the corresponding production of a response (and thus the capacity and apparatus of subjectivity) from the side of the subject" (Hall 2000, 25). This is, then, a matter of reproduction. Locating the question of reproduction in this space between the hail and the turn (and/or its incomprehension) (Hall 1985), Hall explains that this precise conjuncture can be understood as an "articulation" (Hall 2000, 19), which he defines elsewhere as "a connection or link which is not necessarily given ... but which requires particular conditions of existence to appear ... [and] has constantly to be renewed" to remain emotive (Hall 1985, 113–14n2; and see Hart 2016).[12]

The "concrete lived individual" is over-determined (Hall 1985, 108–110) in the sense that she cannot be reduced to any one discourse or representation but is "fixed" as subject within sets of contradictions at particular moments and places and into "particular condensed social positions" (Hall 1985, 111). Thus, explaining political subjectivity requires analysis that builds from the "concrete," those relations in particular "social sites" (Hall 1985, 99, 103; also Hart 2016). Change consists of struggling to establish new meanings for categories, and thus of disrupting chains of meanings, "of dis-articulating [the old category] from its place in a signifying structure" (Hall 1985, 112). These are "subjects-in-struggle" (Hall 1985, 112). "Reproduction," then, more properly can be described as a process of constant shifting (Hall 1985, 113) and of enduring.

"New subjects" (Hall 1985, 112) are born in contests over meanings of existing categories. As this book describes, abasebenzi emerged in retailing in the 1970s and 1980s (see Chap. 3). I find Jacques Rancière's (2010; and see Davis 2010, 84) notion of subjectivation useful to help emphasize the dramatic "rupture" of this particular moment, but I follow Hall's emphasis, such that any break must be understood as part of the process of rearticulation in the longer history that I trace. Thus, black workers in the 1970s and 1980s were not simply opposing conditions of exploitation but were using the constituted site of labour relations to assert a new political subject and way of relating. In this way, subjectivation is not an identity claim, but a contestation of the semantic and material fields (Davis 2010, 86).

Thus, this contingent notion of articulation within a field of historically structured relations and significations is key to understanding why retail workers continue to act at this site. This was a consistently iterative process, in which forms of state interpellation, capital investment and expansion, social imaginaries around polity and belonging, notions of respectability, skill, caring, consumption, adulthood, personhood, and participation "condensed" into "social positions" in places and times and through articulations of race, class, and gender (Hall 1985, 111). The category abasebenzi has to be understood as a concrete articulation of race-class-gender relations rather than reductively as simply worker identity, structured only through an overbearing binary (agent or victim; liberal subject or its antithesis, object/thing). If understood as the constitution of meaningfully articulated relations in time and space, then abasebenzi, as a collective subjectivity, simultaneously upends those relations and reproduces them.

In this book, I consider retail worker politics in the present by undertaking an examination of the dynamic shifts in retail worker politics from the 1930s onwards. I argue that the collective political subject abasebenzi became significant on its own terms, to make demands around forms of relationality within the retail workplace, itself a space of national imaginary. Thus by the present day, as Gillian Hart explains for South Africa, "escalating struggles over the material conditions of life and livelihood are simultaneously struggles over the meaning of the nation and liberation, as well as expressions of profound betrayal" (Hart 2008, 680). Recurrent claims of worker politics confronted global restructured retail capital and rearticulated forms of participation in a post-apartheid polity and market, but they also did so under changing conditions in ways that have implications for the future.

The isiZulu word abasebenzi means "workers," with the suffix "aba" designating the plural noun category of human beings (sing. *um-*). This collective noun, referring to a group of people, must have developed in relation to an earlier word for worker, *isisebenzi*, a noun class that denotes objects (*isi-/izi-*).[13] In South African local languages, words for "wage labour" – brought about in the violent historical context of migrant labour – referred to an alienated condition of labouring for someone else. These ascriptions were distinguished from words for "work," which signified a constitutive, materializing labour that brought into being social relations and ties of obligation and belonging (see Comaroff and Comaroff 1987; Moodie and Ndatshe 1994 for the seTswana lexicon). Thus in isiZulu, *isisebenzi*, with its linguistic prefix *isi-* marking an object, meant "worker," but carries the connotation of someone who was enslaved or doing (often degrading) work for someone else (Madondo 2001, 136; Hemson 1995, 134).[14]

By contrast, abasebenzi seems to take its root from another set of connotations: the words *imisebenzi*, little tasks bringing people together with ancestors, and *umsebenzi*, any kind of work or religious practices in which the family relates to the ancestors (Dlamini 2005, 87) both of which emphasize the constitutive properties of "work" (see Chap. 7 for more discussion). I suggest that the self-ascription of abasebenzi can be seen to signify a linguistic reassertion (with the suggestive shift in the noun form from an object to a human designation) of a collective category in which "workers" were associated with work as relational activity, which offered, as this book argues, a process of subjectivation in response to the very experience of wage labour.[15]

Abasebenzi staked a claim to a relational redefinition of labour relations. The use of abasebenzi was not unique to the retail sector; it was a subject mobilized by the labour movement as a whole. But I contend that instead of seeing it as a constitutive subject – in my analysis marked through language and practice – "worker" has been taken for granted as an identity. For retail workers themselves, the political subject abasebenzi came to mean variously: adult, participative, respect-worthy, facilitative of other social relations, skilful, collective, and public. The political subject was at once a constituting claim and one that contested the political community out of particular historical meanings of nation, race, labour, and freedom. The political subject abasebenzi is dynamic, then.

Again, I differentiate four periods in which the political subjectivity of retail workers coalesced in different ways. During the 1930s to the 1940s, white women shop workers enacted a class and gender identity that, by the 1950s and 1960s, became harder to sustain as their respectability became reinforced through race and gender norms, in relation to the state, changes to consumption, changes to the labour process and labour market, and limitations within their union (Chap. 2). By the 1960s, individuated, white women projected affect through their caring labour of service in retail spaces and by affirming their loyalties to families through part-time work. Still, many were working class: while their labour was central to constituting retailing in greater Johannesburg, this disposition condensed into subjectivities which emphasized their difference from black women entering retail work in the late 1960s (Chap. 2).

In contrast, when black women and men entered jobs in retailing in the 1970s and 1980s, they were only begrudgingly recognized as service workers or their positions were reclassified as those of general workers. The Indian and coloured women who first entered service work may have been individually accepted, particularly if they performed gendered norms of respectability, but distrust pervaded shop relations and could erupt with consequence for them. Their unions organized to protect the occupational status of service jobs and ensure their conditions matched standards. For African workers entering service work in the 1970s and 1980s, these were good jobs, requiring higher education than that held by their parents' generation. In Johannesburg, many new retail workers brought political experiences from the student movement into the workplace, which in turn influenced their understanding of racialized relations there. Their union used organizing tactics from predecessor unions but to different political aims, namely to emphasize racial and class inequalities in the shops. Direct engagements with white managers, the white public, and sometimes their white colleagues reinforced a struggle around race and class. Thus the ruptural political subject abasebenzi was not gendered female; it was an explicitly race-class disposition contesting feminization within the labour relations. It confronted legal hierarchies and exclusions and demanded participation and equality as adults therein (Chap. 3). This retail worker politics changed forever the dynamics within the sector.

In the post-apartheid period of the late 1990s and early 2000s, workers gained full formal labour rights and unions assumed political influence within the democratic state, but employers also began to increase casual employment and outsourcing through labour brokers. The story of

Hyperama shows workers' feelings of betrayal around the loss of participatory relations. As the company restructured and capital consolidated, workers were interpellated as inputs, to be managed by computers and surveilled in their everyday interactions. Managers punitively used democratic labour law to discipline and dismiss workers. More and more casuals were hired, and workers felt that they no longer were seen to be "workers" at all (Chap. 5). Yet black workers, now hired through different kinds of employment contracts, still embarked on collective actions to insist on their abiding role in workplace relations, to claim themselves as full-status employees, and to argue for the recognition of their skilled contribution (Chap. 6). In these struggles, however, workers localized their politics to branches and reproduced divisions among themselves, by employment category. This had the effect of reinscribing the "full-time permanent," standard-shift worker as the ideal subject, and displacing what could be seen as workers' common growing precariousness onto a single category, the (feminized) casual worker. At the same time, workers laboured to provide for household members and to build futures for their children, in turn ensuring their own (adult) sense of selves in gendered ways that reinforced the notion of abasebenzi as political subject within workplace relations (Chap. 7).

Finally, by 2013 with expanding global capital investment in South Africa, retail workers faced even greater fragmentation of employment conditions through increased use of labour brokers and "flexible" forms of employment (Chap. 8). In the shops examined, black working-class customers now patiently waited for their baked goods, but service meant less and less to retailers. Shifts extended into longer unsocial hours. Wage underpayment was common. New technologies monitored workers while abetting a lack of transparency in "system" errors. And, the employment contract itself became a mechanism to evade labour rights, as labour brokers falsified information and withheld documents. While managers were now black, workers continued to experience workplace relations as a site of racial domination, where workers laboured for (white) owners and where they understood all too starkly the symbolism of their lack of power. Yet they did not interpret these experiences in terms of individual inadequacies or miseries. They rearticulated a firm collective experience that reinforced the endurance of abasebenzi as political subject, as defined by relations of power to capital and to whiteness. As employers rehire contract workers into part-time shifts as "general workers," the skill of service is stripped from the occupation (Chap. 8). The reiterated association of blackness with bulk labour supply – in labour broking and in a flexible workforce of generic workers – exacerbates forms of precariousness and also reasserts the purchase of the labour relation as a political terrain, even while the site is becoming more tentative.

*   *   *

This book is based on 20 years of engagement with retail sector workers in and around the greater Johannesburg region, South Africa's economic centre.[16] In the chapters covering the apartheid period, I speak of the Rand ("Ridge"), short for the Witwatersrand, or the extended area around and including the city of Johannesburg, defined originally by the contours of its gold reef. In the post-apartheid period, I use the broader term Gauteng Province, the current administrative and geographical unit (Fig. 1.1).

Chapter 2 examines the constitution of the retail sector through the labour of white women from the 1930s to the 1970s in service to a "white public." A gendered and racialized notion of service became central to directing expanding consumption under apartheid. Working-class white women organized into their union to contest poor conditions in stores, but a class identity became harder for them to maintain under apartheid. Their experiences were often individualized, and they reproduced social hierarchies within shops while securing these spaces of consumption for their customers.

Chapter 3 turns to black workers entering service jobs in retailing in the 1960s to 1980s. Black women were discriminated against in shops in a number of ways, which marked their difference in status and presumptive skill from white women. By the late 1970s and early 1980s, they organized and contested their marginalization, defining abasebenzi as a militant political subject, in contrast to white women. This race-class subject was a potent signifier, a particular response both to an already constituted labour process and to a realm of consumption defined through white women's labour.

Chapter 4 examines the socio-legal history of the category of "employee" in the retail sector. It describes the relationship between the categories of employee and that of servant/native/labourer in law. It then traces the shifting uses of casual, part-time, and contract labour, key employment categories defining the retail sector through its history from

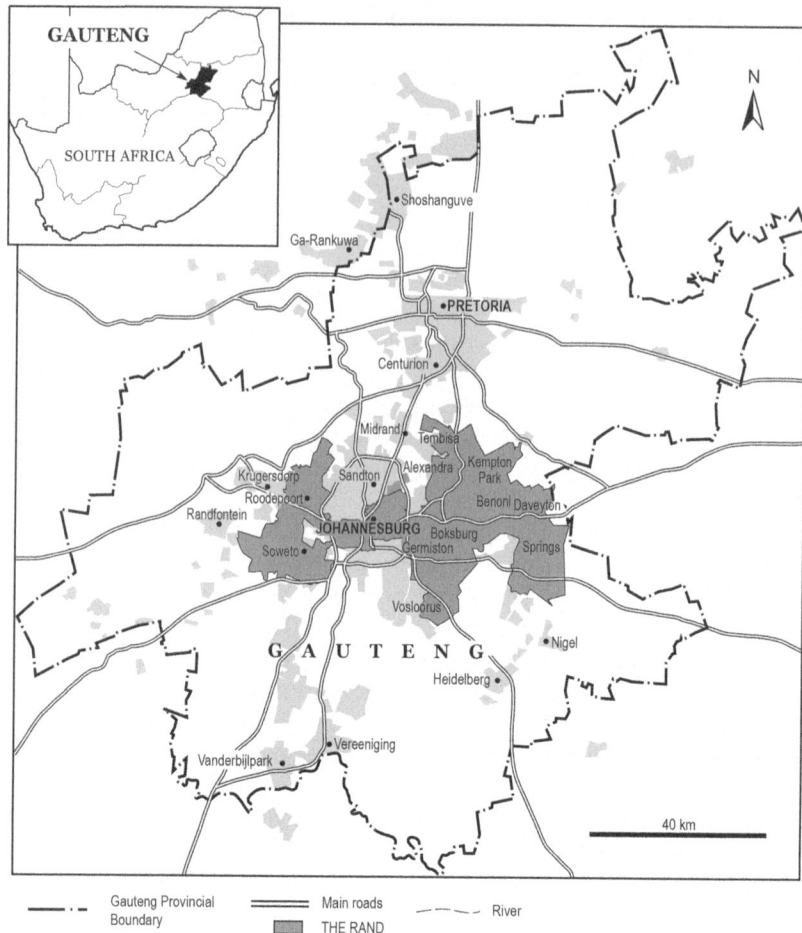

Fig. 1.1 Map of Gauteng and the greater Johannesburg region (Map by cartographer Wendy Phillips)

the 1930s to the post-apartheid period. The chapter shows how workers' claims to labour rights developed in relation to legal categories with affective histories. It tracks how the full-time, permanent worker became the ideal category. Gendered and racialized legal categories conditioned the collective political subject emerging in workers' struggles.

Chapter 5 details the expansion of retail capital through the format of the "hypers" in the 1970s and the 1980s on the Rand, as sign of modern living and national progress. In the 1990s, these arenas underwent restructuring as retail capital concentrated and consolidated domestically. Under democracy, workers confronted what they perceived to be a betrayal of built-up relations, which they had enacted to effect a participatory realm. They narrated experiences of loss and objectification in the face of a neoliberalizing corporate culture. These formulations suggest how these workplaces continued to be terrains of relationality.

Chapter 6 looks at worker actions occurring in these shops in the 1990s and 2000s, including wildcat strikes and go-slows. It traces how workers in different forms of employment both reaffirmed the collective political subject abasebenzi and reproduced divisions.

Chapter 7 examines the discursive symbolism of the ubiquitous phrase "to sit at home and do nothing," in order to interrogate how spaces outside of the workplace helped define the meaning of work for these retail workers. Workers' stories of household precariousness and the "praxis of providing," expressed through gendered anxieties and futurity in children, help to explain the endurance of a politics focused on workplace relations.

Finally, we end our story in Chap. 8 with the US multinational Wal-Mart's acquisition of South African listed Massmart Holdings. Wal-Mart, the world's largest private employer, is well known for wage theft, work intensification, eroded benefits, and anti-union practices (Lichtenstein 2006). This chapter juxtaposes the low-price consumer, to whom Wal-Mart expresses loyalty and who signifies democratic market inclusion, to the low-wage service worker, employed through labour brokers and as "general workers," in order to examine the reproduction of retail worker politics redefining abasebenzi, race, and skill in a fraying relationship of labour to nation.

The retail workplace has become the new frontier for young people, who as workers peddle the promise of mobility to consumers while confronted with the betrayal of economic scarcity. Retail workers, like Ruth and Ninah, whose stories began this chapter, offer a particularly salient view that focuses analysis of gender, nationhood, race, consumption, and belonging toward a single point: the meaning of the dead-end job that yet holds so much promise. This story centres on the history of political desire, on the embodied imbrication of blackness with labour, and on the endurance of collective imaginaries constituted through long-term struggles at a key site of power, not just for those in the wage relation but for all those tied into its circuits.

Insisting on a longer history, from the 1930s to the present day, this book charts a path for understanding precarious labour politics in contemporary South Africa. Precisely because of retail workers' inability to fix their belonging securely through their labour politics, its appeal endures. Retail workers' continuing fight as abasebenzi cannot be reduced to its organizational and institutional dimensions in trade unionism nor should it be so readily dismissed as obsolete (or delusional). The politics of precarious labour today cuts both ways, then: it reinvests older signifiers of political subjectivity with life, and it reconfigures the terrain of politics.

Notes

1. I follow the practice in South Africa of referring to "black" as including all oppressed by the apartheid regime in terms of their "race." In this situation, however, the workers were specifically "African." Official census classification maintains the following categories: Black-African, Coloured, Indian, and White. For a critique of ongoing racial classification in the post-apartheid period, see Maré (2014). "Township" refers to a residential area that had previously been legally segregated to black people.
2. All names are pseudonyms, except in the case of public figures. Ruth Ngobeni, interviewed by Bridget Kenny, Daveyton, July 10, 2005.
3. Focus group interview with contract workers by Bongani Xezwi, Johannesburg, May 19, 2013.
4. Focus group interview with shop stewards by Bongani Xezwi, Johannesburg, September 29, 2013.
5. There are too many references to list, but for a range of work, see Kenny and Bezuidenhout (1999), Valodia (2001), Desai (2002), Lund (2002), Bramble and Barchiesi (2003), Samson (2003), Miraftab (2004), Webster and von Holdt (2005), and Neves and du Toit (2013). See Seekings and Nattrass (2015, 54, 63–67) for a critique of research that argues for the "informalization" of the South African labour market. They emphasize improved regulation and wages in key sectors, such as the public sector, and for higher-skilled workers. They argue that in the post-apartheid period, there are some "winners" within the labour market and offer a corrective to generalizations which focus on the "losers" (67). By contrast, this book contributes a long-term and qualitative portrait of workers' experiences in a sector where multifaceted processes have indeed affected the nature of the work.

6. The official unemployment rate measures those not employed in the previous six months. The expanded unemployment rate, which includes discouraged work seekers, rose from 31% to 35% in the period from 1994 to 2015 (International Labour Office 2015b; Statistics South Africa 2015). In the first quarter of 2017, this increased to 36.4% (Statistics South Africa 2017). This measure is widely regarded as the more accurate record.
7. Because social welfare grants in South Africa have come to serve an essential stopgap in household survival, particularly for households without access to employment, some argue that South Africa cannot be characterized as a neoliberal state but must be seen as a southern example of a hybrid/redistributive state (see Seekings and Nattrass 2015). For the apartheid context, see Beittel (1992), who argued that wage levels determined household provisioning.
8. This literature is extensive. For example, see Knights and Morgan (1990), Fuller and Smith (1991), Leidner (1993), Gutek (1996), Smith (1996), Macdonald and Sirianni (1996), Wharton (1996), Bulan et al. (1997), Frenkel et al. (1999), Crompton and Birkelund (2000), Gutek et al. (2000), Korczynski et al. (2000), Pettinger (2004, 2015), and Grugulis and Bozkurt (2011).
9. For discussion of the consumer as citizen, see Soper (2004, 2007), Zukin and Maguire (2004), Bauman (1998), and Featherstone (1991). For South Africa, see Iqani (2016), Comaroff and Comaroff (2003), and von Schnitzler (2008).
10. For studies in which human rights discourse relates to social movements and popular struggle, see von Schnitzler (2016) and Robins (2008). On disorder and the law, see Comaroff and Comaroff (2006).
11. See also Butler (1997, 2004), Fraser (1997), Benjamin (1988), Brown (1995), McNay (2008), Fanon (1967), Ahmed (2006), and Arendt (1958, 2005).
12. Also see Hall's (1980) much more detailed discussion of articulation.
13. The original word for worker was *isisebenzi* (singular) and *izisebenzi* (plural). For instance, Bryant (1905, 565) lists "isi-sebenzi" as "workman" and "umsebenzi" as "work, of any kind" but does not include abasebenzi (thanks to Mark Hunter for discussion around my effort to periodize abasebenzi). In isiZulu, noun prefixes that relate to human beings are in classes 1/1a and 2/2b (*ama-*; *aba-*). This suggests that there would have been a shift from using *izisebenzi* (class 4, which designates the category for an object or body part) to abasebenzi, which represents a category of human being (Innocentia Mhlambi, personal communication, May 23, 2016). While I cannot date the shift precisely, abasebenzi became the preferred term by the 1970s workers' movement. For

instance, in 1971, the first issue of the magazine *Isisebenzi* of the Durban Wages Commission was published (http://www.sahistory.org.za/article/isisebenzi, accessed June 21, 2017). In November 1975, a brief newsletter of the African National Congress *Abasebenzi* promised to help workers in Cape Town (http://www.sahistory.org.za/archive/abasebenzi-november-1975, accessed June 21, 2017). By the 1980s, abasebenzi was used throughout pamphlets and publications of the labour and liberation movements. We see in Chap. 3 how abasebenzi was used to refer collectively to retail workers by this time.

14. Madondo (2001, 136) writes that "The original word-form *isisebenzi* has been discarded by workers because of its negative use by many people as they say it no longer refers to a worker but an enslaved worker so they came with *umsebenzi* [the singular form]." Hemson (1995, 134) comments in passing similarly that "The word *isisebenzi* refers to work which is of a humiliating and degrading kind" such as being a servant or looking after someone else's cattle, and thus primarily marking forms of subordination.

15. (Thanks to Mark Hunter for referring me to Dlamini 2005). See also Gunner (1986) for an analysis of oral tradition in union songs, which invoke a collective identity for workers and link it to a common history and tradition through the idioms and expressions used. See Phadi and Manda (2013, 205) for a discussion of the now common use of abasebenzi for "workers."

16. Research for this project is based on several extensive periods of in-depth research between 1997 and 2017. From 1997 to 2002, I conducted ethnographic fieldwork in three branches of a major South African retailer, with follow-up interviews performed between 2003 and 2005. This included 24 focus group interviews with casual, contract, and permanent workers between 1998 and 2000, 59 life history interviews with workers in 1999 and 2000, and 242 semi-structured workplace interviews which formed two non-representative surveys in 1998 and in 2000. Nathaniel Ndala, Vivienne Ndatshe, and Cambridge Manzini assisted me with some of the interviews and with interpretation from isiZulu and seSotho. Phineas Riba assisted with transcriptions and translations of several key life history interviews. In the same period, I conducted interviews with industry experts, branch management and former managers, and SACCAWU officials and shop stewards. Where interviews were conducted in people's places of residence, I have listed these, but where interviews were conducted at stores, I have listed the wider metropolitan area to protect interviewees. Between 2007 and 2015, I conducted life history interviews with another 25 people, mostly women, who had worked in Johannesburg chain and department stores from the 1930s to the 1970s. Venessa van der Walt assisted me with Afrikaans interpretation in a couple of these interviews. I also conducted

archival research in a number of South African archives, including the Historical Papers Research Archive at the University of the Witwatersrand, the National Archives, and the Mayibuye Archives at the University of the Western Cape. I also commissioned interviews from Matlhako Mahapa and Fatima Mathivha of people who shopped in Johannesburg stores in the 1960s to the 1980s. These are referenced accordingly. In 2013, a team of researchers and I conducted a non-representative survey of 109 workers from six Gauteng branches of a Massmart subsidiary as a project for SACCAWU. In addition, we conducted seven focus group interviews (one per branch and one with shop stewards from across the branches). Project researchers included Zakhele Dlamini, Tlaleng Letsheleha, Ntsiki Mackay-Anderson, Matlhako Mahapa, Zivai Sunungukayi Mukorombindo, Lesego Ndala, and Bongani Xezwi. Bongani Xezwi led the focus group interviews. Interviewee names are pseudonyms except where public figures were interviewed. Finally, I have worked with SACCAWU over this period, including on casual labour in the sector and most recently in support of the Africa Massmart/Wal-Mart Shopsteward Alliance.

CHAPTER 2

Servicing a Nation: White Women Shop Assistants and the Fantasy of Belonging

> *I enjoyed my customers because they always came back. Those years we used to even scrub our floor and polish it and shine it up. Mr. Levine used to come and stand at the entrance of my [department] and he says, 'You could eat off this floor!' But it was such a pleasure because we put everything into our work.*
> *Ingrid du Toit, shop assistant at OK Bazaars, 1940s and 1950s.*[1]

White-women shop workers founded modern retailing in South Africa. The discourses of white femininity, so closely tied to the constitution of the nation under apartheid, defined these women's experiences through the affect of city shops, the labour of service, and the elisions of class. In turn, their work reproduced gendered hierarchies with male managers, a locus of belonging in "familiarized" market relations with white consumers, tropes of gendered difference underpinning state power, and, indeed, themselves as subjects. These articulations of race, class, and gender, then, constituted the workplace, the marketplace, the polity, and political subjects.

Discursively, white womanhood has long buttressed "the nation" in South Africa. Colonial power, intra-colonial contestation, and apartheid state-making relied variously on the images of respectable femininity and motherhood to activate appeals to nationalism, to bound and bind the nation.[2] The sign of the sacrificial white woman unified South Africa

© The Author(s) 2018
B. Kenny, *Retail Worker Politics, Race and Consumption in South Africa*, Rethinking International Development series, https://doi.org/10.1007/978-3-319-69551-8_2

through what Anne McClintock (1993, 71) has called a "fetishistic displacement of difference." Such a discourse recognized the power of white women and yet contained it "within an iconography of domestic service," which integrated women through social lineage as daughters, wives, and mothers and made men into agents of progress and politics (McClintock 1993, 72). In the process, white women's labour was erased, and they were associated with a time out-of-history, with tradition (McClintock 1995).

What, then, do we make of white female shop assistants who, despite a context discouraging white women from working,[3] nonetheless laboured and thereby contributed to their household incomes, facilitated "progress" and modernity precisely by expanding markets and commodity culture, and did so through public everyday interactions, visible to all? While McClintock and others have emphasized the semiotics of nation requiring white women be constituted as wives and mothers,[4] and while labour in its association with manual work was imbricated with blackness, as we will see in Chaps. 3 and 4, white women not only formed a critical labour force, but did so by tempering the ambivalence towards working through service to a white public.

The register through which white women could be considered workers required a domestication of their economic role, as shown below. As service workers, they claimed skill while reinforcing limits to their authority and, in many instances, reproducing an infantilized status in relation to white men. Yet, their incorporation as a respectable workforce required ongoing effort that indicates the interplay between daily relations and forms of representation. Ultimately, white women themselves reaped a reward (in McClintock's terms, were complicit) in playing to the meanings available, thereby securing their respectability. Still, an underlining uneasiness with their options tells us something too. As Carolyn Steedman (1987) argues, the excision of a category of belonging ("working class white woman") meant that these women through their own assertions reproduced their legitimacy, yet with an excess, a gap, something overdetermined that had no place to go. For some, it became shame and for others it reinforced racism. And, in broader terms, it redirected these women's identification towards other markers, such as consumer (see Chap. 5).

In this chapter, I emphasize two points that explain the significance of women's service labour in the period from the 1930s to the 1970s in and around Johannesburg, an area called the Rand at this time. First, actual white women as historical beings cannot be reduced to the discourses describing white womanhood (Stanley 2013; Steedman 1987). The gap between the hailing of them and their turn to the hail, in Stuart Hall's (2000) terms, pushes us to theorize the relationship of social imaginaries to race–class–gender relations in practice.[5] These dialogics of discourse and identification played out in places (i.e., not only in the aesthetic arenas of advertising and novels): in the space of retail shops, which materialized meaning in workplaces and in city streets. These were active stories of nation, which set limits to the daily lives of Rand residents.

Second, accruals from these engagements worked in multiple, potentially conflicting directions. Women's labour in shops cannot be said simply to reinforce forms of colonial/apartheid power *tout court* (Bannerji 2000), but instead we can track competing affective effects. Moving back and forth between home and town, returning on trams and buses with sore feet from a day of standing at the counter, at other times carrying packages or children, white women produced a fantasy of belonging under conditions of settler colonialism, but through disjunctures with white male managers, husbands, retail capital, National Party politicians, other shop "girls," and their customers. In the process, these stores became emotive sites, places where workers, city residents, and political beings contested relations and, as such, ensured that relationship mattered there.

Retail Capital, the City and White Belonging

In 1952, Janice Tomlinson started working at Anstey's department store as a shorthand typist in the office. She described downtown Johannesburg in the 1950s:

> In those days, town was the main shopping centre … Generally people went into town. They went into town by bus and the buses operated into the night … All the shop assistants were white, the bus drivers were white, the lift operators were white. The menial jobs were black. Obviously the street sweepers, the toilet attendants, that sort of thing, remained black. The main part of town, Eloff Street was the street … the shopping area where they had quite upmarket shops … Anstey's, Stuttafords and John Orr's … If I was going shopping, I would go to town to shop. There were no malls. You'd go into town to shop … The buses were very reliable and on time. They always dropped you at your bus stop. They were punctual and strict. The bus drivers were white men … Very few black people were shopping. Look, there was total segregation. The black people were not allowed to sit on the

same benches with us. They had separate buses than us ... [They did] the manual, heavy labour if there were things to be moved. Black people were around but they were very few.[6]

To its white residents, Johannesburg's city centre was in many ways defined by its majestic shopping district, which symbolized modernity through the combination of metropolitan culture and racial exclusivity. Retailers commandeered the corner of Pritchard and Eloff Streets, the block with the city's highest land value, making it the "premier shopping corner not only in Johannesburg, but in South Africa as a whole" (Beavon 2004, 158). Other retailers and department stores were located around this core. Eloff Street was renowned for its fashion, styles, and shops, reminiscent of the world's greatest cities (Chipkin 1993, 96). Indeed, when South Africa's version of the game Monopoly came out, Eloff Street was ranked as its most expensive property.[7] Reinforcing its status conversely, as Veit Erlmann (1998, 16) discusses, the song "Eloff Street," written in 1940 by the Dundee Wandering Singers, offered the perspective from migrant workers first entering Johannesburg: "*Safika eGoli sabona intombi nensizwa zehla ngo Eloff Street*. We arrived in Johannesburg and saw ladies and men walking down Eloff Street. *Sanibona siyanibingelela*. Greetings, we are greeting you." Erlmann (1998, 16) suggests that these lyrics portrayed not benign wonder at a bustling metropolis, but "a space hinging on the experience of shock." For black inhabitants, Eloff Street with its crowds of shoppers marked the very centre of alienation in Johannesburg.

The shopping district was sustained by ongoing capital investment, tax laws that levied property sites rather than improvements, thereby encouraging upgrading and new construction, as well as by the proximity of an elite and middle-class market of white consumers in surrounding suburbs who travelled to town to shop, meet in tea rooms, and relax at bioscopes (Beavon 2004, 153–54; Chipkin 1993; Beall et al. 2002, 46–50). Architecture concretized the city's character, and department stores contributed to this "Johannesburg style," a mixture of modernisms overlaying each other and drawing on global influence (Chipkin 1993). From the Edwardian OK Bazaars building to the 17-storey Anstey's skyscraper built in the late 1930s, retailers enhanced Johannesburg's claim to modern cosmopolitanism (42,146–49). In towns along the Rand as well, branches of these shops offered equally extraordinary architecture (120). Apartheid state policy spatially segregated and limited the growth of Indian and Chinese business to the far west side of town, such that downtown

Johannesburg was by law white-owned (Beavon 2004, 153; Swilling et al. 1991). The geography of the city could be plotted in part by its city-centre shops and the pathways of its shoppers.

As early as the 1920s, many of these stores were branches of chains. South African retailing expanded through chain stores, or what the industry sometimes called "multiples." Chains lowered prices by standardizing merchandise and ensuring better product availability to growing urban markets (Cook 1975, 102–3; Kaplan 1986, 326). This model included "bazaar trading," most famously represented by OK Bazaars, defined through cash sales, discount prices, and mass marketing techniques (Kaplan 1986, 326–27). While at the turn of the nineteenth century on the Rand retailing pivoted on the local male merchant's professional skills – his "intimate knowledge" of stock and of the "requirements of the inhabitants of the district"[8] – by the 1930s and 1940s, "modern retailing" was in full swing, and it was the retail chain that solicited loyalty. Its operations were organized through retailing systems adopted from England and the United States. As immigrants from these countries, retailers had direct experience with their home country practices and actively sustained transnational networks through industry journals and associations, which circulated trends in design, layout, and systems operations. Like in Australia, New Zealand, and Argentina (Humphrey 1998; Laurenson 2005; Milanesio 2013), settler colonialism brought metropolitan retailing practices swiftly into circuit to shape the city and reflected claims to national modernity through consumer culture.

Countertops displayed clearly price-tagged commodities behind glass (Joyce 1981, 283; Kaplan 1986, 326).[9] Like elsewhere in the world, South African retailers used packaging and advertising innovations to standardize products. South Africa's first chain, Ackermans, succeeded because of mass marketing ideas – copied from the American F. W. Woolworth's and Britain's Marks and Spencer chains – for instance, a single low price of "1/11" (spoken as one-and-eleven) was introduced, as was the notion of the sale (Ackerman 2001, 19–20; Kaplan 1986, 321).[10] Wealthy shoppers could entertain themselves with a trip to one of several elegant department stores, with branches in major towns; the more "thrifty housewife" could budget with cash sales and discounts from chain bazaars (Joyce 1981, 283). Customers bought commodities from around the world, such as "American dresses, beautiful dresses of crepe de Chine."[11]

Chain stores introduced shoppers to expansive trading areas. By the 1940s, the gross sales area in many towns along the Rand had doubled to between 60,000 and 75,000 square feet in multi-storey buildings (Cook 1975, 100). While specialty stores and a range of smaller shops serving different economic brackets diversified city streets, by the 1940s Johannesburg's definitive stores were larger ones run by bigger workforces (101).

These chain retailers concentrated power. In the early twentieth century, the cost of imported goods operated as significant barrier to entry for smaller merchants. By the time the local production of food and other commodities became more important than imports, larger wholesalers and retailers controlled supply through trade associations (South Africa 1958a, b; Legassick 1977, 189–90; O'Meara 1983). While smaller, particularly Afrikaner, capital invested in commerce in the interior, it remained petty in nature and relegated to lesser towns and rural areas (O'Meara 1983, 213–14). Disparate and uncoordinated interests and a fragmented set of laws that regulated monopolistic conditions before 1955 meant that little political pressure was brought to bear on powerful retailers.[12] While a diverse sector, by the 1950s larger firms had become central to distribution especially in cities, with this trend towards consolidation continuing.[13]

This ordering of the city through relatively concentrated capital, chain stores, large buildings with impressive architecture, and a wealth of commodities on display was imbued with a powerful affect for many white residents. The "trip into town," nostalgically remembered by many interviewees, signalled belonging to and affinity for the city. Regardless of their economic background, residents described the ritual of travelling into town for Saturday morning shopping, dressed in their finest.

Becca van der Walt, who worked for John Orr's in the 1950s, outlined a class difference mapped onto the physical environment. People shopped at John Orr's or OK Bazaars. The clientele of these emblematic stores differed by standard markers of class, and yet they came and went within the same few blocks:

> [T]here were a lot of young people in OK Bazaars. John Orr's was elderly, stately … stiff upper [lip]. There were different classes of people, the way they dressed, the way they behaved. So OK Bazaars was very casual, noisy. John Orr's was very quiet. It wasn't a shop that you would go and take your children … They didn't like it. It wasn't the thing to do. But OK Bazaars, everybody shopped [there].[14]

As Hanalie Erasmus, who worked at John Orr's in the early 1950s, recalled: "We used to buy something small just in order to get a John

Orr's bag, after which we went shopping at OK."[15] These shop assistants crossed the streets during their lunch breaks to shop and wander, both consumers and workers in this downtown world in which white residents of different classes intersected (Photo 2.1).[16]

Photo 2.1 OK Bazaars in downtown Johannesburg, 1956 (Image by Museum Africa)

By "everybody," then, Becca meant white people. She explained, "And [there were] hardly any black customers. We didn't have black customers. If you saw a black person in the shop, it was like, 'What are you doing here?'" She continued, "Joburg used to be very white. I actually don't know where the black people used to shop. It never entered our heads. You didn't think about it."[17] In fact, when in town, black people shopped mostly in the western area of the city (Beavon 2004, 159). As one black resident described for Johannesburg in the mid-1960s:

> Shops such as Stuttafords we were totally not allowed to enter. OK [Bazaars] also, we used to buy from a small window where you could buy a little something. Food we bought in the location. Things such as blankets we bought them at the Indian shops on Market Street. And [for] clothes we used to go to [places] like Sales House. Sales House was like the shop that we were allowed to buy in.[18]

Although people were present as workers and to do their errands, a segregated mapping for white residents became part of the affective attachment of the city.

Becca then evoked the meaning of this premiere shopping district within the sociality of white life in Johannesburg in the 1950s:

> OK Bazaars was noisier and younger. And you had lots of families shopping there. Because you could go there and you could buy a cheap meal ... And they had a place for you to sit. John Orr's had a tea room with music. [T]here was a guy who had a piano and he used to play, and they used to drink tea and have cake ... [At] OK Bazaars ... they had little tables and you could sit with your family and you could have, I tell you, the most fantastic fish and chips. Wow it was nice. And cold meats and salads.[19]

These stores offered white Johannesburg a space for socializing and an experience of consumption that mirrored life in a European or American city. The thrill of these spaces depended on the symbolism of modern architecture and the demonstration of progress and plenty on the trading floors, but also in how they built an everyday belonging into experiences of the city. These affective impressions circulated – between shop and bus stop, between tea room and countertop, past plate-glass and through turnstiles – and relied on the erasure of black people; they constituted the semiotics of these stores and the city in ways that were particularly material. As we shall see, this city sentiment relied on the labour of white women retail workers.

White Women's Service Labour

White working-class women entered retailing in and around Johannesburg in the first decades of the twentieth century and in increasing numbers from the 1930s.[20] At first, they were young and unmarried, and many worked to assist families or, in more dire situations, to support themselves. Maureen Williams had grown up in an orphanage after her father left and her mother could not provide for her on a waitress's wages. At 16, the orphanage sent her to a women's lodging house "on the cheap side of town," where she was expected to pay for her keep. The orphanage helped her find work in a millinery shop in the centre of town, sewing flowers on hats. Her level of education led to a better job in the regal department store Stuttafords as a shop assistant in the early 1930s. Living on a small income, Maureen sewed her own clothes, as many of her colleagues did: "We had to look like somebody special, you know, very special at Stuttafords, because it was a beautiful shop." The young women who worked with her were "all the same kind of girls as me. Once you were old enough to work, nobody would keep you. You had to go to work."[21]

In contrast to newly proletarianized women coming from farms and entering garment factories at this time, shop assistants had a relatively high level of education with schooling up to Standard 8 (Grade 10), the ability to read and speak English, and a good command of mathematics, necessary for customer service in retail.[22] They had to look presentable and demonstrate poise like shop workers around the world (Albertyn et al. 1932, 208–9); or, in Maureen's words, "we had to make ourselves absolutely perfect."

Ingrid du Toit, whose words opened the chapter, left school and went to work part-time at the age of 14 and then full-time when she turned 15 in 1944: "[W]e were six in the family and I didn't have a dad, and my mom was dressmaking at the time … [I got a job] to get extra money."[23] Like others, she wore her best clothes to work at OK Bazaars, even if they were second hand, which her mother altered with a little collar or a frill. Johanna Coetzee, too, lived with her mother when she worked at OK Bazaars in the late 1940s. She explained that many young women did the same. She would wake in the early morning, pack her own lunch, and walk to the store.[24] At 17, Becca started working in shops in the 1950s to assist her mother who herself worked as a shop assistant in a sandwich shop while her father worked on the railways.[25]

These women joined male colleagues who had different designations: white men who worked as sales assistants and salesmen were merchants-in-training, while black men were employed as distributive workers lifting and sorting stock in backroom warehouses and delivering orders.[26] The shop "girls" were often directly supervised by older white women. Working as counter-hands and shop and sales assistants, they assisted customers by weighing and measuring goods or recommending fabrics and clothing styles. They kept their counters clean and themselves neat.

These female entrants were working class and yet leveraged educational advantage to gain access to higher status jobs than those in factories. Still, in the articulations of race, class, and gender that would play out, they would both contest and reinforce hierarchies evoking their subordination within the structure of feeling of white life.[27] Over the decades, these white women would produce relationships that constituted both workplaces and a wider social imaginary of the nation. In these spaces, white women workers negotiated class identities and gendered respectability, and also affirmed for themselves, their employers, and their customers an experience of the city where race held a class order intact. While women's experiences show how these relations were reproduced, they also suggest ambivalences, places where they confronted this order, and others that left them invisible and individualized.

Skill and Status

Pauline Schmidt first worked at Paramount stores, owned by OK Bazaars, in Johannesburg in 1943 to earn some pocket money during school holidays. When she left school, she found there were few job options available to her: "It was only sales, or you had to go do typing, and typing was just typing, you're either bored or you're not, you know."[28] Her sister, a supervisor in the shop, helped her to get a full-time job. The store was divided into departments with one or two women working in each section. Pauline started in the ladies' underwear department, advanced to other departments, and described her work thus:

We had counters where we'd serve people ... On top of the counters were bins; things were in [each bin]; and we had drawers. And you would walk up to me and say, "I'd like a blouse, have you got one in this shade?" or so, and I would say, "Yes!" or something, and I would take out my whole drawer and show you all what's in there.

Pauline emphasized her role in understanding her clientele and enjoyed helping them:

[Y]ou attend to the customer, and you recommend something ... Already I'd know what cloth and style. When you see the customer you'd already see what kind of person they are, or they [would] say, "I'd like something for a cocktail party or work or just for casual" ... But it was nice, a pleasure to show the people.

Women commonly remarked on the skill of selling to other women in these decades, both in the grander department stores and in the bazaar shops. Johanna, who worked at OK Bazaars in Benoni in the 1940s and early 1950s, recalled of customers: "Often they wanted to ask me the price of things ... and they called me and [would] say, 'How much was this?' and 'How much was a tin of [that].' And I was quite proud to be that way and help them."[29] She remembered how her supervisor would phone her mother to ask her to do extra shifts because she was such an effective salesperson. She saw herself as being good at her work because she supported her customers: "Well, if [my supervisor] always put the old stuff in front of me, I would say [to the customer], 'Rather try this.'" A modest woman, who flushed as she recounted her abilities, Johanna quickened when she said, "And I'm telling you, the people were sitting waiting in the queue at the orders counter, when I was at the orders, for me to come and help them. I must really not say that, but I was very, very proud of that. That was the main thing, being nice to people and advis[ing] them." For many young women, feeling their competence and having it acknowledged by supervisors and customers became an important experience of affirmation tied into service work.

Aware of the subtle affective labour she extended to her more wealthy customers, Johanna explained how she sometimes safeguarded them. When her store manager's (immigrant) wife phoned her to order a package of Boudoir biscuits, "she really couldn't pronounce the words or spell the words out to me. And I used to say, 'There's a lot of noise here, do you mind repeating it?'"[30] In another instance, she rescued an older customer's dignity when the elastic of her underwear broke while she was shopping. Johanna had bought herself a pair of panties that very morning and, quick-thinking, offered them to the mortified customer. She explained, "It was only one and six ... And she was so nice. Every time she'd come in she said, 'Thanks for the pantie.'" The service worker enacted the care of the domestic within her workplace, offering a gift even within the very heart of the marketplace. White women were over-determined as "familiar" sights (Du Plessis 2011) – both comfortable presences and "of the family," protecting relations in the public space of the shop.[31] This role offered respectability to many.

The National Union of Distributive Workers (NUDW) formed in 1937, and organized this workforce of women workers.[32] By the early 1940s, women occupied branch and executive union positions.[33] In representing its membership, the NUDW emphasized the skill of sales, portraying the wiles and patience of shop assistants in its newsletter. Selling was difficult, wrote one employee from OK Bazaars, for to convince a customer to buy something besides what she had in mind "may mean a battle of wits, where the salesgirl actually induces her customer to change her plan in every detail."[34] Shop assistants expressed great knowledge of the commodities they sold. As Pauline explained, "You had to know your merchandise very well, and you had to know the materials."[35] Ingrid, who worked across several departments, explained, "And you've got to know what you've got in stock. And placing your own orders, you mustn't run out of an item especially when it's a popular line."[36] Women's interpersonal grace and their physical propriety combined with an extensive, often self-taught knowledge of what they sold.

The union advocated for the work of women. An active female leadership mobilized its white female membership in a historic strike against OK Bazaars for recognition and improvements in wages and conditions in 1943.[37] Pauline participated in the 1943 strike. She joined the union when she started her job because it was expected, and her sister, the supervisor, was a member. As a "junior," her role was to block the entrance to the shop:

> The senior ladies and the supervisors didn't go on strike. They were union members but they didn't go on strike. But we youth, we did. We were told to go, but we enjoyed it. We thought it was a big joke actually. We used to picket the doors only. We used to sit in front of the door and we would stop

the people from entering the building. We wouldn't be violent. If they wanted to go to work, they may.[38]

Pauline is careful to indicate their restraint. Yet, while acknowledging norms of respectability – the senior women delegated the picketing to their juniors and the juniors allowed them to work – they affirmed themselves as workers and made for a visible signal to customers. Bessie White, a striker at another OK Bazaars subsidiary, reflected on the outcome: "The shop assistants began to believe in themselves – pride and self-assurance – and they took more interest in their work because they were working under proper conditions. They couldn't just be told, 'you're going to do five hours overtime.'"[39] The union gained recognition, limits to overtime, improvements in annual leave and wages, organizing facilities and procedure to consider grievances and dismissals, and through an extension of the agreement by arbitration award, these gains applied to most of the major chain retail employers within the sector (Herd 1974, 126–32).[40]

By the end of World War II, female shop workers were more often married women, and the NUDW represented this membership against the shifting tide of public opinion towards employed women (Kenny 2008). As part of its ongoing efforts to emphasize occupational integrity, the union played down the difference in status between a "young lady" in department stores and the "shop girl" in bazaar outlets, and it bargained to build a career path of shop work defined by tenure and qualification.[41]

By the 1950s, the NUDW represented members through lobbying the Wage Board around wages and conditions in the sector and by taking up individual branch-level member grievances (Herd 1974, 134–38).[42] These jobs were better paid than those of their grade in other sectors at this time (Mabin 1955). Pauline became a shop steward, and explained how they bargained with their management: "There was communication ... You would say 10%; they would come back with 5%, and it would go like that. If you could show why you needed that amount, then they would go for it."[43] Ingrid also was a union member: "We belonged to the union. In case of a job loss or things like that. [But] those years everything went so smooth, hey. We never had problems."[44] The union played an important role to legitimate women's experiences as service workers. It bolstered conditions and wages in the sector and measures of respectability to define the work in meaningful ways for many women.

Still, by the 1950s, with the National Party in power and its curtailment of militant unionism (Alexander 2000), the idioms through which the union sustained its defence of this female workforce shifted from championing women as class subjects towards arguing for the stabilization of working conditions in order to protect "our mothers, sisters and wives" (Kenny 2008, 378). By the 1950s, white household income rose and husbands benefitted from apartheid protections. For many of these women, though, they kept working either because they had to or because they wanted to. As Hall (1985, 111) suggests, race, class, and gender articulate and coalesce into positions. These women accrued status from their white-collar work, the skill of service, the affect of recognition within their daily relations with customers, and through the work of the union. In doing so, they troubled the discourse of white women and national belonging. Internal to the shops, however, these complex relations were reproduced in other ways.

Rules and Respectability

Shop work was organized through a hierarchical labour process in which male managers controlled operations, made decisions and gave orders, senior women directly supervised younger women in departments, and black men did packing in storerooms, managed by white men. Becca remembered her floor manager: "you had to go and report to him, and he used to be the one who used to come talk to you. So there was a woman [who supervised]. The women used to work and the man was like the boss."[45] At OK Bazaars, too, as Ingrid explained, white men occupied the key management positions and women acted as supervisors and floor walkers in charge of shop assistants.[46]

Tenure in the occupation carried legislated seniority with differentiated wage scales. "Junior" shop assistants worked for four years before becoming "qualified" and earning the higher rate. Years were portable within the sector, such that women who remained in the sector advanced to qualified status. Some became buyers, making decisions about what a department sold, but at this time, women did not often rise to the level of manager. Furthermore, the wage determinations stipulated a higher wage rate for white men in relation to white women in the same occupation.

This order acted, in particular, to discipline younger shop assistants. Pauline recounted that at Paramount in the 1940s, they had social workers in the store: "[You] would tell them your problem, and they would help you." She described how they intervened when a "young girl" was smoking, explaining that "We weren't allowed to smoke at the counters."[47] In the 1950s, in department stores like John Orr's, senior women monitored younger women's behaviour. Becca described the atmosphere: "You know you had to [purses lips and pulls facial expression of being prim and proper] to work there."[48] Shop assistants' dress and appearance were scrutinized, as was their timekeeping: "But you had a strict dress code. If you weren't dressed properly, you were soon told, you know, this is not acceptable ... And they were very strict with times. You had ten minutes to have tea. And you used to clock in and out."[49]

Moira Campbell immigrated to South Africa from Scotland as a young woman in the early 1960s and got a job at Woolworths. She was fired from her job there for wearing what was regarded as an improper blouse:

> I get a new outfit for work. And I'm so proud of it. Everybody's looking at me, I don't know why. Everybody! But nobody's saying a word ... And the personnel officer, a lady came up to me and took me to her office for the first and last time. She said to me, "What do you think you're doing?" and I said, "I don't know what I've done, what have I done?" And I didn't know: [The blouse] is see-through! And I am serving the public![50]

She was devastated that none of her colleagues had told her. And yet she walked across the street to John Orr's and got another job. When she was fired again for taking a day off sick without permission, she was "blacklisted by word-of-mouth." An informal disciplinary system worked to shame her.

Other forms of control infantilized women, as when fathers were called in to make decisions on their part or husbands determined when they worked or stopped. Hanalie left work in 1955 when she had her first child because her husband insisted that she stay home to raise her son.[51]

In some contexts, discipline was exercised in more subtle ways, as with language marking class differences. Thus, Becca, who grew up speaking Afrikaans, felt a division in the shop between English- and Afrikaans-speaking women: "It was very cliquey. They [the English speakers] didn't like you to join in with them."[52] Not all experienced the use of language as excluding, however. Johanna, working at OK Bazaars in Benoni, felt that the exercise of speaking English with customers offered her a measure of respectability: "That's where I picked [up] my English, there from the customers I had. Sometimes I'm ashamed of myself when I want to speak English and this person is English. And I don't know ... this helped me such a lot."[53] These daily measures of gender and class difference infused notions of what working meant to these women (see Skeggs 1997).

In a particularly poignant example belying the apparent status of even those older qualified women, Janice spoke of the senior women who worked the counters on the floors below her office at Anstey's in the 1950s: "As I walked through the various departments, I noticed that many of the sales assistants were quite elderly, and I realized that many of them, as it was in those days, were genteel women, not trained for any more lucrative positions."[54] These authoritative older women, with decades of experience, had limited career paths. She continued, "As an example, one dear lady with whom I chatted had a twin sister. They were both spinsters from England, who lived in a flat in the dense suburb of Hillbrow. I was shocked to see in the newspapers one weekend that the two of them had gassed themselves in their dingy flat, leaving behind their few possessions and obviously almost empty pantry." Janice found the hidden class realities surprising, a sharp sign of the difficulties of survival for many single women, which went unremarked behind the public presentation of shop work, but she also attested to the fine-grained distinctions between service and office workers in the same firm.

White women constituted retail relations on multiple levels. They sold desire and progress in commodities; they affirmed customers and white sociality in these spaces; they performed comforting femininity; they enacted workplace hierarchies; yet, they also contested some of these associations in their claims to skill, income-earning, and union action. These complicated articulations reproduced some meanings of white womanhood even as many of these women absorbed the contradictions. In the next section, we will see how changes to the sector by the 1960s began to deskill their jobs and to alter white women's experiences.

Retail Expansion, Deskilling, and Racial Reorganization

From the 1950s but especially in the 1960s, retailers expanded by opening new branches and extending and refurbishing current branches. For instance, between 1955 and 1964, OK Bazaars opened 38 new branches, revamped older stores, and purchased new sites for future development, often next to existing stores in anticipation of branch extension.[55]

Retailers' new site developments extended the numbers of branches without affecting older branches by moving outward from the centre of towns to new neighbourhood shopping districts. This trend was bound up with the extension of capital investment into property development and the planning of new suburbs beginning in the 1960s in South Africa (Beavon 2004, 179–80; Tomlinson and Larsen 2003; Mabin 2005, 48; Mabin and Smit 1997; Cook 1975, 84).

The general move for chain retailers in this period was to build even greater economies of scale: the large-scale retailers reduced profit margins on individual commodities by increasing supply and reducing the time of stock turnover, and by gaining substantial discounts through bulk buying (Lambrecht et al. 1967, v). One feature of this set of practices was the opening of the first supermarkets in South Africa in the 1950s and their proliferation in the 1960s.[56] Retailers also shifted towards self-service in the 1960s in South Africa, taking up a trend that became popular in the United States and England as well as in Australia by the late 1950s (Humphrey 1998, 63), which required "improved display facilities … which has added to capital costs," explained a sector analyst at the time (Lambrecht et al. 1967, v). These expansionary moves required substantial investment and favoured the ongoing concentration of capital in chain retail companies.[57] By 1972, according to the state's own investigation, 10% of firms in the wholesale and retail trade accounted for 77% of turnover in the sector (South Africa 1955a, 30).

These developments changed the labour process of retailing operations in two ways: they increased the professionalization of retailing management, and they exacerbated the fragmentation and deskilling of frontline service work. The increases in branch numbers and branch sizes enlarged corporate hierarchies and required a different type of retail manager. In 1963, OK Bazaars' Managing Directors noted for the first time the importance of "the Company's senior and junior executives," and extended the training programmes of these "future executive personnel."[58] This went along with building increasingly sophisticated retailing "systems": from merchandising to supply chain to display, the management of retailing gradually became a modern "science" (Bowlby 2001), and with it came male managers bestowed with abstract skills.

For the white female shop assistants, this increasing bureaucratization deskilled their work in three ways. First, self-service shopping not only reduced the immediate relationship between shop assistant and customer, a site of autonomy for many women as we saw, but also moved the emphasis to marketing, display, and merchandising, areas commanded by male managers (see Humphrey 1998, 67). Second, a range of new job classifications were added in the 1960s. For instance, branch-level personnel officers were introduced to process staff wages.[59] With the advent of supermarkets came cashiers, situated at the end of the shopping experience at separate till points. The wage determinations from this period graded counter-hands, seen as merely serving customers, lower than cashiers who carried more responsibility by taking money.[60] Now differentiated, a till supervisor managed at least six cashiers while a till controller handled fewer. Administrative systems were broken up, and separate clerking jobs were graded on the basis of minute differences.[61]

Finally, employees experienced work intensification, a point that led to large numbers of complaints by the 1960s and further downgraded the respectability of women's work. As the assistant branch secretary of the NUDW wrote to the store manager of OK Bazaars Boksburg in 1968: "Complaints were made to us that one employee is expected to handle two or three counters which means considerably more work for them, and furthermore, that such an employee must then cash up two or three tills and this means that they do not finish work until 5:45 p.m."[62] A newspaper article from 1967 reported on a high level of absenteeism among shop workers, an indication of a significant drop in morale and loyalty among workers (Smith 1967).[63]

Women workers expressed these changes in terms of declining standards and took up grievances indicating that the respectability that they relied on to sustain their work was beginning to fray. In 1962, union members complained about a lack of sick bay, tea room, and changing room facilities: "A few days ago somebody fainted and she was carried upstairs slung over a man's shoulder with her underwear showing!"[64] In another instance, women workers were aggrieved to use "chipped and cracked" cups in the staff canteen and, the union official wrote to the company, "request that these be replaced with new ones."[65] In 1975, women's lockers were seen to be too small to accommodate "an average size handbag," to which the union's branch secretary added in his appeal to the company manager, "you are no doubt aware of the trend towards the use of oversize handbags, these days."[66] By the 1960s and 1970s, thus, the union and women shop workers raised issues symbolizing changes to an order of propriety which had secured women's status. These affronts to respectability took on further signification through racial divisions.

In the late 1960s, OK Bazaars reorganized its shops to reduce the number of general workers employed. This restructuring intensified work for cashiers and sales assistants. In the 1960s and early 1970s, the union received many complaints from white women having to carry heavy stock or to clean their tills, already showing the distance from the time when Ingrid relished keeping her station clean. The women asked the union to confirm that these were the tasks of black general workers.[67] The union defended the occupational skill categories, but nevertheless recognized that the division between service and general workers was also racially coded in the eyes of its members. For instance, in 1970 the union wrote to a distressed shop workers' mother that "The Manager assured me that it is not normally necessary for white ladies to push heavy skips, and that the shop employs two Bantu for that purpose."[68] The union's white women members were angered by having to do the "manual" job not just of general workers, but also of black men. The racially stratified occupational segmentation in shop work reinforced the respectability of white women's work in a context of its declining status. The NUDW was interested in maintaining grade differences in order to retain a hold on the integrity and respectability of service work.

While white women became supervisors and line managers by rising through the ranks of shop work, many others remained ordinary shop assistants.[69] Along with deskilling, gendered hierarchies continued to operate to subordinate women regardless, more so with added layers of authority based on abstract managerial skill. In a grievance the union pursued in 1972, one experienced shop assistant was fired for being "cheeky and insubordinate" towards a new young male store manager: "It seemed to Mrs. K that the new Manager resented her superior knowledge of matters appertaining to her particular department, of which she was an expert."[70]

The increased differentiation of skills in the retail sector naturalized the gendered job hierarchy, as shown by recruitment advertisements (see Acker 1990). For instance, in 1971 an ad for managerial posts at a major food retailer solicited "responsible men" and offered "top salaries, medical aid fund, pension scheme, and opportunity for advancement,"[71] while a notice for cashier jobs "call[ed] all ladies" to apply and promised "Free Transport," "Early working hours," and a "Free hairdo each week."[72] In addition, retail wages had declined for white women relative to other sectors.[73]

Male managers continued to depreciate women shop workers as young girls. A Wits branch organizer described a worker's complaint against her manager: "Mr. Smith had called her to his office and told her that he wanted her to leave that day … He then said if she was a wise girl, she would sign [a resignation letter] and go, and if she insisted on staying, he would make her life a misery."[74] Other women complained that a manager at an East Rand OK Bazaars store was in the "habit of calling them 'stupid' and of making such remarks as 'you are falling asleep' and 'your brains are sawdust.'"[75] Some women whom I interviewed intimated at a milieu of normalized sexual harassment.

When black workers, first Indian and coloured and then African women, entered frontline labour market jobs in Rand shops in the late 1960s and 1970s, many white women workers interpreted this as a further degradation of their jobs. They remarked to the union on the "congestion caused in their canteen as a result of the non-White employees congregating there for the purpose of fetching their meals."[76] They were ruffled by the "African women employees [who] are said to be using the European canteen, to the extent that they leave their handbags there. These handbags are allegedly placed by the African women on the shelves where the cups and saucers are kept, and these cups and saucers are said to be coming into physical contact with the aforesaid handbags."[77] Members raised "Bantu employees using the same cups as whites" as a problem.[78] At one store, "The African staff have a cooking stove situated in the canteen of the White staff, hence the White employees are being disturbed by the cooking activities carried on by the Africans."[79] Handbags, tea cups, and cooking, all markers of domesticity, now became the battle line to defend class status and respectability of white women workers.

At one level, these complaints voiced grievances against the blurring of legally prescribed racial separation of facilities in workplaces. Companies had to provide separate entrances, lifts, canteens, and bathrooms for black and white employees.[80] At another level, anxieties over social space, which extended to the shop floor, masked white women's sense of loss of gendered respectability in these jobs. Many of their grievances centred on what they perceived to be infringements of an order of cleanliness, particularly threatened with their physical proximity to black women, as they began to be hired (see Swanson 1977; Burke 1996; Ally 2013; and see Douglas 1966). In this period, service work was deskilled, and white women's respectability was challenged. They reasserted it through claims to racial (and racist) difference even as articulated through gendered and class ambivalences. As a whole, these changes to the labour process portended a shifting labour market and reconfigurations in the nexus of retailing and national belonging.

The Necessary "Familiarity" of White Women's Labour

Throughout the 1960s, South Africa's economy grew at unprecedented rates and with it urban centres (Mabin 1991).[81] Retail expanded in this context. By the late 1960s and the early 1970s, a number of contradictions began to emerge, such that this period represents a moment of change in the social relations of shop work. First, consumption increasingly became a marker of status for white households. Greater access to credit encouraged white consumption, but this produced concern in the National Party, which feared that growing cosmopolitanism might undermine its specific support in a race–class alliance (Grundlingh 2008; and see Hyslop 2005, 176). Second, black women began to be hired as service workers, which destabilized the affective publics of shops. The importance of the relationship between the white public and its service workers surfaces in this moment of change.

With the growing economy, the demand for white-collar work increased during the 1960s and 1970s (Crankshaw 1997, 75). Yet, as a result of the decline in the status of shop work outlined above as well as expanded opportunities elsewhere, younger white women increasingly chose jobs in finance and the public sector. As Herd writes of the 1970s from concern for the NUDW's loss of membership, "A large proportion of the young women currently recruited by the trade in recent years have no intention of staying with it … There are others who regard employment in a shop as a useful time filler while they wait for an opening in a bank, building society or the Public Service" (Herd 1974, 234). Faced with white labour shortages, retailers began to hire black workers in service and clerical jobs (see Chap. 3). This trend was true more generally of white-collar employment and because the supply of qualified black workers had increased due to educational reforms in the 1970s (Crankshaw 1997, 76–79; Hyslop 1999). Thus, Fig. 2.1 shows the total employment in retail trade growing since the 1940s. African men, largely as general workers, along with white men and white women made up the biggest component of employment in the trade overall. From the late 1960s, however, there is a sharp increase in employment of black women, particularly African and coloured women (see Fig. 2.1).

Looking specifically at the job of shop assistant, Fig. 2.2 shows an even more dramatic increase in black women's service employment in the 1960s and 1970s along with the relative decline in white women's employment

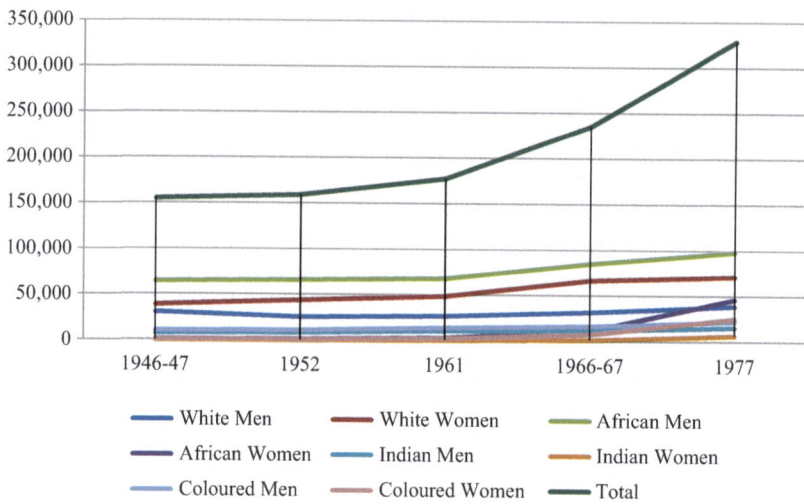

Fig. 2.1 Employment in retail trade by race and gender, 1946/47–1977. Source: Own analysis of Census of Distribution and Service Establishments (see South Africa 1952, 1960, 1967, 1973, 1981)

in these jobs. Thus, white women and men made up 70% of these frontline service jobs in 1966/67, but less than 40% by 1977. By 1977, black women (Indian, coloured, and African) surpassed white women as a total percentage in these jobs (see Fig. 2.2), continuing into the 1980s, as we will see in Chap. 3.[82]

These early signs of changes to the racial composition of the labour market provoked a call for job reservation, which would bar the employment of blacks in service and clerical work, by the ruling National Party in 1969.[83] In the case of shop assistant jobs, the National Party contended that black workers replaced white workers, received preferential hiring, worked next to white workers, served white customers, and so threatened "separate development."[84] It framed its appeal in terms of the danger posed to white women: "White girls were working alongside non-Whites – 'and they even call each other by their first names' … 'This is terrible.'"[85] The NUDW leadership opposed job reservation along with employers and Chambers of Commerce. In fact, the Ministerial investigation determined that there was no evidence that Indian or coloured workers were displacing white workers. Instead, they were being hired into positions for which

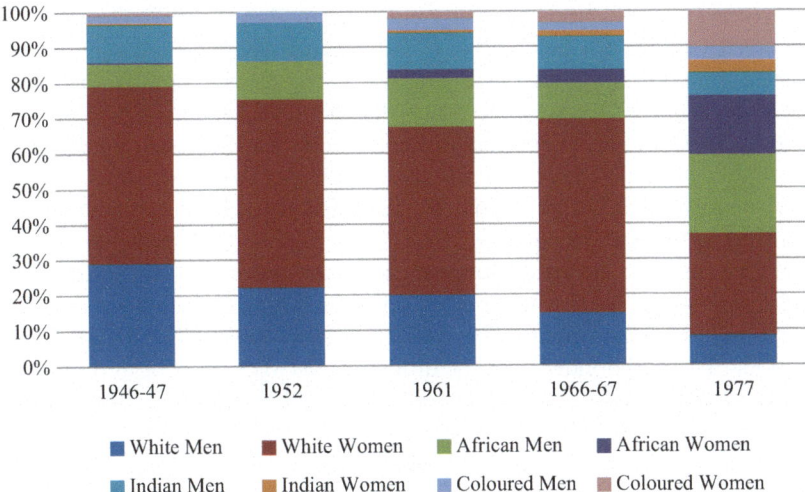

Fig. 2.2 Shop assistants in retail trade by race and gender, 1946/47–1977. Source: Own analysis of Census of Distribution and Service Establishments (South Africa 1952, 1960, 1967, 1973, 1981)

no white workers were applying. The Minister thus ruled against job reservation.[86] These anxieties resurfaced, though, in the early 1970s as some NUDW members agitated for protection from the union against replacement by African workers. Again, the NUDW's Johannesburg leadership firmly rejected such a position, but warned its executive that members "do in fact feel quite unsafe. For this reason many of the White workers are restless, and they are determined that the Government should introduce job reservation."[87]

The National Party proposed an amendment to legislation covering African workers, a clause giving the Minister of Bantu Administration and Development the power to introduce job reservation with respect to them, and to do so giving one month's notice and without requiring a hearing, as the Minister of Labour was required to convene under industrial relations law.[88] The issue used to frame this amendment in Parliamentary debate was the very complaint that "African women have been serving behind counters, have been acting as clerks and typists in offices, and that these are displacing white women" (Suzman, in South Africa 1970, 1584). The Bantu Laws Amendment Act was signed into law in March 1970, although job reservation was never properly enforced in shop work.[89] This debate occurred one month before the 1970 national election, and opposition parties argued that the National Party was trying to win votes by "protecting white women" (Suzman, in South Africa 1970, 1584).

An opposition party representative explained that the issue evoked anxiety in the ruling party precisely because, in the spaces of shops and offices, service work implied that "contact takes place at [a] level of human relationship, at the level of equality," in contrast to private homes where black domestic servants provided longstanding care work and an "intimacy" existed between "a Bantu servant" and her white household members (Suzman, in South Africa 1970, 1603; see Ally 2009; Cock 1980). The National Party responded that the difference between an African domestic servant working in one's home and a "Bantu clerk or shop worker" serving a white person was that, in a shop, relations were defined formally in employment law (Le Grange, in South Africa 1970, 1598). The state argued that white women were required to work in shops in order to preserve the integrity of the consumer market, whereas black women's presence would confound these spaces by blurring intimacies and the public. As we have seen, however, the very core of service work in the marketplace, its emotional labour (Hochschild 1983; Mills 1956), was predicated on white women's affective labour. By presenting white women as subjects in formal relations, the state actually exposed the necessity of their specific affective bond with the white public that maintained market relations and cemented cross-class racial affinity. It naturalized white women's labour in these relational spaces. Only by keeping white women in service labour, argued the National Party, would these emotive spaces of belonging be preserved.

* * *

The service work of white women directed towards a white public constituted the nation in these retail arenas. These working-class women laboured to build both these spaces of consumption and the place of the city. The shops could be what the messier city could not be – a space of white civility (and sometimes colonial cosmopolitanism), affirmed by the reassuring presence of the woman shop assistant. In so doing, white femininity became a condition of consumption in chain store retailing. Women's service work not only proffered the decorous distribution of commodities to a settler population and respectability for these white working women, but it also constituted these workplaces as sites of relationship where practices and meanings of race, class, and gender worked in and through one another to project ideas of the nation. A reification of "white womanhood" into a singular discourse obfuscates the "social relations of power that create the difference" (Bannerji 2000, 36). Instead, in its over-determination, the ambivalences and ambiguities of white women's labour itself defined belonging in shops.

Service offered by these shop assistants "made familiar" these spaces of consumption. And so, service labour was a critical lineament to apartheid relations of modernity, urbanity, and work and labour. A gendered and racialized notion of service became central to directing expanded consumption under apartheid as well as to defining labour relations. In the opening words of Ingrid du Toit, that working-class girl whose seamstress mother sewed her uniform, work was so pleasurable because it offered status through tropes of femininity, domesticating workplaces and relations with customers. Yet, as conditions changed with the expansion of retailing in South Africa's growing economy and deskilling of labour by retailers, the place of these working women shifted: their racial privilege became a starker signifier even as it belied their economic vulnerability.

When black women entered service jobs in the late 1960s and 1970s, they confronted not merely racism, but also a set of relations and meanings dependent on an experience of service carried out by obliging white women, as we will see in Chap. 3. By the late 1970s and 1980s, they became the new workforce in retailing and asserted a very different class politics.

Notes

1. Ingrid du Toit, interviewed by Bridget Kenny, Benoni, August 21, 2007.
2. See, for example, McClintock (1993, 1995), Hyslop (1995), Hofmeyr (1987), Kruger (1991), du Toit (2003), Brink (1986, 1987, 1990), du Plessis (2010, 2011), Vincent (2000), Boehmer (1992), and Walker (1995). See Hassim (2006) for a discussion of the complex relationship of the women's movement to nationalism in relation to such tropes in a later period. Tiffany Willoughby-Herard's (2015) history of the Carnegie Commission and its work tying "global whiteness" to forms of nationalism through governing white poverty and labour is also relevant, as white women were both symbols of what she calls "white vulnerability" and targets of reform (51). For a broader literature linking gender to nation, see Bannerji (2000), Yuval-Davis and Anthias (1989), and Scott (1988).

3. During the first decades of white women's employment in South Africa, general prejudices and in some sectors legal bars operated against the employment of married women (Berger 1992, 33, 56, 74–75). Partly as a result of wartime labour shortage, in the 1940s shifts in policy opened up the employment of married women (Berger 1992, 142, 178; Marks 1994, 113). But, in some sectors, such as the public service, these bars operated into the 1950s and 1960s (Walker 2001), and the attitude toward white married women working fluctuated: for instance, see Mooney (2006, 91) for a rise of concern over juvenile delinquency in the 1950s which was linked to working mothers.
4. See literature cited in endnote 2, above. That is not to say that white women did not resist this interpellation. Brink (1987), for example, discusses the class identity ("factory meide") of Afrikaner women garment workers in the 1920s and 1930s in relation to the notions of respectable motherhood. During the 1930s and 1940s, these working-class white women made claim to an alternative notion of *volksmoeder* (mother of the nation) to assert an alternate feminine respectability in worker identity (Brink 1990; Vincent 2000; also Kruger 1991; Berger 1992). I have argued (Kenny 2008) that white women shop workers' capacity to claim a class identity narrowed substantially with the National Party's victory in 1948. At issue here is how these service workers in complex ways constituted notions of nation, belonging, and respectability in retail shops.
5. Following Hall (1985, 2000), I contend that subjects are constituted through language, within social relations and through practice in time and place. This precise conjuncture involves a process of articulation which itself "fixes" meaning (Hall 1985, 93) and can only be understood in its "concrete" analysis (Hall 1985, 92). I discuss this conceptualization in more detail in Chap. 1.
6. Janice Tomlinson, interviewed by Bridget Kenny, Johannesburg, October 1, 2013.
7. It was licensed from Parker Brothers in 1963 for the South African market.
8. "East Rand Gossip," *The East Rand Express*, May 11, 1912, 29. Retailing was initially a male occupation, with shops started by immigrants (Gill 1957; Kaplan 1986). See Swaisland (1993, 61–62) for the lack of appeal of retail jobs to British immigrant women in the early twentieth century. On professional male merchants in other contexts, see Humphrey (1998, 57), Bowlby (2001), and Benson (1986).
9. Displaying goods with glass and special lighting signalled a shift to selling desire, which expanded consumption, as discussed formatively for France, Britain, and the United States (Leach 1993; Benjamin 2002; Bowlby 2001, 55–78).

10. "11/1" is 1 s.11d., approximately £0.09 in decimalized sterling. Raymond Ackerman (2001, 20), son of the founder of Ackermans and notable South African retailer in his own right, comments that the term "1/11" became slang for anything cheap. See Bowlby (2001, 80–83) for UK advertising innovations.
11. Pauline Schmidt, interviewed by Bridget Kenny, Johannesburg, March 6, 2007.
12. It should be noted that in this period small Afrikaner traders secured the exclusion of Indian merchants from white areas through the Group Areas Act of 1950 (see O'Meara 1983, 213–18; for the Group Areas Act, see Mabin 1992). South Africa did not use anti-trust legislation to promote competition, as in the United States, where an effect was to divide the national market through regional firms (Wrigley and Lowe 2002; Levinson 2011). Until 1967, the South African state supported Resale Price Maintenance, which legislated price controls on certain items, with the effect of balancing large producers, wholesalers, and retailers. The Regulation of Monopolistic Conditions Act, No. 24 of 1955, prohibited forms of uncompetitive behaviour that were seen to contribute to soaring consumer prices. The first investigation under this act was the grocery trade, and in 1958 the Minister of Economic Affairs prohibited monopolistic practices seen to be operating in the distribution of groceries, such as preferential buyer lists, price trade discounts and profit margin collusion, collective negotiations over trade discounts with suppliers, collective boycotts of non-compliant suppliers, and exclusive dealing arrangements (South Africa 1958a, b). The Steyn Commission in 1977 was a later inquiry on the high concentration in the sector. For Britain, see Shaw et al. (2000), who argue that shifts towards large, national grocery chains in the 1920s and 1930s can partly be explained by changes in competition regulation.
13. Between 1952 and 1960/61, the percentage share of total trading revenue accounted for by the 10 largest retail firms increased from 8.1 to 12.4. By 1966, the largest *five* firms made up 12.8% of the total retail turnover. OK Bazaars was the largest firm by turnover (Horvitch 1970, 43).
14. Becca van der Walt, interviewed by Bridget Kenny, Johannesburg, March 19, 2007.
15. Hanalie Erasmus, interviewed by Venessa van der Walt and Bridget Kenny, Alberton, November 22, 2007.
16. See Milanesio (2013) for working class consumers in this period in Argentina under Peron.
17. Becca van der Walt, interview.
18. Dinah Nhlabatsi, interviewed by Matlhako Mahapa, Johannesburg, January 20, 2013. Sales House was acquired by the department store Edgars in 1965. It marketed itself to black consumers.

19. Becca van der Walt, interview.
20. As early as the South African War and World War I, war brought women, particularly those on the Rand, into shop work as men went to fight. Their employment increased in the 1930s and during World War II (Gill 1957, 28; Berger 1992, 57). Household poverty also sent women out to work (Herd 1974, 21; Berger 1992, 34–35). For the general trend of white women entering wage labour during this period, see, for example, Berger (1992), Brink (1986, 23–54), Hyslop (1995, 61–62), Pollak (1932), and Vincent (2000). Indeed, the Carnegie Commission was set up in the early 1930s to report on the "Poor White problem" of proletarianizing rural whites. It was particularly interested in the phenomenon of young women entering factories to support their impoverished families (Albertyn et al. 1932; Grosskopf 1932; and on the Carnegie Commission, see Willoughby-Herard 2015). For women's entry into retailing in other places, see, for example, Benson (1986), Leach (1993), and Johnson (2007) for the United States; Humphrey (1998) for Australia; Lerner (2015, 110–25) for Germany; McBride (1978) for France; Young (1999) for Japan; Sanders (2006) for Great Britain; Randall (2008) for Soviet Russia; and Hanser (2008) for a much later period in China.
21. Maureen Williams, interviewed by Bridget Kenny, Johannesburg, March 7, 2007.
22. South African shop assistants had relatively high levels of education, possessing a minimum of Standard 6 (Grade 8) education, and often as high as Standard 8 (Grade 10) (Malherbe 1932, 105–7).
23. Ingrid du Toit, interview.
24. Johanna Coetzee, interviewed by Bridget Kenny, Benoni, May 18, 2007.
25. Becca van der Walt, interview.
26. On black distributive workers, see Hirson (1990, 93–98), Harries (1981), and Hellmann (1953). It is important to note that coloured and Indian women made up a minority of the female population on the Rand in this period, in contrast to other areas like Cape Town or Durban, where more coloured and Indian women respectively entered service employment (see Berger 1992, 34–35). For a discussion of the limits to African women's formal employment options on the Rand at this time, see Bonner (1990a), Eales (1989), Berger (1992, 58–67), and Hyslop (1995, 62).
27. Raymond Williams (1977) used the term "structure of feeling" to articulate the less-than-conscious relations structuring categories, possibilities, and limits within ordinary everyday practices to explain the ambivalences and affect underpinning inequalities, sometimes reproducing them and other times offering resources to challenge them (see also Steedman 1987).
28. Pauline Schmidt, interview.
29. Johanna Coetzee, interview.

30. Johanna Coetzee, interview.
31. Irma Du Plessis (2011) argues that the figure of the domestic worker and her "familiarity" in South African apartheid social imaginary tied the nation to the intimacy of the family. She uses the word "familiar" to invoke both senses. For the long-established relationship between family and nation, particularly with reference to Afrikaner nationalism, see also Hofmeyr (1987) and McClintock (1995).
32. Regional unions merged in December 1936, and the new national union was registered in 1937 (Herd 1974, 38–40). The NUDW was a relatively progressive union with regards to race (Berger 1992, 138; Alexander 2000, 62). However, union officials were split between the more conservative, white South African Labour Party and the "non-racial" Communist Party of South Africa. This division meant that the union reached limits on its position towards black workers, especially as the state increased restrictions over black trade union membership (see Alexander 2000; Desai 1997, 105). In areas where Indian and coloured women served as shop assistants, such as Cape Town and Durban, the union initially organized these workers within its main branch. When the NUDW was formed, the national conference endorsed a policy of parallel, "B" branches under which to organize Indian and coloured workers (Desai 1997, 105–7; Herd 1974, 92). The African Commercial and Distributive Workers Union (ACDWU) organized African warehousemen, packers, and deliverymen (Hirson 1990, 93–98; Alexander 2000, 44–45, 62, 66–67).
33. Desai (1997, 109–13).
34. "Trials and Tribulations of Selling – As our Readers See Them," *New Day*, November 1948, 14; G1; National Union of Distributive Workers (Natal Branch) Records 1937–1978 (AH1202); Historical Papers Research Archive, University of the Witwatersrand (hereafter cited as AH1202).
35. Pauline Schmidt, interview.
36. Ingrid du Toit, interview.
37. The strike lasted 17 days and involved nearly 3000 workers across the Rand and in Cape Town. It involved many women strikers, and strike leaders and government ministers had to step in (Herd 1974, 116–23, Alexander 2000, 65–68). The NUDW was joined by the ACDWU, which organized black men (Alexander 2000, 67). An earlier OK Bazaars strike in 1942, also joined by ACDWU members, won resumption of shop committees, a closed shop (which employers reneged upon afterwards), and wage increases for black distributive workers (Hirson 1990, 97, 108; Alexander 2000, 44–45; Herd 1974, 96). Led by Daniel Koza, the ACDWU was active in this time, and won gains in wages for black male workers (Alexander 2000, 44–45, 62, 66–67; Herd 1974, 102; Hirson 1990, 96–98; see also "Good News for Distributive Workers," *New Day*, October

1945, 28; G1; AH1202). However, unions organizing African workers, varying by sector, started weakening from around 1943/44 (Alexander 2000, 80–85) (see Chap. 4 for more detail).
38. Pauline Schmidt, interview.
39. Bessie White, quoted in Alexander (2000, 68). For women shop workers' unions and resistance in other contexts that combined awareness of respectability with affirmation of themselves as workers, see Frank (2001), Opler (2007), Benson (1986), Ziskind (2003), Johnson (2007), and, more broadly, Enstad (1999), Cobble (2004), and Kessler-Harris (2007).
40. Throughout the 1950s and 1960s, this multiple-company agreement was automatically extended by "gentlemen's agreement" (Herd 1974, 138).
41. See "The Distributive Trade as a Career" by Ruth Boonzaier, *New Day*, July 1949, 25; "Women's Legal Disabilities," *New Day*, September 1949, 28; "'Men Must Work and Women Must Weep' – The NUDW Says 'No!'," *New Day*, June 1949, 33; "Discrimination Against Married Women?," *New Day*, March 1949, 15; G1; AH1202.
42. The Wage Board was a statutory commission which reviewed Wage Determinations in particular sectors through a process of public hearings (see Chap. 4 for more discussion).
43. Pauline Schmidt, interview.
44. Ingrid du Toit, interview.
45. Becca van der Walt, interview.
46. Ingrid du Toit, interview.
47. Pauline Schmidt, interview.
48. Becca van der Walt, interview.
49. Becca van der Walt, interview.
50. Moira Campbell, interviewed by Bridget Kenny, Johannesburg, March 4, 2008.
51. Hanalie Erasmus, interview.
52. Becca van der Walt, interview.
53. Johanna Coetzee, interview.
54. Janice Tomlinson, interview. These quotes are taken directly from written reflections which she prepared for me for our interview. By "genteel" she means well-mannered.
55. OK Bazaars, Ltd., "Directors' Reports" in company annual reports for 1954, 1955, 1956, 1957, 1958, 1959, 1960, 1961, 1962, 1963, and 1964; F1900/P/(a)51 National Accounts, Public Companies (SAB, SES); National Archive of South Africa (NASA) (hereafter cited as NASA F1900).
56. OK Bazaars opened a supermarket in Kenilworth, Johannesburg, in 1955 (OK Bazaars, Ltd., Directors' Report in company annual report, 1955; SANA F1900). The first Pick n Pay supermarket opened in 1967 (Joyce 1981, 283). The NUDW organized "supermarket workers" in 1961 (see

"Calling Supermarket Members of C.T.C. Bazaars," 1961; Qa 3.1; National Union of Distributive Workers (Witwatersrand Branch) Records 1939–1984 (AH1601); Historical Papers Research Archive, University of the Witwatersrand (hereafter cited as AH1601)). Supermarkets were larger than conventional grocery stores, with average sales areas of 12,000–15,000 square feet (Cook 1975, 100), which reduced costs in terms of unit margins (see also Humphrey 1998).

57. At the same time, the state increased controls placed upon black township stores in 1968, adding 25 separate regulations governing these shops (Cook 1975, 126).
58. OK Bazaars, Ltd., Directors' Report in the company annual report, 1963; SANA F1900.
59. Letter from A. Fife to R. Altman, July 4, 1960; Ua 41.2.2; AH1601.
60. Letter from F. Botten to The Branch Secretary, National Union of Distributive Workers, February 13, 1964; Ua 41.2.2; AH1601.
61. Letters from M. Kagan to D. A. Smith, December 14, 1971, and May 3, 1972; Ua 41.1.2; AH1601. Letter from M. Kagan to Mrs. Van Aswegen, April 7, 1971; Ua 41.2.6; AH1601.
62. Letter from D. Hartwell to Mr. J. Mitchell, October 9, 1968; Ua 41.2.3; AH1601. See also "Minutes of Meeting of OK Bazaars Orange Grove, June 19, 1962"; Ua 41.3; AH1601. Letter from D. Hartwell to Mr. P. Chadwick, October 9, 1968; Ua 26.2a; AH1601.
63. A letter from the Wits branch secretary to the national secretary of the NUDW in 1968 reported that one branch of OK Bazaars with 677 whites on the payroll lost 647 man-days due to absenteeism during April of that year. The branch secretary wrote that "the problem is of lesser magnitude in respect of the Coloured staff and is not a problem at all in respect of African staff" (Letter from B. Robarts to R. Altman, May 29, 1968; 41.2.3; AH1601).
64. "Minutes of meeting of OK Bazaars, Orange Grove, June 19, 1962"; Ua 41.3; AH1601.
65. Letter from M. Kagan to The General Manager of Greatermans, February 25, 1971; Ua 26.2.b; AH1601.
66. Letter from M. Kagan to Mr. H. Fonn, July 3, 1975; Ua 26.2.c; AH1601.
67. Letter from M. Kagan to F. Botten, April 11, 1969; Ua 41.2.4; AH1601. Letter from M. Kagan to H. B. Kampf, July 21, 1969; Ua 41.2.4; AH1601. Letters from M. Kagan to D. A. Smith, February 4, 1972, and May 3, 1972; Ua 41.2.7; AH1601. Letter from M. Kagan to D. A. Smith, May 23, 1975; Ua 41.2.10; AH1601. Also, see Letters from D. A. Smith to M. Kagan, August 28, 1972, and August 31, 1972; Ua 41.2.6; AH1601.
68. Letter from M. Kagan to Mrs. Steyn, February 9, 1970; Ua 41.1.1; AH1601. "Bantu" refers to African workers.

69. In retail, when black women—at first Indian and coloured and later African women, as we will see later—entered service jobs in Johannesburg, they entered the same jobs that white women occupied. In manufacturing, by contrast, there was an "upward floating colour bar" when white and coloured workers moved up as African men entered semi-skilled work in the 1970s (Webster 1985; Lewis 1984).
70. "For Publication in New Day: Union Member gets her Job Back, but says, 'No Thank You'," c. 1972; Ua 41.1.3; AH1601.
71. Pick n Pay advertisement for job of manager, *The Star*, May 3, 1971, C13; Ua 43.3; AH1601.
72. Pick n Pay advertisement for job of cashier, *The Star*, November 3, 1971, B2; Ua 43.3; AH1601. Women were also offered medical aid and a pension fund.
73. Darcie Hartwell, "Counter Attack," *Personality*, March 27, 1969; Pa; AH1601.
74. Letter from B. Roberts to R. Altman, March 9, 1969; Ua 41.2.1; AH1601.
75. Letter from D. Hartwell to Mr. J. Rose, October 9, 1968; Ua 41.2.3; AH1601.
76. Letter from M. Kagan to Mr. R. Duggan, July 14, 1976; Ua 12.2.6; AH1601.
77. Letter from M. Kagan to Mr. L. May, March 17, 1971; Ua 26.2.6; AH1601.
78. Letter from M. Kagan to The Manager, June 16, 1970; Ua 43.2; AH1601.
79. Letter from M. Kagan to Mr. R. Duggan, November 20, 1975; UA 12.2.6; AH1601.
80. Separate facilities were regulated by the Shops and Offices Act.
81. South Africa's GNP grew at an average rate of 6% annually during the 1960s (Gelb 1991).
82. See also Berger (1992, 253) for the shift between white and black women in sales jobs. For the broader trend of changes in the racial and gender composition of routine white-collar employment, see Crankshaw (1997, Figs. 5.1–5.3).
83. J. R. Altman, NUDW Press Statement, May 23, 1969; Pa; AH1601. Industrial correspondent, "Shopworkers in direct appeal," *Rand Daily Mail*, June 3, 1969; Pa; AH1601. Paulette Dupree, "Inquiry into 'Mixed Serving in Shops'," *Sunday Express*, October 5, 1969; Pa; AH1601. Job reservation was legislated by section 77 of the Industrial Conciliation Act.
84. Paulette Dupree, "Inquiry into 'Mixed Serving in Shops'," *Sunday Express*, October 5, 1969; Pa; AH1601. See Letter from M. Kagan to Mr. K.B. Hartshorne, August 27, 1973; Ua 41.2.9; AH1601. NUDW Case Record C25/73, March 8, 1973; Ua 12.1; AH1601. "Questions and Answers in Parliament: Minister Denies White Workers Replaced," *New Day*, May 1970, 8; G1; AH1202. "Separate development" was the policy

of the National Party that aimed to separate the population according to race and provide "appropriate" services corresponding to their hierarchical place in society.
85. Paulette Dupree, "Inquiry into 'Mixed Serving in Shops'," *Sunday Express*, October 5, 1969; Pa; AH1601.
86. "Editorial: The Effective Rate for the Job," *New Day*, August 1970, 2–3; G1; AH1202. Industrial correspondent, "Shopworkers in direct appeal," *Rand Daily Mail*, June 3, 1969; Pa; AH1601. Express reporter, "Stores Reply: 'Not enough Whites'," *Sunday Express*, 1969; Pa; AH1601. In the mid-1970s the concerns over African workers serving white customers in public places, such as bars, were also being tested legally (E. Galli from the Witwatersrand Liquor and Catering Trade Employees' Union, "To Serve or not to Serve," August 3, 1976; Rb2; AH1601).
87. Letter from M. Kagan to Mr. A. Fife, August 10, 1970; Ua 41.2.5; AH1601.
88. Bantu Laws Amendment Bill was debated furiously in Parliament. The Bantu Labour Act, No. 67 of 1964, consolidated laws regulating the employment of African workers, and was ministered under the Department of Bantu Administration and Development rather than the Department of Labour since Africans were excluded from the definition of "employee" (see Chap. 4).
89. See Section 20A, Bantu Laws Amendment Act, No. 19, 1970, *Government Gazette*, March 6, 1970, No. 2657; Department of Bantu Administration and Development, No. R 531, Employment of Bantu in Certain Classes of Work, 1970, *Government Gazette*, April 3, 1970, No. 2679.

CHAPTER 3

Rupturing Relations: Abasebenzi as Collective Political Subject

By 1986 when a landmark strike against OK Bazaars was in full swing, black service workers had organized into their own union, the Commercial Catering and Allied Workers Union of South Africa (CCAWUSA), and had mobilized the now majority black workforce as well as black consumers in their defence. As this strike pamphlet proclaimed:

> We the 10,000 workers at over 100 OK concerns throughout the country are demanding what is rightfully ours. We've had enough of unfair dismissals, starvation wages, poor working conditions, sexist and racist behaviour. The bosses at OK refuse to listen. IT IS NOW TIME FOR ACTION.[1]

In their declarative demand, "We the 10,000 workers" asserted their collective political subjectivity in terms of a new articulation of race, class, and gender in relation to changes in retailing from the late 1960s: they were abasebenzi (workers). A 1987 play, called "Exploitation is not O.K.!," put on by OK Bazaars/Hyperama workers, dramatized the strike:

> Manager turns and walks out. Organizer goes out to [sic]. As mamager [sic] leaves, group of workers move forward and sing strongly …
>
> "*Manyanani Basebenzi*" [Unite Workers]

© The Author(s) 2018
B. Kenny, *Retail Worker Politics, Race and Consumption in South Africa*, Rethinking International Development series,
https://doi.org/10.1007/978-3-319-69551-8_3

Whilst they are singing, police come in ... shouting, swearing, demanding silence. Workers carry on singing. Policemen are shouting – in Afrikaans.[2]

The singing of "*Manyanani Basebenzi*" called on this collective abasebenzi against (white) managers and police.

In commerce, black workers, including many women, experienced the imbrication of race and class as a formative antagonism, as we will see in this chapter. They levelled a critique of their subjugation by mobilizing through a robust labour politics, one that intersected with white women's experiences and yet, ultimately, offered a very different politics.

From a membership of 1,000 in 1977, CCAWUSA grew to 5,000 in 1981, 33,000 in 1984, and more than 50,000 in 1985. When the Congress of South African Trade Unions (COSATU) was launched in 1985, CCAWUSA was the second largest union to join after that of the mineworkers (Baskin 1991, 55).[3] In 1987 Johannesburg was CCAWUSA's "oldest, largest and strongest branch" (Baskin 1991, 202). This new conjuncture of retail worker politics took hold.

As examined in this chapter, black women and men entering service jobs between the late 1960s and the 1980s engaged with management, fellow workers and the unions active in the sector. When they came to organize into their own union, they demanded access to the same conditions as their white colleagues and to the status of "employee," as we shall see in greater detail in Chap. 4. Yet these claims encompassed not only a material dimension, to some extent consistent with white women shop assistants, but also an affective content – substantive, structured feeling directing vectors of attachment, as Lauren Berlant (2011) puts it – located in the very premise of relationships in shops.

Women and men responded to trade union mobilization due to common experiences in this time and these places, but why those articulations condensed in the form that they did requires closer attention. Stuart Hall (1985, 108) explains that the "concrete lived individual" is not coincident with the ways of representing her. She is over-determined within the various relations and discourses. But attempts at struggle "to win a new set of meanings for existing terms or categories" (112) produce new collective subjects, which in turn alter languages for thinking with and through. This chapter focuses on how this new workforce became "subjects-in-struggle" (112) which in turn altered discourses and relations in South African retailing.

Workers' expressions of collective intervention were "ruptural" in that they demanded not simply better treatment, but asserted their say, contesting relations of domination and, in so doing, formulating a new collective political subject (Rancière 2010, 32–39). Through their actions and contestations, the "very existence of that subject as subject" (Davis 2010, 83) materialized and thus disrupted a set of presumptions about relations at these workplaces, in turn reinforcing this space as a "scene of relationality" (87), and as such, as shall be argued in later chapters, a site of enduring affective attachment.

Retail workers defined abasebenzi as a militant collective political subject that re-symbolized worker politics. The chapter shows that the potent signifier abasebenzi was a particular collective subject responding both to an already constituted labour process and to a realm of consumption defined through the femininity of white women. Through workers' struggles, abasebenzi came to focus on the ability to engage actively within workplace relations and to contest forms of subjugation there, which intertwined skill, gender, and race in contradictory ways in these sites.

The chapter first examines work relations during the period when Indian and coloured women entered service labour in the late 1960s and 1970s. The second section then turns to an overlapping period in the 1970s and 1980s when African women and men entered service work to detail their experiences. Finally, it investigates the late 1970s and 1980s, with the formation of CCAWUSA and the articulation of black worker politics in retailing.

BLACK WOMEN'S SERVICE WORK: DISCRIMINATORY CONDITIONS AND RACIST RELATIONS

As we saw in Chap. 2, black women and men entered higher-skilled service jobs in the late 1960s and the 1970s because demand grew as retailing expanded, fewer white women wanted to do this work, urban black secondary education meant that young blacks now met employment requirements, and the consumer market itself was becoming more diversified. And yet, as we sense from Chap. 2, those entering in this period were subjected to discrimination as their presence invoked discomfort in white workers (and the National Party).

The very transition from white to black service workers itself marked, according to commentators, a visual and gradated change by skin tone in an industry relying on the presentation of the shop worker to her public. By the 1960s on the Rand, retailers began employing Indian and coloured women. One National Union of Distributive Workers (NUDW) organizer, who later moved to CCAWUSA, explained that "job grading and colour closely interlinked. It was a gradual process of deracialization. It varied from geographical region to region, depending on demography." He continued, "The closer you got to the supervisory level, the lighter the workers became." He said that the union always alleged that certain companies deliberately chose lighter skinned workers because of an impression that they would be more palatable to customers.[4]

In 1969, a newspaper covering an inquiry into job reservation in retailing reported the Minister of Labour's opinion that the "ultimate aim" was to have "a system of each race group serving only those people of their own race." Yet alongside the article, it offered several photographs: "A typical scene at counters in department stores – non-Whites serving White customers" as well as portraits of several black shop assistants, one Indian man and two coloured women. In captions, the testimony of "Mrs. Nellie Olifant, Coloured assistant" working at a fruit juice counter at a major store was quoted: "I am accepted by customers as just another sales assistant, in spite of my race." Demurely pictured with the caption "18, a Coloured shoe assistant," Miss Valerie du Toit, too, affirmed that "Satisfied White customers ask to be served by me when they call again" (Dupree 1969). With these visual representations, this news story contradicted the Minister's claim to separate development. The very visibility of "race" signified that the transition was underway, and the efforts to represent coloured women as respectable and compliant, like their white colleagues, worked to assuage white public opinion.

Within workplaces, however, retail managements formally discriminated against these workers in ways that confirmed the logic of the existing order. For instance, as the NUDW noted in 1970, OK Bazaars "requir[ed] the Coloured employees to work the maximum hours permitted under the Wage Determination, whereas White employees in the same occupations work from 2 to 2 ½ hours per week less." The company "frequently pa[id] Coloured employees the bare minimum wages for the job, whereas Whites are mostly paid much more," the NUDW complained.[5] Coloured shop assistants were neither given a pension nor medical aid, unlike white workers.[6] In union notes entitled "Complaints lodged against Pick n Pay (White and Coloured Employees)" from around this period, the NUDW listed differences pertaining to transport when staff finished late at a suburban branch: "NOTE:-White employees are taken in the firm's van to the centre of the City, from where they must find their own way home, but Coloured employees have to take taxis from the shop."[7] To several retailers it complained that "half days off," considered to be a "fringe benefit," were granted to white shop assistants but not to coloured staff.[8] It noted John Orr's differing long-leave policies, in blunt comparison: "Whites: three months after 10 years; Coloureds: four weeks after 25–26 years."[9] The NUDW found that "In at least one instance Coloured workers wore a different colour uniform or overall but were often also made to wear caps to distinguish them even more from the Whites."[10] And it accused OK Bazaars that "large numbers of your Coloured employees had been misclassified [as general workers] in such a way that it resulted in their being underpaid."[11] Thus in multiple ways, retailers drew differences with white staff even as they came to rely more heavily on black staff for service work.

In other cases, service workers were made to do general workers' duties.[12] In 1969 and 1970, the NUDW Transvaal Regional Secretary wrote to the Personnel Director of OK Bazaars to object "to the practice of the two-tier system in regard to working conditions, as between white workers on the one hand and non-white workers on the other, in the Commercial Distributive Trade." He went on to detail several instances in which workers had reported this practice to the union. In the restaurant of one East Rand branch of OK Bazaars, he relayed, "the Coloured cook, Coloured counterhands and Coloured Cashiers are required by the local management to clean the Coloured staff cloakroom." The union official argued that this request would never have been made of white workers: "no White assistant, cashier or cook has ever been required to (nor is ever likely to be required to) clean the White staff cloakroom." The union accepted the principle that "Coloured general workers" might be called upon to clean, but objected in principle to "cashiers, counterhands, cooks and other employees of similar grades being called upon to perform such menial tasks, regardless of whether they be White or Non-White."[13]

The Personnel Director, in turn, explained that the branch had required all "Coloured female staff" to clean because they "had failed to learn how to maintain a cloakroom in spite of assistance given in cleaning it; and in order to help them learn they were put on a roster basis to assist with the cleaning." He assured the union that "the same would be done with White staff to teach them to keep their cloakroom clear," if required.[14] In a follow-up letter, he clarified that it was a matter of decorum and domesticity: "The point at issue is that all the staff using the cloakroom, which we like to think of as part of their own domestic quarters, were asked to assist in keeping it clean for themselves."[15] As Deborah Gaitskell (1990) has described for young African domestic workers being brought into domestic service in the nineteenth century in South Africa, colonial schools insisted on training women and their bodies toward proper demeanour. In 1970, the OK Bazaars manager offered coloured staff what he deemed beneficent assistance toward their personal development. These black workers were to be trained to become adept female subjects within the workplace order.

The NUDW, however, reasserted its principle of grading, in which it drew a line between occupations requiring "menial work" and those "traditionally non-menial jobs" of service work.[16] It articulated its practice to protect the integrity of the occupation. In discussions with the company, the union stressed the "effective rate for the job," aiming to maintain existing job hierarchies and prevent the undercutting of its core membership by a new workforce: if these were shop workers, they must do shop work, or they begin to pollute the job grading.[17] In mobilizing these arguments, though, the union stressed management's inherent racism: "the moment a Coloured person is engaged as a cashier, counterhand or cook, etc.[,] she is expected to do just that [perform menial tasks]."[18] It was her race that explained the duties, not her job description. Racism that structured shop floor relations projected affective attachments: from management of infantilized young women trained to feminine responsibilities, and from the union, of redressing a specific wrong within employment relations. It should be noted that by this time, to comply with labour law amendments, the NUDW had created a separate union, the National Union of Commercial and Allied Workers (NUCAW), to organize Indian and coloured workers in the sector.[19] The NUDW worked closely with NUCAW to defend this workforce, in evidence in these examples, as it represented both unions to management. In the end, the union won an acknowledgment from OK Bazaars that it was not company policy to discriminate against coloured employees.[20] Its emphasis was similar to how it operated with its white membership (Chap. 2), insisting that the company meet existing legal standards in the sector.

Nevertheless, these pervasive and readily documented examples of formal discrimination only describe one measure of the experiences of early entrants. There were also the informal means by which retail managers asserted control through race and gender. Workers complained, in particular, of various means of bullying and harassment.

Inflicting additional security measures onto black workers was a common practice. In 1969, John Orr's responded to the NUDW branch secretary that "The decision requiring Coloured staff to put their bags in the parcels room was made for security reasons and we are not prepared to vary it."[21] In 1972, a group of 27 coloured women workers from a suburban OK Bazaars complained that their tills were "checked three/four times daily ... They are being questioned by Mrs. Edelman – 'Where do you Get the money?'" The union organizer for this branch reported to her superiors, "Workers feel that they are under a constant cloud of suspicion and conditions were unpleasant."[22]

In the same year, the NUDW and NUCAW pursued a wrongful dismissal case for Mrs. Marjorie Smith, a salesperson at the Hillbrow branch of OK Bazaars who lived in Riverlea, a coloured township of Johannesburg. She had worked for the branch since 1964, advancing from counter-packer to sales and then becoming a cashier in the showroom in 1971. She reported she was respected informally as a supervisor when the section manageress left without being replaced: "[T]he staff used to come to me for permission to go to the toilet, to go for personal shopping, and so forth. Even the White staff on the first floor used to treat me as being in charge of them."[23] Nevertheless, her story disclosed a chain of events that concluded with her arrest and dismissal. In late 1971 she reported that "two African girls" came into the shop. She recognized one of them as someone she suspected of being "a regular shop lifter." She asked the customer if she needed help, and "she said: 'I don't want to buy anything in this department, go and do your work.'" Mrs. Smith continued to monitor them and, indeed, "the two girls went around 'prowling' in the showroom." The saleswoman then served the "two girls" by showing them some blouses, which they did not buy. "Suddenly," her affidavit declared, "I saw the tall girl leave" and "I found Mrs. von Molket standing and pointing a finger" at the other one. Her colleague told her that "she had caught this woman in the act of pushing a red skirt, which she showed to me, into a pocket under her own dress." Then, her colleague told the "African girl" to leave or "she would call the Manager." Mrs. Smith was met with a "dirty look" from the "African girl" who then left the shop.

But, that was not to be the end of this customer. Mrs. Smith reported that in the afternoon her manager brought the same "African girl" to her when she was busy "serving a White customer." The alleged shoplifter accused Mrs. Smith in "a most fantastic story" of giving her a bag filled with stolen merchandise to deliver to an accomplice. Mrs. Smith's manager had corroborating evidence that the "African girl" had left the OK Bazaars with a parcel of unpurchased store items. Incredulous, Mrs. Smith asked her manager to confirm the customer's story with her colleague Mrs. von Molket, but "he did not reply, he just looked at me." A few days later, Mrs. Smith was arrested for the theft. Her case took several months to come to court, during which time she was put on unpaid leave.[24] When her case came to court, she was acquitted, with her colleague Mrs. von Molket giving evidence in her defence, but the company still dismissed her. The NUDW official called it the "the worst case I have ever experienced in 25 years." He wrote that she was "the victim of a diabolical scheme by a professional shoplifter who was bent on taking revenge" on her for attempting to prevent the theft. In his letter to the OK Bazaars personnel director, the union official exclaimed his shock that she was fired instead of being rewarded for her loyalty.[25] In the end, the union only managed to get back pay to compensate her.

This story maps racial relations that existed in retail stores such as at OK Bazaars at the time. The coloured shop worker was given greater responsibility but was not promoted in line with it. Both black and white staff on the floor recognized her authority in practice, thereby affirming her professional capacity, a point which the union emphasized repeatedly in her defence. She executed her job as a dedicated employee would, acting to quell a threat from two dishonest customers, at a time when black consumers began to have a bigger presence in these stores. That the report on the incident caricatured the suspicious customers as "African girls" who "prowled" the store without buying, and glared at the shop assistant without engaging in reciprocal transference of good feeling between shopper and service worker, affirmed an ambivalence to their belonging in this space. The store manager did not bother to check Mrs. Smith's story with her (white) colleague, which also indicates the limit to white women's authority and decision-making. The manager's decisiveness was required to restore order. Mrs. Smith's case demonstrates the exposure and vulnerability that characterized the work space for black women in the early 1970s. Even with seven years of dedicated service to her company and with the union stridently objecting to her treatment, the affect shifted quickly from belonging to distrust, when Mrs. Smith was linked with the "African girls" in a paranoid story of consumer collusion.

Other kinds of hostile experiences surface in union testimony. In 1972, a group of coloured women cashiers from an OK Bazaars branch in Johannesburg held a temporary work stoppage and complained to their union about a range of issues, including several instances of bullying. One of their colleagues had been dismissed when she refused to sign a confession saying she had stolen R50, which she denied. Another colleague was given a final warning for missing work on a Monday, accused of taking "a long weekend," even though she informed management that she had attended her brother's funeral.[26] The women also "complained about a certain Mr. Odendaal, who used vulgar language." The store manager told the women that they should have raised their issues with him, even after they explained "that he was unapproachable and did not like to discuss matters with them."[27] The ambivalence of line managers toward them spurred these young women to seek out union protection.

Miss Hawa Mohamed of Lenasia, an Indian township in Johannesburg, wrote to the union in 1970 to ask if her manager at a branch of OK Bazaars, where she had been working for two years, could force her to work overtime to do stocktake on a Saturday afternoon. She had been attacked one night returning home alone from the cinema, and she feared having to travel late from work. She asked the union not to intervene to exempt her from overtime hours, but ultimately to ensure that she got her "leave pay, my reference and my unemployment card. For I don't want to go back to the OK Bazaars. I must risk my life for R1.48?" Her manager's uncompromising attitude instead led her to take her chances to find another job even though she was the "breadwinner."[28]

The issue of sexual harassment emerges as a concern throughout this period. In 1976, black staff at another retailer alleged that "the Bantu and Coloured female personnel are being stripped for the purpose of being searched without getting the permission of the employee concerned."[29] In other case notes, we learn that a white salesman and member of the NUDW had worked in the "Gents shirts" section at OK Bazaars, Eloff Street, for eight years when he was dismissed in 1972 "for allegedly having misbehaved with some of the female employees, while on duty." The union was unsuccessful in getting his dismissal overturned. When it investigated the case, it found that he had sexually harassed women colleagues and customers, in particular coloured women, and did not obey instructions. The unionist's handwritten notes list: "a strong remark (sexual)"; "last incident on Monday/Tuesday. 4 Col. Girls. Yesterday"; "A white woman is a witness"; "3rd case of breech of criminal law"; and, "He apologized for touching a woman's breast – in public." A note from 1966 recorded that he had argued, used "foul language" and "fiddl[ed] in the till." In 1971 he received a warning for swearing and threatening assault. His case culminated in "over-amorous behaviour (Col. Girls)," with the unionist's underlining emphasizing the seriousness of the charge. The mass of evidence made clear to the union that his dismissal was justified. His case suggests that his harassment of women had gone on for several years with little response by management, until his behaviour became too persistent to ignore.[30]

White female supervisors also persecuted junior employees over whom they exercised authority. At John Orr's in 1969, the union complained that a "New supervisor, Miss Wright, [was] alleged to use foul and abusive language. She is responsible for the arrangement whereby some Coloured staff eat with African men in the toilets on the roof."[31] Cynthia Petersen, residing in the "Coloured Section, Germiston," in 1972 described her uncomfortable working relations at Checkers to the branch secretary of her union: "The Managers are all friendly toward us but there is a supervisor that [is] always finding something wrong in me ... She is forever picking on me." She felt so harangued that she stayed home from work and requested the union to find her another job.[32] Rather than challenging how her supervisor treated her, like Miss Mohamed, this young woman simply decided to leave. Abusive treatment from colleagues and supervisors characterized these women's daily working relations. The articulation of race and gender explained the affective relations in these stores, in which colleagues and superiors sexualized black women (which very likely happened to white women as well) as well as directed distrust, humiliation, aggression, and their own anxiety toward them.

Even the union's organizers reported harassment from store-level managers. In one instance in 1971, the organizers of both the NUDW and NUCAW visited the same store. In a letter to the regional personnel manager of OK Bazaars, the NUDW regional secretary described an "unsavory incident" that ensued when the two organizers "happened to meet in the staff canteen," which catered for both coloured and white employees, though the tables for eating were reserved only for white employees. The NUCAW organizer "bought a colddrink [soft drink] which she drank in a standing-up position," while the NUDW organizer sat down at one of the tables. The two women "exchanged the normal pleasantries and discussed some Union business," whereupon the NUCAW organizer sat down for a short while with her white colleague "who was sitting all by herself." When she returned "to the COLOURED cloakroom, which is separated from the food canteen by a partition," the store manager exclaimed to the NUDW organizer "at the top of his voice, words to the following effect: 'Look here, if I see you with a COLOURED girl sitting at the same table again, I will not only throw her out, but I will throw you out as well.'" He shouted it so loudly that everyone in the room could hear, including the NUCAW organizer behind the partition.

Segregated cloakrooms, canteens, and rules about who could sit where represented the spatial and symbolic racial order in these workplaces. This store manager appeared frustrated with the crossing of these boundaries. While the company had an agreement for the two unions to have access to their members, the branch manager interacted with the organizers aggressively exposing the gender and racial order in which humiliation served as a form of control. In the report, the NUDW official counterposed the manager's ill decorum to "the ordinary decent human behaviour displayed" by the two organizers to each other.[33]

In these cases, the union appealed to the company manager to right the wrongs of each individual instance of discrimination as it came up, arguing that racism was preventing an order premised on recognition and civility from operating. While it served individual workers, its ameliorative orientation maintained the chain of authority – with the regional secretary writing to the company director to request his intervention. The effect was to insist on the equal treatment of Indian and coloured workers within the existing structural hierarchy. In the next period, however, from the mid- to late 1970s and in the 1980s, black women and men in service and clerical work, including a majority of African workers, would take a different approach to deal with poor conditions and racism, and the independent union CCAWUSA would organize to defend them. The next section examines the rupture effected by these workers' politics. Black workers organized collectively to insist on their substantive participation within these workplaces.

Refusing Erasure, Rupturing the Logic of Relations: Abasebenzi Emerge

Amos Tshabalala worked in Hyperama, a subsidiary of OK Bazaars, from its opening in 1976. At this point most Africans were shelf packers and cleaners, with a small number doing clerical work in the receiving sections and the buying departments. A few black [African] ... females received token promotions in the cash department, although the promotion did not affect their salaries. A few blacks [Africans] were promoted to positions of supervisors, although they could not supervise white workers.[34]

Masoka Makeketlane was appointed to a position in the customer service department of a suburban Woolworths branch in 1978 when she was 20 because the company thought she was coloured. She described the tiered racialized hierarchy:

> It was whites at the top and they were mostly students as well. Preferences w[ere] whites, coloureds, Indians and then blacks [Africans] were the last ... Packers were black [African]. In the butchery, it was blacks [Africans]. And in the storeroom it was blacks [Africans]. Because obviously it's hard labour, they've got to pick up things. Hard labour was meant for blacks [Africans]. At customer service they preferred coloureds, Indians or whites. And then obviously cleaners were black [African].[35]

Tembi Motlhamme worked alongside white women in the administration office of a Shoprite branch in the early 1980s. When African workers began to enter clerical jobs, "maybe the white ladies would be supervisors ... but the blacks [Africans] ... maybe you would be the line supervisor ... You were very fortunate if you were working in the office as a black [African]."[36] Black workers repeatedly described these divisions, which were a definitive marker of working relationships in the retail sector. It was a racially marked hierarchy, with "manual" hard work considered the lowest level work and associated with African workers. It also corresponded to pay differentials, as reported in a survey of female retail sector workers published in 1982: white women earned on average R80 per month more than coloured women and R120 per month more than African women (van der Walt 1982, 35).[37]

The affective relations crisscrossing these hierarchies involved distrust and suspicion. Amos described that "Generally management, which was ... 100% white, treated black [African] employees with contempt and mistrust, which was standard practice."[38] As a customer service worker, Masoka experienced difficulties with the white upper middle-class consumers at her branch: "So you found that the attitudes of the white customers towards the black [African] servers, it was like they didn't trust you in whatever you were doing. They wouldn't prefer to be served by a black [African] and in most cases they'd always, whenever you try to assist them, they'd always demand to see the manager ... You know that when you approach [them,] the manager is going to be involved in one way or another."[39]

As more African workers were hired, managers tried to keep them individualized. This happened, for example, when offering pay increases, as described by Mary Nkosi who began working as a cleaner in the warehouse at Hyperama in 1981:

> I earned 154 [Rands per month]. That was the basic salary for everybody who was new. In June, [management] called us in individually to tell us that we will get R20 or R40, between 20 and 40. We were told not to tell others what increase we got [laughs]. Whites were heartless [*bebekhohlagele abelungu*] because there were no unions during that time.[40]

This sense of manipulation and victimization was pervasive. Workers emphasized the relational implications of this harsh treatment: *bebekhohlagele* indicates "evil" and heartless behaviour, having no feeling, or being "corrupt" – in other words not engaged with workers in any kind of reciprocal relationship. Tembi explained that workers' grievances mainly focused on wages and conditions of employment, but that these material demands were entwined within a regularized set of relations in which managers engaged with staff punitively and personally. One key early grievance of women was treatment when female workers became pregnant. Often, Tembi explained, women had to leave to have a child without any guaranteed job security: "Sometimes they'll tell you that the company didn't decide for you to be pregnant. It's you who decided to be pregnant."[41] In the 1980s, Thandile Ziyane explained, women's main grievance was "victimization, managers who are rude. They fired without reason."[42]

Coloured and Indian workers could join the parallel union NUCAW, but African workers did not have a union until 1975, as we will see in the next section, and once established did not achieve union recognition by many retailers until the early 1980s. Thus, in the late 1970s and early 1980s, African workers were particularly exposed to discrimination.[43] Shop work meant carefully negotiating one's daily tasks while challenging relationships with managers, supervisors, and customers on hostile terrain.

CCAWUSA AND COLLECTIVE LABOUR POLITICS

CCAWUSA was initiated by the NUDW in 1975 in order to organize African workers. Its first branches were in Johannesburg and on the East Rand. The legendary Emma Mashinini became the first organizer and president of the union. Though not a shop worker, she was recruited and trained by Morris Kagan, the NUDW regional secretary, because of her reputation as a unionist.[44] The NUDW rented offices for CCAWUSA and provided start-up money and office furniture (Mashinini 1991, 32).

Following NUDW's lead, Mashinini focused initially on recruiting members and on obtaining audiences with retail management in order to facilitate access to shops. CCAWUSA's first member worked at OK Bazaars. In 1977, Checkers in Benoni went on strike over an unfair dismissal and workers came to the downtown Johannesburg CCAWUSA offices for assistance. Mashinini (1991, 36) marks this as the first real victory for the union in negotiating on behalf of the workers. The first (informal) recognition of the union was in the same year with Pick n Pay (37).

CCAWUSA focused on organizing the large chain stores, and it used some of NUDW's tactics, such as comparing actual conditions to minimum standards provided in the wage determinations. A union official remembered how this technique worked differently in the late 1970s and early 1980s to organize black workers. He said, "I came in at an interesting time. I just caught the darkest days of apartheid at their most impressive worst on the retail shop floor. Class barriers were definitely drawn. It was a white working class shop floor and white bourgeois management. These lines were clearly drawn." He explained that the unions used wage determinations to compare conditions to stipulated minimums across grades and across race: "It was effective. There was little compliance [by employers] ... I could also use non-racialism around wage rates and grading as an organizing tool. The unions' main focus was not minimum rates of pay, but what black workers' actual wages were. African workers would be at the minimum, and Coloured/Indian workers above the minimum for their grading."[45]

On the Rand, many African workers joined CCAWUSA, as did some coloured and Indian workers; effective in mobilizing workers, the union used basic conditions as a means to raise deeper issues about the fundamentally unequal relations within shops. In a 1982 interview, CCAWUSA's president Issac Padi explained that the union was attractive to workers because

The treatment [of] workers was not so good. Management had a tendency to terminate staff for no apparent reason ... In some cases, a manageress would phone the area manager to complain about one of the staff, and the area manager would readily say, "Kick her out." [They] wouldn't even bother to come and find out from the person concerned, what the cause was ... or is it true what the manager claims ... People can't be treated like this. There must always be a reason at least. Tomorrow I'll be the victim.[46]

It was against this form of arbitrary and despotic treatment that workers organized (see also von Holdt 2003). The refusal to be cast as having no voice or capacity to engage in itself provoked workers' resistance.

In Johannesburg, and in what was called the Wits region, this politics was particularly inflected through an active consciousness of the interpenetration of race and class in black workers' lived experiences. Many black workers entering the retail sector at this time were young, recently out of high school and urban based; and many were women. Like their white female predecessors, they met the level of education required in the sector, so that most had Standard 8 (Grade 10) education, had a basic maths competency, and spoke English. They were a unique segment of black working-class people. As discussed in Chap. 2, educational reforms to black secondary schooling increased the available labour supply for white-collar employment (Crankshaw 1997, 79), but relative to the rest of the working class, the number of those achieving this level of education was small. In 1985, only 8.1% of the African population had a Standard 8–10 level of education (80, Table 5.4).[47] In contrast to shop workers, for instance, young metal workers on the East Rand at this time often left school earlier to get jobs (Sitas 1983, 330). This generation of service workers were the children of parents who had moved to Johannesburg and nearby towns in the 1940s and 1950s looking for work in the Rand's expanding manufacturing economy.

Like young white women in the 1930s and 1940s, black women and men entering retailing in the 1970s and 1980s came out of school to work for their families, but at a time when economic growth was slowing and, of course, with apartheid barriers to job and housing access. Mary left school in 1977 after completing Standard 7 (Grade 9) because her family lacked resources, despite the fact that her father had a steady job as a municipal worker for an East Rand local council: "I went to look for a job as the situation was not good." She got her first job in a Boksburg shop, and her second as a full-time employee at an East Rand Hyperama in 1981 when she was 18, after having taken time off to have a baby.[48] Vuyiswa Xaba, too, left school due to economic necessity; her mother was the sole breadwinner in her family after their father left them. Leaving school after Standard 8 (Grade 10) in 1975, she took a job at a factory for five years but left because "the money was too little." She then found a job as a sales assistant in 1981, when she was 24 years old.[49] Buhle Bhengu left school in 1984 when she was 20 years old, after completing Standard 8 (Grade 10), to help her mother and older sisters provide for their household after the death of her father. She said, "We did not leave school because we liked, it was poverty."[50] These stories were common among those who began working in the 1970s and 1980s.

Still other young people entered the labour market after the birth of a child, often cared for in their parents' households. In this generation of retail workers, the birth of a child drove them into work, rather than out of work as was the case for white women in previous decades. As Zama Ntuli said, "It was just because of the situation. I was interested [in returning to school] but the problem was money."[51] She left school in 1986 when she was 16. With the expenses involved with having a child, she could not afford school. Thabang Moloka also left school in 1985, at the age of 23, because of the birth of a child. He had completed Standard 9 (Grade 11), but when his girlfriend fell pregnant, he needed to "take responsibility. So I said, it's better I go and look for a job."[52] Compelled to find work, black retail workers in the 1970s and 1980s then entered shop work.

In Johannesburg and surrounds, this generation of African service workers was part of the 1976 student movement, and many had been exposed to the Black Consciousness Movement (see Hirson 1979). Prior political experiences and the memories and burdens of parents and families informed their encounters in the workplace. Tembi, who grew up in Tembisa on the East Rand, described how her experience of student politics later directed her to the union:

> I was very strong [in the union] because I knew from the school that to fight for something that you want, you'll get it ... Because during the march of June 16 [of the Soweto student uprising] ... on the 17th we gathered in Tembisa High, and then we started marching from there, township burnings ... everything was burned down during that year ... You know, we were called by a very young boy, young guy, and he was killed ... He just gathered everybody in the ground[s] and said, "Today, we are not going to the

classes, but instead, we are going to march." And we were strong; we were marching on the police. The police were going on that side, parallel, and we were on this side, but we were not scared, instead we were shouting at them ... [From this experience] I had that courage to join the union.[53]

They had participated in political action and had been part of a cohort debating what it meant to be black and working class in South Africa. As one CCAWUSA organizer and worker leader in the Wits region explained,

> [W]e were lucky because most of our members were in urban communities. They had matric. They were forced to work because they did not have an option to go to university. I never dreamt of going to university. My father and mother worked to get me to matric, and I was grateful. Most of our members were forced to work. Essentially they were people with ambitions of a better life; they were literate; they were current with the news. And the BC [Black Consciousness] movement was strong. There was a political consciousness ... When you close people out, you make them want to come in and they organize themselves to come in.[54]

The young women and men of the late 1970s and 1980s rejected a mode of relating in which blacks were assumed to fit at the bottom of an order of domination. They experienced and consciously spoke of this subjection through the imbrication of race and class. These young people understood their experience as common, claimed it as collective, and refused to abide by the "consensus" (Rancière 2010) of apartheid, thereby showing up the order as arbitrary and contingent. White women often experienced low pay and degrading conditions at work, responded to their union and sometimes identified collectively. Black workers, however, linked workplace conditions to wider political exclusions and degradations (see Seidman 1994), regardless of their political orientations. In Tembi's tale, the students marching parallel to the police is a powerful metaphor of their confrontation with being "hailed" into predominating positionings (Hall 2000; Althusser 1971). Theirs was a political struggle that ruptured workplace relations, and it did so by disputing their naming, positioning, and participation within the relational order.

CCAWUSA was independent of the major federations at the start. In particular, it did not align to the non-racial Federation of South African Trade Unions (FOSATU) primarily because of strong political divisions across branches. It was loosely associated with the Pan Africanist Council of Unions of South Africa (CUSA) until it helped to form COSATU in 1985. In the

1970s and 1980s, its regions acted fairly autonomously politically, displaying the full spectrum of political positions during this time. Thus, while some regions organized from the Congress tradition, others like the Wits region and Johannesburg were aligned to left socialist and Pan Africanist groupings. These (opposing) political traditions would be negotiated in what became known as the "unity talks" to form COSATU, but they also served to add to the political fervour of the time.

In Johannesburg, the union consciously organized its membership as "black workers." Thus, in her memoire Mashinini (1991, 33) described the broader context of the period after 1973:

> There were other black trade unions that were being set up at that time. Every union was busy getting on its feet, and although their focus wasn't on the particular industry we were representing, at least it was on other problems that we shared, like legislation or recognition. That was very helpful and good – to work as black unions together, not just with [NUDW] which was registered and recognised. Even when we worked with unions belonging to FOSATU, for example, we weren't tempted to federate with them because the FOSATU leadership was dominated by white intellectuals, and although we valued the support of its unions we did not want to be swallowed up by their way of thinking.

Mashinini (1991, 39) argued that she defended the separate mobilization of African workers when the NUDW and NUCAW proposed merging with CCAWUSA in the wake of labour law reforms after 1979[55]:

> Our problems were very different from the problems of those white and Coloured workers, and this was vital to us as a group, to keep together in order to tackle injustice. We felt this in 1979 when the chance came to join with NUDW and NUCAW. They could not have included us before and stayed registered, but when the law changed they began to tell us they wanted to form a single union … It is hard for black workers in South Africa to identify with other workers' problems. Other workers are seen as human beings, and the black workers are seen as underdogs.

While CCAWUSA actually allowed coloured and Indian workers to join, her quote suggests the nature of debate at the time. The context of union organizing more broadly in South Africa, with new formations emerging and with debates specifically about race and class, influenced workers' activism (Buhlungu 2006; Sitas 1983). Like other contexts where workers organized under conditions of rapid industrialization, authoritarian states, and exclusion from political participation, black workers in South Africa merged workplace activism with political organizing (Seidman 1994). Still, it was relatively unusual for commercial workers to be part of this groundswell in other contexts. Born from a tradition of occupational unionism (Cobble 1991), similar to retail workers in the United States, Britain, and Australia, retail worker politics for white workers resembled organizing in those contexts. But, when the new black workforce confronted the conditions of its own exclusions, they broke from this trajectory. Retail workers in South Africa in the 1970s and 1980s claimed a specific political subjecthood, as a collective within relationships in workplaces, based on a strong sense of solidarity and common experience. As a Johannesburg branch official recalled, "For us the struggle for national liberation coupled with this struggle for bread and butter issues … The union was actually giving them some sense of belonging to a group of people with common problems; one that was doing something."[56]

Mobilizing shop floor-level organization, which countered NUDW's practice by this time of officials representing workers, CCAWUSA built a network of active shop stewards. These structures fed into company councils that "assisted in organizing because workers were able to talk to workers. It accelerated unionization and organization."[57] According to Vivian Mtwa, organizer and Mashinini's successor as CCAWUSA General Secretary, retail workers were particularly capable of engaging in debate and in strategizing because of their higher education levels, making them less reliant on officials (Mtwa, quoted in Forrest 2005, 48). This was born out in the 1986/1987 OK Bazaars strike when shop stewards stepped forward to carry the strike after CCAWUSA officials were detained by the state (Forrest 2005; Bonnin and Hurt 1987).

In an interview conducted in 1982, Mongezi Radebe, at the time a CCAWUSA organizer on the Vaal and an African National Congress (ANC) supporter, explained how he engaged with branch-level managers in smaller towns, in this case Sasolburg:

> I never talk Afrikaans in spite of the fact that I'm good in it … Once you start talking in their language, their superiority complex becomes worse. It's as if you are their subject. They become very authoritative … But the moment you don't talk their language, it's as if their pride falls … They feel threatened, despised … It keeps them in check all the time. Some are not even very clear in English. We are equal in the language … His nervousness

will help lower his superiority complex … Sometimes I do allow them to talk Afrikaans if they cannot express themselves in English. But I'll answer back in English for the sake of keeping their complex at a reasonable level.[58]

Thus, organizers and workers displayed a level of confidence of their abilities and a clear sense of the symbolism of employing their knowledge within public arenas.

The NUDW organized to secure occupational status, as we saw in Chap. 2. Because general workers in retailing were historically black men and in the 1940s members of a different union, the workforces of distributive and service workers had been segmented in practice. The NUDW and NUCAW signed up and represented (white, coloured, and Indian) individuals from these job grades, but it was not until CCAWUSA that this group of workers was brought en masse into a union again with shop assistants. They proved to be a militant vein of membership, particularly when united with service workers. In 1982, for instance, a strike by warehouse workers and service workers achieved a recognition agreement with OK Bazaars (Bonnin and Hurt 1987). Thus CCAWUSA bridged the divide between general workers and service and clerical workers.

Finally, the union also made major advances on issues important to women workers. The first maternity rights agreement in South Africa was brokered at OK Bazaars in 1983 (Bonnin and Hurt 1987; Appolis 1998; Tshoaedi 2012). It was a landmark agreement that allowed one year unpaid leave and, crucially, job security for the woman returning to work. Given the pressures on women to provide for families, the issue of job protection was fundamental and mobilized still more workers to join the union (Photo 3.1).

By the mid-1980s, black workers felt their union protected them. Tembi said she felt more secure than many of the white women with whom she worked because they "would take instructions from the managers. They were like … puppets."[59] She was a supervisor and could join CCAWUSA, but the white women supervisors were torn between their own declining conditions and their status affirmed through affective ties with managers. Tembi argued that CCAWUSA offered her solidarity to counter divisions of occupational stratification. As a supervisor and a higher status clerical worker, she felt her interests rested with other black shop floor workers.

Workers rejected the racial hierarchy in stores, which posited authority in white managers. As one worker stated clearly in 1982, "I've joined the

Photo 3.1 Women workers meeting during Edgars strike, 1985 (Image by Paul Weinberg/South Photographs/Africa Media Online)

union because I saw it suits [me] to join the union. I'm one person who can't take unlawful accusations ... They accuse you of intending to go and steal that thing ... We had such hassles, and I'm one person who can't say 'yes' to everything."[60] This dialogic assertion was definitive of workers' resistance. Being subjected to abuse often brought workers into the union. Makhulu Ledwaba, who would become president of CCAWUSA in 1984, started working for Metro Cash & Carry as a filing clerk in 1981. He became involved in CCAWUSA when he assaulted a white worker who was "racially abusive" to him and he required legal protection. After his own case was finalized, he began to organize Metro workers (Baskin 1991, 63). The response to an egregious act, often through a collective call to public action, was critical to the constitution of workers' political subjectivity.

Amos, the shop steward in Hyperama cited above, described the union actions of retail sector workers in the 1980s (Photo 3.2):

> At that time we were already involved in civic matters and underground activities which politicized some of us greatly. We began to take this

Photo 3.2 OK Bazaars strike, 1986/87 (Image in personal collection of Kally Forrest (photographer unknown))

politicization onto the shop floors … Our pickets were very militant in front of the store and sometimes turned violent against … scab labourers … Indirect intimidation also took place at the homes of the counter-revolutionaries. We also donated and collected donations to support struggling strikers and their families in [the] form of food packages and small sum[s] of monies for travelling and edibles. There was huge support for the [1986/87 OK Bazaars] strike by workers.[61]

These markers of solidarity defined rules of participation and regulated relations among workers. Common experiences protected workers at stores. As Masilo, a CCAWUSA shop steward, explained in 1982,

> While I was alone I was always ... now and then threatened about being chased away, inciting other workers, and all that ... I was not safeguarded at work ... I decided to join and organize the workers ... Because it is not easy for the company, just to say to 50 people, "just get out like that."[62]

By the 1970s and 1980s, the consumer public had also begun to change. In the 1960s and 1970s, the Rand's black population had become an increasingly stable urban working class employed by a growing manufacturing industry (Bonner 1995; Hindson 1987). Its standard of living began to improve and African families began to shop in city-centre retail outlets. Retailers noted the growing importance of the "African market" (Lambrecht et al. 1967, vi–vii) and saw an increasing need to hire African front-line workers to service these new customers (Martins 1988; Crankshaw 1997, 82). By the early 1970s, 42% of African trade in groceries was spent in central business districts, primarily in chain stores (Cook 1975, 124). The consumer market was becoming more diversified on the Rand.

This changing consumer base provided another layer of support for workers who organized in these stores. In Johannesburg, black residents experienced consumption in these stores not as a leisurely activity as did white customers, but as an uncomfortable engagement. Being served by white cashiers, as was still often the case, could be an intimidating experience, as one shopper said of those days: "But there was that thing with white people, you know, they don't have time. So you would go there, you pay and you go. That's why sometimes people would even find it difficult if the thing were expired or not fresh. People would even be reluctant to take it back just to explain that this was not right."[63] Consumers readily supported boycotts of stores when workers called on them. The nation of retail shops maintained through white women's labour (see Chap. 2) had been disrupted by the mid-1980s.

* * *

The OK Bazaars strike, with which this chapter opened, began in December 1986 and spilled over into 1987. It was the largest retail strike in South

Africa that had happened up to that point. It was also one of the largest national strikes of the period; it was supported by a consumer boycott of OK Bazaars and a solidarity strike in several suppliers. CCAWUSA argued that "the Directors of OK are paid high salaries. Workers should not be victimized and the gap between salaries of management and that of workers should be lessened."[64] In the context of a state of emergency, strikers were arrested and charged with violence and intimidation and union leaders were detained. After more than ten weeks,[65] the union won a record across-the-board increase and the reinstatement of many dismissed workers (Baskin 1991, 169–71).

By the time of this strike, black retail workers' political subjectivity defined lines of solidarity. When asked what the most important actions of the 1980s had been, Tembi identified the OK Bazaars strike, even though she worked at a different retailer: "It was in OK, 1987 …We had to support them. We had to support them as an injury to one is an injury to all … The stay-aways had an impact … Everybody is at home. Sometimes the store will close. The solidarity was part of the experience of being a worker then."[66]

The workers in the play performing the OK Bazaars strike at the start of the chapter sung "*Manyanani Basebenzi* [Unite Workers]." The stage direction described, "Whilst they are singing, police come in … shouting, swearing, demanding silence." And then, very simply, "Workers carry on singing."[67] This political subjectivity, defined by the unifying symbol abasebenzi, and enacted by workers and by CCAWUSA in the 1970s and 1980s, was underpinned by several defining features. First, it was collective in nature and acted against the individualizing and denigrating practices of white management and in relation to NUDW (and NUCAW) traditions of protecting workers through individual cases to meet minimum standards in the sector. Second, workers rejected an association of blackness with unskilled labour, instead building "subjects-in-struggle" (Hall 1985, 112) out of a common experience of relationality in shops. Finally, black workers contested unequal relations in shops by identifying themselves as speaking and acting subjects against the order imposed by white managers and constituted out of the associations of white women's labour. Defying managers' rules, workers countered with their own logic. In Jacques Rancière's (2010) terms, this moment was "ruptural." The collective political subject of black retail workers fundamentally contested relations within shops and modes of participation therein.

Notes

1. OK Strike Bulletin 1, p. 1, hand dated December 20, 1986; 21.4; Congress of South African Trade Unions (COSATU) Papers, 1984–1997 (AH2373); Historical Papers Research Archive, University of the Witwatersrand (hereafter cited as AH2373).
2. CCAWUSA News, Vol. 1, No. 11, July 1987, p. 8; M5.3; Original SAHA Collection (AL2457); South African History Archive (SAHA) (hereafter cited as AL2457).
3. After various unions merged to create one union per industry, CCAWUSA became the fourth largest union after the National Union of Mineworkers (NUM), the National Union of Metalworkers of South Africa (NUMSA), and the Food and Allied Workers Union (FAWU). CCAWUSA's membership subsequently grew to 56,000 by the 1987 COSATU national congress (from 50,345 at COSATU's launch in 1985) due to its own mergers (Baskin 1991, 213).
4. Jeremy Daphne, national organizer and negotiator for CCAWUSA and SACCAWU, interviewed by Bridget Kenny, Johannesburg, August 15, 2001. Msokoli Qotoli told me similar stories of stores in Cape Town (personal communication, September 29, 1999).
5. Letter from M. Kagan to Mr. A.H. Fife, August 3, 1970; Ua 41.2.5; National Union of Distributive Workers (Witwatersrand Branch) Records 1939–1984 (AH1601); Historical Papers Research Archive, University of the Witwatersrand (hereafter cited as AH1601).
6. "Effective Rate for the Job Urged," *New Day*, July 1970, 6–7; G1; National Union of Distributive Workers (Natal Branch) Records 1937–1978 (AH1202); Historical Papers Research Archive, University of the Witwatersrand (hereafter cited as AH1202).
7. "Complaints Lodged against Pick n Pay (White and Coloured Employees)," n.d., estimated late 1960s; Ua 43.3; AH1601.
8. Letter from M. Kagan to Mr. A.H. Fife August 3, 1970; Ua 41.2.5; AH1601. See also "John Orr & Co. (TVL) Ltd.: Matters requiring further attention," September 23, 1969; Ua 32.2; AH1601.
9. "John Orr & Co. (TVL) Ltd.: Matters requiring further attention," September 23, 1969; Ua 32.2; AH1601.
10. "Effective Rate for the Job Urged," *New Day*, July 1970, 6–7; G1; AH1202.
11. Letter from M. Kagan to Mr. A.H. Fife, August 3, 1970; Ua 41.2.5; AH1601.
12. "John Orr & Co. (TVL) Ltd.: Matters requiring further attention," September 23, 1969; Ua 32.2; AH1601.

13. Letter from M. Kagan to Mr. A.H. Fife, March 31, 1970; Ua 41.2.5; AH1601.
14. Letter from A.H. Fife to Mr. M. Kagan, May 18, 1970; Ua 41.2.5; AH1601.
15. Letter from A.H. Fife to Mr. M. Kagan, August 4, 1970; Ua 41.2.5; AH1601.
16. Letter from M. Kagan to Mr. A.H. Fife, August 3, 1970; Ua 41.2.5; AH1601.
17. "Effective Rate for the Job Urged," *New Day*, July 1970, 6–7, G1; AH1202.
18. Letter from M. Kagan to Mr. A.H. Fife August 3, 1970; Ua 41.2.5; AH1601.
19. The NUDW maintained a position that supported organizing black workers throughout its existence and had at various time Indian and coloured members varying by region. In 1956, when industrial relations law was amended (see Chap. 4) to require coloured members to either leave registered unions or to separate out into parallel "B" branches, which had to be led by white officials and which could not meet with white branches or members, it was forced to create B branches in all regions. In 1966, with the support of the NUDW, the Cape Town B branch split to found its own union, NUCAW, to represent coloured and Indian shop workers. It organized other cities and continued to work with NUDW (Herd 1974, 212–19). See also Letter from J.R. Altman to Mr. L. Miller, June 20, 1966; Ua 41.2.2; AH1601. After Wiehahn labour law reforms, NUDW and NUCAW reunited into the National Union of Distributive and Allied Workers (NUDAW). As discussed below, NUDW started CCAWUSA in 1975 to organize African workers.
20. Letter from M. Kagan to Mr. A.H. Fife, August 10, 1970; Ua 41.2.5; AH1601.
21. Letter from H.E. Gover to The Branch Secretary, National Union of Distributive Workers, October 30, 1969; Ua 32.2; AH1601.
22. "OK Orange Grove, Temporary Work Stoppage," by Z. Farrah, May 15, 1972; Ua 41.7; AH1601.
23. Affidavit signed by M. Smith, May 22, 1972; Ua 41.1.3; AH1601.
24. Affidavit signed by M. Smith, May 22, 1972; Ua 41.1.3; AH1601.
25. Letter from M. Kagan to Mr. A.H. Fife, May 23, 1972; Ua 41.1.3; AH1601.
26. "OK Orange Grove, Temporary Work Stoppage," by Z. Farrah, May 15 1972; Ua 41.7; AH1601.
27. "OK Orange Grove, Temporary Work Stoppage," by Z. Farrah, May 15, 1972; Ua 41.7; AH1601.

28. Letter from Miss Hawa Mohamed to "Dear Sir/Madam," May 2, 1970; Ua 41.2.5; AH1601.
29. Letter from M. Kagan to Mr. J. Usher, January 30, 1976; Ua 12.2.6; AH1601.
30. Case Record, Office Ref C54/72. Date of interview August 3, 1972; Ua 41.1.3; AH1601.
31. "John Orr & Co. (TVL) Ltd.: Matters requiring further attention," September 23, 1969; Ua 32.2; AH1601.
32. Letter from Cynthia Petersen to Miss D.M. Hartwell, August 23, 1972; Ua 12.2.5; AH1601.
33. Letter from M. Kagan to Mr. E. Lawrence, February 16, 1971; Ua 41.2.6; AH1601.
34. Amos Tshabalala, former shop steward, interviewed by Bridget Kenny by telephone, Tembisa, August 11, 2000.
35. Masoka Makeketlane, interviewed by Fatima Mathivha, Johannesburg, August 30, 2014.
36. Tembi Motlhamme, interviewed by Bridget Kenny, Germiston, May 16, 2007.
37. African workers in OK Bazaars in 1978 were earning less than R200 per month (Mashinini 1991, 38).
38. Amos Tshabalala, interview.
39. Masoka Makeketlane, interview.
40. Mary Nkosi refers to the organization of African workers into trade unions. Her comment refers to the early 1980s when CCAWUSA was organizing stores but did not yet have a presence everywhere (Mary Nkosi, interviewed by Bridget Kenny, Daveyton, August 26 and December 3, 1999, and September 7, 2000). Another worker described this practice: "They used to call it 'Don't tell the others'" (Sara Dlamini, interviewed by Bridget Kenny, Soweto, June 19, 1999).
41. Tembi Motlhamme, interview.
42. Thandile Ziyane, interviewed by Bridget Kenny, Daveyton, February 22, 2000. The "apartheid workplace regime," as von Holdt (2003) has called it in the context of the manufacturing sector, operated through despotic authority vested in white managers who maintained it through frequent dismissals, the threat of violence and fear, and arbitrary procedure (and reinforced by state regulation).
43. In retailing, companies introduced liaison committees, in line with the existing apartheid law in the period. African workers could not belong to a recognized union in the 1970s. But the Bantu Laws Amendment Act enabled works committees to be set up in branches to serve as communications forums. The NUDW did not oppose these liaison committees, but argued that African workers needed to be included within a single industrial

relations system and thus to be allowed to join unions that could bargain on their behalf (National Union of Distributive Workers (NUDW) Head Office Circular No. 33/BN/77, Memorandom to Wiehahn Commission, October 28, 1977; 97; Part IV; Karis-Gerhart Collection of South African Political Materials, 1964–1990 (A2675); Historical Papers Research Archive, University of the Witwatersrand.)

44. Emma Mashinini (1991, 24–25) worked as a garment worker as a young woman and then for the Garment Workers Union, in 1962 becoming elected to the national executive of the merged National Union of Clothing Workers, where she served for 12 years.
45. Jeremy Daphne, interview.
46. Isaac Padi, president of CCAWUSA, interviewed by Jeremy Baskin, April 17, 1982; C2; Jeremy Baskin Papers 1982–1988 (AH2920); Historical Papers Research Archive, University of the Witwatersrand (hereafter cited as AH2920).
47. This figure was 11.1% for coloureds and 25.7% for Indians (Crankshaw 1997, 80–81, Tables 5.5 and 5.6). See Sitas (1983, 328) for the perception by East Rand African workers of the higher status of jobs in "offices and commerce."
48. Mary Nkosi, interview.
49. Vuyiswa Xaba, interviewed by Bridget Kenny, Daveyton, August 27, 1999.
50. Buhle Bhengu, interviewed by Bridget Kenny, Daveyton, August 27, 1999.
51. Zama Ntuli, interviewed by Bridget Kenny, Daveyton, December 1, 1999; Thandile Ziyane, interview.
52. Thabang Maloka, interviewed by Bridget Kenny, Daveyton, August 13, 1999.
53. Tembi Motlhamme, interview.
54. Kaiser Thibedi, former CCAWUSA organizer, interviewed by Bridget Kenny, Johannesburg, July 25, 2005.
55. The Wiehahn Commission, appointed in 1976 in the wake of strikes and an upsurge of black labour militancy from 1973, examined the industrial relations system with respect to incorporating black workers. It reported in 1979 and argued that black workers be allowed to join registered unions. These reforms, while subject to fierce debate within the labour movement, ultimately enabled trade union growth among black workers in the 1980s. It also meant that membership to unions was no longer racially limited. CCAWUSA only formally adopted a policy of "non-racialism" with the founding of COSATU.
56. Kaiser Thibedi, interview.
57. Kaiser Thibedi, interview.

58. Mongezi Radebe, Vaal branch secretary for CCAWUSA, interviewed by Jeremy Baskin, June 23, 1982; C2; AH2920.
59. Tembi Motlhamme, interview.
60. Diana, Checkers, Vereeniging, joined CCAWUSA in 1981, interviewed as part of 3 CCAWUSA shop stewards by Jeremy Baskin, April 17, 1982; C2; AH2920.
61. Amos Tshabalala, interview.
62. Masilo, Edgars Marketing Services, Jeppe, joined in 1979, interviewed as part of 3 CCAWUSA shop stewards by Jeremy Baskin, April 17, 1982; C2; AH2920.
63. Linda Mofokeng, interviewed by Fatima Mathivha, Alberton, August 1, 2014.
64. "OK Strikers Picket 50 stores," *The Sowetan*, Friday, January 9, 1987.
65. "Deadlock in OK Bazaars strike," *The Sowetan*, Tuesday, January 6, 1987.
66. Tembi Motlhamme, interview.
67. Excerpt from play "Exploitation is not O.K.!" by OK Bazaars/Hyperama workers, 1987; CCAWUSA News, Vol. 1, No. 11, July 1987, p. 8; M5.3; AL2457.

CHAPTER 4

Regulating Retail: The Category "Employee" and Its Divisions

Where the last chapter established the constitutive political subject abasebenzi born out of struggle and in relationships within shops, this chapter examines the meaning over time of the legal category "employee" in South African retailing through several divisions: those that split it externally – servant/native/labourer and contract worker – and those that separated it internally, part-time and casual worker. Regulatory histories of these forms of employment reproduced specific race, class, and gender assumptions that informed workers' and trade unions' ideal of the standard-bearer of rights. As we will see in later chapters, in the postapartheid period, workers' politics came to be premised on a prescribed political subject – a particular notion of "worker" – the full-time, permanent employee. Thus, historical articulations producing these specific legal categories shaped the terrain of workers' politics and subjectivity.

Worker has defined a citizenship category in South Africa, a logic for securing inclusion and relation to the state and polity (Mamdani 1996; see also Barchiesi 2011). Yet, this chapter deconstructs the privileged positionality of employee to suggest that the very divisions in the legal category contributed to workers' enduring political claims. The Bifurcation of "employee" and "servant/native/labourer" split the category on the basis of presumptions about race and skill. Within retailing, part-time and casual employment also came to define the normative subject of labour rights – the full-time worker – invested in because of its relation to adult "social

© The Author(s) 2018
B. Kenny, *Retail Worker Politics, Race and Consumption in South Africa*, Rethinking International Development series,
https://doi.org/10.1007/978-3-319-69551-8_4

life," as discussed below.[1] Finally, once the employment contract had been unified in post-apartheid South Africa under reformed legal dispensation, the use of labour broking again divided it, reintroducing ambiguity through associations of contract labour as "unskilled" work again. The law was a medium through which the state, trade unions, and employers worked to contest a terrain of power. As legal scholar Duncan Kennedy (1979, 212) puts it, "We are implicated in what we would transform, and it in us." These battles reaffirmed the category of full-time permanent employee as the standard-bearer of rights, as political subject, with implications, as we will see in the remaining chapters.

Subjects of Employment Law: "Employee" and "Labourer"

South Africa's labour regime was defined through a racially bifurcated system of industrial conciliation for white workers and coercive control for black workers. As Martin Chanock (2004b) argues, South Africa's "legal culture" was not one of two "systems," but of the constitutive relationship within this apparent duality of forms of control. A key implication was racial and gendered segmentation of the labour market (see Crankshaw 1997; Berger 1992; Webster 1985; Cock 1980; Davies 1979). The various instruments used to shape the labour markets and labour relations of black and white workers in South Africa, as we will see, effected two intersecting discourses in which "employee" as the privileged category of labour relations was bound to other categories – variously, "servant," "native," "labourer" – describing manual, unskilled work, coterminous with blackness. In addition, the category of employee held within it other divisions, marking the secondary status of white women and of youth.

The legal definition of employee was consolidated in the 1920s. The state introduced the national industrial relations framework in 1924 as a response to several violent strikes by white workers, and culminating in the 1922 Rand Revolt carried out by white workers.[2] The state moved to discipline, institutionalize, and incorporate the white trade union movement by establishing a system of statutory bodies called industrial councils to mediate industrial disputes. It prohibited the right to strike during an agreement. Where industrial councils did not exist, parties could apply for a conciliation board to hear a dispute.[3] Trade unions were thus refigured to "industrial purpose" focused on wage bargaining (Chanock 2004a,

362). To be represented within its scope, a worker had to belong to a registered trade union and to be an "employee." The definition of employee within the law of dispute resolution excluded "pass-bearing natives" or African men, and later African women (Chanock 2004b, 437–38). While they could belong to unions, through this definition of employee, African workers were denied representation by legally recognized trade unions, and hence direct participation within the national industrial relations system. Thus the definitive division in law separated employee from "native."

Instead, African workers were regulated principally by laws administered under the Native Affairs Department, which focused on ensuring an adequate supply of labour that did not disrupt production.[4] For instance, the "pass" (an identification document Africans were obliged to carry) registered an African worker's legal movement into an urban area for the purpose of work (see Hindson 1987). Pass laws were variously developed out of older colonial vagrancy laws that regulated the movement of Africans, coloureds, and ex-slaves (Chanock 2004a, 340–41). In general, the colonial state introduced a wide range of measures – from poll and hut taxes to control over movement, residence, and land ownership – to ensure a supply of black labour to mining and agriculture, and to the manufacturing industries that emerged alongside these (Wolpe 1972; Legassick 1974). Resistance to incorporation into wage labour was frequent and proved a frustration to colonial administrators, in turn affecting these legal frameworks (Cooper 1996).

Pass laws supplemented earlier masters and servants laws that punished desertion and other breaches of contract of service as criminal offences (Chanock 2004a, 346–47). Masters and servants laws derived from the British statute and were imported in various formulations to its colonies and between colonies (Hay and Craven 2004). In South Africa, while "servant" was initially not racially defined but more broadly meant labourer, over time the courts narrowed its application "to keep whites out of the range of definition of servant" (Chanock 2004a, 339; see also 2004b, 444).[5] Chanock adds, "in any case administratively ... proceedings were not normally taken under the Acts [of masters and servants] against white employees" (Chanock 2004b, 444). Thus, masters and servants applied to "unskilled" labour, which in turn elided into referring to African labour. Masters and servants laws were particularly useful to control rural labour and to justify compound labour in mines. In order to control urban African labour, pass laws and regulating access to urban areas became fundamental (Chanock 2004b, 424–36; Duncan 1995, 93–101). In the South African state's legal regime, the coercive measures to regulate movement and ensure a labour force to mining and agriculture melded with the regulation of African workers as "unskilled" labourers, for whom the key purpose was to be bound by a contract of employment to work. This category was, then, not excluded per se, but incorporated as a bulk labour force – not as individuals with rights to enter a contract (as the liberal subject of law), but as a supply of labour, undifferentiated as "unskilled," in contrast to white workers who, through the recognition of free association and the right to bargain, entered an employment contract with a mediated presumption of "equality" with employers.

Unlike in Britain, where masters and servants law was absorbed into the labour contract which united unskilled and skilled workers under one system, in South Africa the "idiom of contract" operated differently for black and white workers (Chanock 2004b, 409). For African workers, it strengthened the relation of master to servant by obfuscating coercion behind the "choice" of contract (Chanock 2004a, 359). The combination of regulations created a regime of control over movement and breach of contract within a frame of an apparent freedom to choose employment. This pattern differed from French African colonies, where forced labour played a more central role, and from non-settler British West African colonies, where peasant production remained stronger (Cooper 1996; Rathbone 2004; also see Anderson 2004). In South Africa, African workers were "free" to choose their employment, provided they had a pass to look for employment. Once they found a job, they were expected to remain in that employment, without striking, and to accept the wages and conditions offered through minimum state "protection." With the industrial conciliation machinery adapted particularly from other white settler states like Canada and Australia (Chanock 2004b, 438, 443; Davies 1978, 74–75), for South African white workers, in contrast, inclusion in turn applied to negotiation around wages and working conditions, while limiting strike action.

For sectors not covered by industrial councils and generally with less cohesive representation of employers and workers, such as retailing, the Wage Act of 1925 introduced an administrative mechanism to regulate basic working conditions and minimum wages (Chanock 2004b, 453). It set up the Wage Board as a statutory body that decided "wage determinations" by sector.[6] The retail industry was not successful at securing an industrial council as the state argued that the sector was too fragmented

(Herd 1974, 134). From the early 1930s, retail employment was regulated through wage determinations on the basis of public hearings at which trade unions and employers presented their positions.[7] In the sector, the 1943 strike mentioned in Chap. 2 concluded the Tribunal Agreement, which established dispute resolution procedure in most major retailers (Herd 1974, 132). In its day-to-day work, the National Union of Distributive Workers (NUDW) monitored that companies applied stipulated conditions (see Chaps. 2 and 3) and more generally lobbied the Wage Board when these determinations were reviewed (Herd 1974). Thus, unlike in sectors with industrial councils, white workers in the retail sector did not so much as bargain collectively as they were recognized as employees through state protection of wages and conditions and daily engagement with employers via the union.

Furthermore, wage legislation stipulated that levels must ensure the ability to earn a wage to support a family in "civilized habits of life," which meant "European" (Davies 1979, 210). As in other contexts, this family wage applied only to white male workers (Chanock 2004b, 460; and see Owens 1993; Kessler-Harris 1982; Folbre 1994; Vosko 2000), a formulation borrowed from Australian law (Chanock 2004b, 452). Firstly, the designation of "civilized labour" became a synonym for white, with the government distinguishing it from "uncivilized labour" which was only concerned with "the bare requirements of the necessities of life as understood among barbarous and undeveloped peoples" (quoted in Chanock 2004b, 452). Initially, then, the Wage Act excluded black men as it defined a white man's wage around family living standards.

Yet the Wage Act used a definition of "employee" which did not specifically exclude "pass-bearing natives" as in the Industrial Conciliation Act (Chanock 2004b, 453). African workers were in practice covered by wage determinations, particularly after an amendment to the act in 1937 brought in unskilled workers (Duncan 1995, 170; Alexander 2000, 13). It did not legislate racially differentiated wages, as such.[8] Instead, wage levels were determined on the basis of occupational and skill categories, as well as years of experience and gender. As a result, "unskilled" and general labourer wage rates were defined in wage determinations and applied to Africans (Duncan 1995, 159; see for debates, Chanock 2004b, 455–59). During World War II, African distributive workers were able to use the Wage Board to improve their basic wages in the early 1940s, although this space was to close by the late 1940s (Hirson 1990; Alexander 2000).

Finally, white women's wages were pegged at two-thirds the wages of men on the assumption that "The supply of female labour is ... of a character totally different from that of men. For women, employment is largely a stepping stone to marriage or better times ... There is reason to assume, therefore, that women are prepared to offer their labour generally at a lower price than men" (Industrial Legislation Commission of 1935, quoted in Chanock 2004b, 461; see also Lewis 1984, 54). Debate led to concerns around white women undercutting men. Instead of equalizing wage rates, policy makers argued that "it would be better for men to seek higher-grade work than to try to compete with women, for example in offices and retail trade where they had come to predominate" (Chanock 2004b, 461; also Berger 1992). Gendered divisions then also underpinned South Africa's subject of labour legislation.

The manner in which the Wage Act was formulated and revised over time aimed to achieve a balance between the opposing pressures of those arguing for the market to regulate all wages (a non-racial application concerned to prevent undercutting of white wages) and those seeking explicitly to protect white men (a clause excluding blacks) (Chanock 2004b, 459; Duncan 1995, 163–81). Thus, through legislation that regulated wages and conditions of employees, African men in retailing were tentatively included as labourers, a category defined by skill. The notion of employee, then, was complicated. Legally, only white workers could be "employees" within the industrial relations system, but the reality of the expansion of black employment within urban centres brought other meanings to bear on this category.

With the installation of the National Party in 1948, apartheid-based amendments to legislation introduced in the 1950s more firmly denied African workers the rights to belong to registered trade unions and to strike, and it intensified control over their movement. These changes played out as conflicting concerns to control urbanization, to provide a workforce to urban employers, and to ease dissatisfaction of a growing labour force within the context of apartheid rule (Lichtenstein 2005; Posel 1991; Evans 1997).[9] By the 1950s, labour relations within retailing serviced by urban workers became formalized through a racially bifurcated labour market. White workers fell under standard employment relations, with full-time hours (45 hours per week), sector-minimum conditions and wages, and representation by a recognized trade union. White women mostly filled different occupational categories to white men and their wages were legislated at lesser "female" rates. For both women and men, however, qualified rates of pay for each occupational category were defined by years of experience, counted by time in the industry. This ensured white workers' long-term security and loyalty within the sector (Kenny 2008).

In contrast, African men were employed as manual labourers. Through wage determinations, they earned a minimum wage set for the "general worker" job category that, in contrast to white workers, did not accrue higher wages through experience. Thus, the description of these jobs outlined in the 1946 government yearbook was to apply for the next two decades: "Many [Africans] work in and about shops and warehouses as cleaners, warehousemen, and porters, while a large number are employed as drivers, packers, etc. Natives are much less skilled, and consequently do most of the rough manual labour." Furthermore, these labourers were paid at a "standard rate of wages" for unskilled workers (Union of South Africa et al. 1947, 58). Thus, African men performed generalized manual jobs of packing, lifting, and scrubbing in warehouses and stores (Hellmann 1953, 3). Employers enjoyed great flexibility in assigning tasks to them between departments, jobs, and floors (Hellmann 1953). The manual labour force was relatively stable in tenure – with African retail workers in Johannesburg reportedly staying longer in their jobs than those in manufacturing. Still, insecurity was built into their jobs with punitive surveillance, no advancement to other occupations, and no representation by unions (Hellmann 1953, 9). The workers themselves, in turn, highlighted the difficulties they faced with keeping their "passes in order" (Hellmann 1953, 3).

Thus, the category of employee was defined against three meanings, and in a chain of signification: "servant" (in contrast to free labour), "native" (as a labour supply), and "labourer" (as a skill category). These three divided the legal subject "employee," defining African workers in relation to white workers, at the same time that they were brought into employment. Within the definition of "employee," too, white women were legally defined as being secondary earners. The rest of the chapter discusses further differentiations within the category of employee in retailing: first, through part-time and casual employment under apartheid and, second, through contract labour in the post-apartheid period. The development of these complications would have a significant impact both on the conditions of full-time employment and on union and worker resistance to changes in these conditions.

Part-Time Employment: From Responsible Motherhood to Monstrous Deprivation

Part-time employment was introduced into labour statute in the commercial and distributive trade in the 1950s. Its aim was to encourage white women shop workers to remain in the industry by recognizing and providing time for their housework and childcare responsibilities (notwithstanding that much of the actual care work was done by black women).[10] In a context in which the apartheid regime attempted to define the role of women as located within their families, the recognition of part-time work allowed the NUDW to defend the respectability of married white working women by reinforcing (at least discursively) their roles as mothers and caregivers.

The first mention of part-time work was in the Wage Determination No. 170 of 1953 for commercial and distributive workers. With both the NUDW and employers noting with concern labour supply problems, the Wage Board introduced this form of employment in two occupational categories filled by white women: shop assistant and clerical worker. The reason for its introduction was reports of "exceedingly high" "labour turnover among female shop assistants" (South Africa 1955b, 27). While the NUDW worried that part-time assistants could "prejudice the position of full-time employees" (Herd 1974, 135), it also recognized the need to stabilize white women as service workers, a key membership, as we saw in Chap. 2.

The 1953 Wage Determination (No. 170) defined a part-time employee as someone who worked 24 hours per week, spread either over five or six days in the week, and who had to be paid at least 60% of the weekly wage of the full-time equivalent. It limited part-time employment to a maximum of one part-timer for every two full-time workers employed. In subsequent wage determinations, the NUDW pushed for improvements in these conditions. For instance, the Wage Determination No. 302 of 1968 increased the minimum wage for part-time employees in proportion to that of full-time workers. Over time, wage determinations also enabled the greater use of part-time employment through the addition of several more job categories, an increase in the working hours to 25 per week, and an increase in the ratio of part-time to full-time employees (Wage Determinations No. 223 of 1961; No. 302 of 1968; and No. 356 of 1973). Part-time employees were granted benefits and conditions of employment proportional to those enjoyed by full-time workers.

By the 1960s, part-time workers had come to be a core constituency of the NUDW. The stability of this category was premised on a notion of the regular part-time work of white women. NUDW correspondence from 1963 told how the most common shift for part-timers was "11:00 to 3:00," suggesting that women preferred these hours because of domestic and child care duties.[11] Public opinion on women working had changed since the 1940s, as widely publicized anxieties around juvenile delinquency focused debate on women's "unnatural" participation in the labour market (Mooney 2006, 82; Clowes 1994, 23), and so in this context, the union had recognized the appeal of these jobs for white women.

By the 1970s, some women continued to desire part-time employment to balance their personal life and work. Union member Mrs. S. M. de Lange, for example, converted to part-time hours in 1975 "because of personal reasons."[12] The union's effort went toward securing the correct wage rate for her new status.[13] Other women complained about employers pressurizing them to work full-time when they did not want to. Thus, in 1974 Mrs. H. C. Olsen, part-time employee of a Johannesburg Greatermans, a subsidiary of OK Bazaars, complained to the NUDW that she had been underpaid during a week in which she worked full-time hours on request of her supervisor, whereas she normally worked part-time hours of "11 o'clock in the morning, till 3 o'clock in the afternoon."[14] In a letter to the company, the union regional secretary referenced the wage determination to demand that Mrs. Olsen be paid overtime.[15] Mrs. Olsen, on the other hand, reconsidered employment with the company as she was miffed that she was asked to work full-time and was "thoroughly disgusted" that the company had not paid her appropriately.[16] Similarly, another shop worker did not want her job to be converted into a full-time position: "This did not suit Mrs. Van R" as she "wants to carry on mornings only."[17] The union attempted to broker a transfer of employment to a different store for her, but she left rather than wait for this to happen. These women exited retail jobs when employers tried to push them to work full-time hours; they preferred part-time jobs to meet their other responsibilities.

Work intensification introduced in the 1970s made working conditions at shops less attractive, and white women came to have better employment options elsewhere (see Chaps. 2 and 3). From the outset, part-time work took its significance from the association between white female labour and discourses of domesticity. As in other contexts, gendered assumptions of the family wage and women's reproductive roles shaped the regulation of part-time employment as well as trade union politics (see Vosko 2000; Fudge and Vosko 2001; Cobble and Vosko 2000). Not only was part-time work appealing to its white female constituency, but it also offered a way to legitimate white women's wage labour in apartheid South Africa. The union's approach to regulation, then, affirmed women's right to work, as responsible mothers. In this manner, part-time work acted as a sub-category of "employee" in retailing, with proportional wages and benefits and inclusion in union membership, but also reinforced the gendered secondary status of this category.

In the 1968 Wage Determination, changes "allowed employers to make greater use of part-time employees."[18] At the same time that the first black workers began to be employed as service workers on the shop floor, employers attempted to increase their use of part-time employment even as they also wanted to expand the working hours of part-time white women. Black women who entered service jobs, however, resisted part-time hours. In 1969, union correspondence documents a case of coloured catering workers at an OK Bazaars branch in Port Elizabeth who were informed that "they will be on part-time work."[19] While the union's response was to check the minutiae of notice periods and payment amounts to investigate the legality of the decision, the correspondence reveals that the change to part-time hours was not preferred by these black women. One worker only reluctantly acceded to the new conditions as "her husband had advised her to accept," and the line manager "gave [her] the assurance" that "'I am telling you this won't last forever. The first full time workers we need, you'll get first preference.'"[20] The NUDW branch secretary bluntly described the decision in a telegram to the national union official as "DISMISSING FULL TIMERS REEMPLOYED AS PART TIMERS."[21] The workers preferred to work longer shifts and understood that part-time employment was a way for management to cut costs.

In 1985, Pages, a subsidiary of the Foschini Group, decided to "convert" the positions of 200 full-time Commercial, Catering and Allied Workers Union of South Africa (CCAWUSA) members to part-time employment. By this time, the union had a recognition agreement and defended black workers within industrial relations law. In this case, workers were extremely unhappy at the cut to their working hours, and the union declared a dispute. Unlike white women, black workers regarded "part-time as a monster to their social problems," calculating that their salaries would be cut by one-third. The union stated that "CCAWUSA and its members see part-time as a form of depriving one's social life."[22]

Black working-class women fought for full-time employment. In an economic context of high inflation and low wages, they had no desire to work part-time.

Working class respectability and reproductive constraints operated differently for these women than for white women. A full-time income was necessary to activate "one's social life" as a household member. Neither black women nor their union invoked the need to protect their reproductive role as mothers. Rather, calling in expert advice from lawyers and academics, the union resisted the reduction of workers' hours.[23]

These early efforts by employers to alter working hours portended important changes to come. In the late 1980s, retailers would increasingly draw on forms of employment that allowed them to schedule workers outside the standard shift. It would not be through using the category of part-time, however. Instead, they used "casual" labour. Underpinned by very different meanings, this employment category was more palatable to unions and workers than part-time work, because it was seen as temporary and conducted by young people. Those articulations held quite important consequences for the developments in the sector in the 2000s.

Casual Employment: Student Labour, Extra Help, and Scabs

A second category of non-standard contract existed as a core feature of employment in retail in South Africa. "Casual" labour was legally permitted in the industry from the very first Wage Determination in the sector (No. 38 of 1931) when it was listed as a separate classification. The utility of this form of contract to employers rested in its temporary status. Initially it was defined as employment for not more than 14 days in three months; by the late 1930s, it had shifted to not more than two days per week (Wage Determination No. 70 of 1939). By the 1950s, the sector had normalized the category of "casual employee" as someone working not more than three days per week (Wage Determination No. 170 of 1953). The 1968 Wage Determination (No. 302) added a clause whereby in addition to the normal three days a week, casual workers could work up to five days per week at the end of the month, a particularly busy period in South African retailing because of the timing of salary pay outs.

While the meaning and use of casual employment varies across contexts (Campbell and Burgess 2001a, b; Bowles and MacPhail 2008; Standing 2008), in South African retailing, casual employment was understood to be seasonal work for a short duration. It is likely to have entered South African retail regulation from its Australian formulation.[24] Indeed, until 1968, various wage determinations stipulated that casuals be paid only upon termination of employment.[25]

In 1975, a NUDW official commented on the position of casual workers or what he called "temporary (seasonal) workers" which retailers employed mainly over the Christmas and New Year period.[26] In South African retailing, casual work was considered a form of temporary employment at the end of the month or on short-term basis during particularly busy seasonal periods. While temporary, workers in this category of employment could be hired for the full eight-hour day and were paid a premium wage of one-and-a third the rate of a qualified person in the occupational category; yet they did not have rights to paid leave, paid holidays, notice of termination or other basic non-wage benefits.[27] This "casual loading," to use the Australian term for the practice (Owens 1993; Campbell and Burgess 2001a, b),[28] was meant both to limit and compensate casual employment (Wage Determination No. 302 of 1968).[29]

Owens (1993, 410) writes that in Australia "casual loading" attracted married women. This reinforced the male breadwinner bias because the wages given were "not to be so high as to attract men to this type of work, but high enough to supplement the wage of the male worker so that he could continue to fulfil his role as 'breadwinner.'" In South African retailing, casual work attracted a different category of worker during the 1940s to the 1970s, namely students. By a similar logic, though, it reinforced the ideal of standard employment through contrast to the temporary labour of young people.

Critically, the social meaning of casual employment was quite different than of part-time work. First, casual workers were not part of the bargaining unit of the union. Second, they were usually assumed to be students or young people entering retailing in order to gain experience in the sector while finishing school.[30] Third, they were more often than not a "male scholar or student."[31] Yet, despite not being organized by the union, casual workers were not viewed as competition by the other workers. For instance, in 1972 the NUDW complained to a retailer that "A number of my members, who have relatives working as temporary hands ... and who are students or scholars, have asked me to take up with you the question of the wages and working hours of these temporary employees." It charged that these casual workers were not being paid the premium wage and demanded that the wage rate be rectified "with absolute urgency, as the employees concerned will soon be terminating their service contracts with the

Company."[32] The social meaning differed between part-time employment, associated with the regular core labour of white women, and casual employment, often assumed to be the "extra" labour of (often male) students.

Like their predecessors, black workers in the 1980s brought their children and relatives into casual jobs to earn extra income.[33] And, like their workmates, unionized black workers continued to associate casual labour with its subordinate status. Mary Nkosi started working for a major chain store in 1981 as a full-time permanent worker. She explained how the store employed her as a bag packer during the week, but moved her to a cashier job on the weekends so that it could bring in "young students" (*abantwana abafundayo*) as packers, in this case (black) students. The use of the word *abantwana* connoted both that these workers needed to support their families and that they were young, "below you, owing you respect."[34] Because of the dependent status of casual workers and because of their low numbers, CCAWUSA (and later its successor the South African Commercial, Catering and Allied Workers Union (SACCAWU)) did not attempt to limit casual employment during this period, and rather focused on organizing and consolidating full-time workers' rights.

Extended Trading Hours

The late 1980s and 1990s saw a key change to the retail sector that brought with it an expansion of casual labour, namely the extension of store trading hours. Longer store hours opened up undesired shifts in evenings and on weekends. This section examines the changes in employment patterns and conditions that this new time regime initiated.

The Shops and Offices Act of 1939 set limits on when retailers could open to the public. Provincial authorities administered it through ordinance, often ceded to particular municipalities. In general, stores could not open on weekdays after 5 p.m., Saturday afternoons after 1 p.m., and Sundays, with some leeway of a half to one hour on Friday evenings. Throughout the decades, retailers repeatedly tried to have the shopping hours extended.[35] Drawing on trends in other countries, they pushed for extended trading hours to expand profits. Retailers and Chambers of Commerce surveyed customers on the benefits of extended hours, many of whom preferred to shop after work rather than during lunchtime or on overcrowded Saturday mornings.[36]

The NUDW won initial restrictions on late trading hours in the 1940s, yet continued to have to mobilize against renewed attempts by retailers.

NUDW pamphlets in the 1950s called its membership to meetings asking, "Do you want to go back to the old days of 'black Friday' when shops stayed open to 9 pm?" and "Are you prepared to work night work or maybe work again Saturday afternoons?"[37] It fought against the extension of trading hours because of the implications this would carry for working hours. For nearly 30 years, it consistently put forward the emotive plea to the white public of the need to protect working mothers' social duty to care for husbands and children.[38]

Aware of a growing popular sentiment for the introduction of extended hours in the 1960s, however, the NUDW began to conceptualize and negotiate trade-offs for its membership in exchange for agreeing to some flexibility of hours. Initially it demanded an extra half-day off per month for full-time workers where stores extended their closing times by half an hour.[39] In 1971 it suggested introducing a two-shift system for full-time workers, with one extending from Monday to Friday and a second from Monday afternoon to Saturday morning.[40] It framed its acceptance of some longer working hours within its broader fight for a 40-hour workweek in the sector. Yet, while it agreed to a minimal extension of hours and negotiated with individual companies for shorter workweeks in specific branches, it was never successful in gaining a 40-hour week.[41]

Critically, these agreements included a growing acceptance of the role of casual labour in working extended hours.[42] Thus, in 1973, a major chain supermarket agreed to NUDW demands regarding the staffing of earlier morning hours: "Store managers have again been instructed to ensure that those coming in on the early shift do so voluntarily and that where permanent staff will not work the early shift, casuals must be used."[43] The underlining in the original memo indicates how the union official marked it for attention of his full-time members.[44]

Several major chain supermarkets extended trading hours in specific branches in agreement with the NUDW through the "use of more casual labour at night and on weekends, and also [by] stagger[ing] working hours so that permanent staff work the same number of hours," using flexi-time and rosters.[45] Thus, while the NUDW agreed to some flexibility in its members' working hours, it protected its membership from the most "unsocial" hours – those when white women would be caring for their families – by agreeing to the employment of casual labour, presumed to be young people.

Union and store publications during this period often presented debates on the benefits of extended trading. In 1977 one union member wrote that "Later shopping hours wouldn't be terribly popular with families because of children's bath times, mealtimes, and, of course, T.V." Another member presented the benefits of later shopping hours to customers: "It would be very popular. Some customers become annoyed when the store is closed at 5.00 p.m. and they haven't finished their shopping." She was of the opinion, however, that "only single staff can be expected to work late, as married women have to look after children and cook."[46] The NUDW focused on protecting its core membership of white women, in conditions of a declining white workforce. It envisioned these hours being filled not by the relatively protected and unionized category of "part-time" work, which could have been crafted to serve additional shifts, but instead by casual employees.

As the labour force changed rapidly to black front-line workers in the 1980s, full-time staff working later shifts were more likely to be black workers. Dulcie Hartwell, a regional branch NUDW official, corrected a member of the public who worried about the effects of extended trading on (white) families. She explained that the assumption that "most if not all, of the [full-time] staff necessary to operate shops during the evening would be Whites, has no foundation in reality. On the contrary, all night services ... have been compelled to make progressively greater use of non-White staff because of the reluctance of Whites to take up night jobs."[47]

In 1981, OK Bazaars advised the NUDW and the National Union of Commercial, Catering and Allied Workers Union (NUCCAW)[48] that it intended "to apply for an exemption from overtime provisions" in order to introduce "so-called flexitime" shifts.[49] This new category, which it wanted to introduce in its Durban stores, would require a full-time work-week as well as evening and weekend shifts. The unions objected to the exemption[50] and a subsequent Wage Board investigation found against the employer.[51] For the NUDW, which had consented to bargain around the standard shift in the 1970s, this type of extended trading hours was a deep threat to the conditions of employment of its white membership. By bargaining with employers to use casual workers or black workers in these shifts, the union reinforced the notion that the norm of full-time employment included a standard shift and, by implication, the right to family and social life. It considered these extended working hours as unsocial and not respectable. It rather argued that these "inconvenient hours" should be covered by casual workers who were young and temporary or by black workers. In the process, the union defined these extended working hours as "extra help," and not as central to the occupation of shop work. It thus reinforced the idea that full-time, permanent employees were the standard-bearers of rights, with variation happening as a contingency. The implication of the introduction of extended hours and NUDW's protection of white workers was, however, pressure on the standard shift for regularly employed black workers, who also did not want to work unsocial hours.

Amacasual – A Separate Group

One meaning of casual employment in the 1980s, then, emerged from its association with student employment in previous decades. A second one, however, emerged in the mid-1980s when casual workers were hired as strike breakers. For instance, in one of the largest national strikes against a major supermarket chain, the three-month strike against OK Bazaars in 1986/87 (see Chap. 3), the stores stayed open by using (coloured) casual workers. It was a common management tactic during this time to bring in workers of different racial categories to break strikes.[52] Some of these temporary workers were kept on as "casuals" after the strike, referred to as *amacasual* by workers rather than as *abantwana*. In this manner the term *amacasual* emerged to describe a separate group of workers, differentiated from the *amapermanents*, the full-time, (unionized) permanent workers (for both terms, the isiZulu prefix "*ama*" denotes a distinct group of people). Both metaphors – young students and *amacasual* – signified a division between this form of employment and the primary full-time, permanent workforce. This line of differentiation began to play a critical role in how unions responded to casualization when it increased significantly in the late 1980s.

By the late 1980s, CCAWUSA's successor union SACCAWU came under renewed pressure from employers when a sustained recession threatened retrenchments and store closures. Employers complained about low staff productivity and pushed unions to bargain around flexibility of tasks and scheduling (Trade Union Research Project 1992; Vally n.d.). To win guarantees against retrenchment, SACCAWU reported in 1993 that its "new approach" was "a process agreement on job security, flexibility and mobility, reduction of casualized work, grading and skilling, customer courtesy, and worker's empowerment" (South African Commercial Catering and Allied Workers Union 1993, 26–27). In 1993, then, SACCAWU negotiated its first agreement around casualization, in which it agreed to flexi-timers working extended hours with pro rata benefits, which was framed within the more pressing problem of retrenchments of full-time permanent staff.[53]

In practice, these agreements rarely improved protection for casual workers. In some cases, in exchange for gaining job security by signing agreements to become flexi-workers, the union also supported employers' applications for exemption from the Wage Determination for higher rates in unsocial hours or premium wages for remaining casual workers.[54] In other cases, workers were simply not converted, and casual workers continued as temporary employees without additional pay. In addition, the terms of agreements were rapidly eroded as retail management used labour conflicts to push conditions down (Qotole 2000; Clarke 2000).

As a result, employers increased the use of casual employment in the late 1980s and 1990s despite SACCAWU and workers' opposition to it. This was possible because its legal definition was based on weekly part-time hours of work, without a limit on the duration for which someone could be employed in this status. On the basis of this ambiguity, casual employees came to be hired for long-term durations while continuing to be viewed as "temporary." At the same time, the protections offered casual workers became subject to exemption, allowing retailers to circumvent the mechanisms intended to impose limits on the use of casual labour.[55] Unlike part-time employment, casual work was not limited by ratios or occupational categories. Campbell and Brosnan (1999, 356) argue that in Australia, casual employment was regulated but left unprotected through "gaps" in its award system, such as through exemptions and special provisions, and casual workers fell into "pockets of non-protection." So too in South Africa. Thus, by the 1990s many people had worked for years for the same company as "casuals" with no job security, no benefits, no basic leave provisions, nor the regulated premiums meant to offset this insecurity, and companies continued to employ them on a weekly "temporary" basis for less than 24 hours a week (Kenny 2001).

This situation allowed retailers to increase the use of casual labour on the shop floor across jobs and for extended durations in the 1990s and early 2000s, even as SACCAWU was focused on trying to stay the worsening of conditions of full-time, permanent workers, its core membership; by unintended consequence, it reinforced the assumption that the political subject was the full-time employee. The changing employment patterns are reflected in government statistics which show that between 1987 and 1997, full-time average employment in the Wholesale, Retail and Motor Trades sector fell from 88% of total employment to 81%, while part-time and casual employment increased from 11.8% of total employment to over 19% (Central Statistical Services 1998).[56]

Contract Labour: Splitting the Category of "Employee" as It Is Unified

Following increased mobilization from black workers' trade unions in the 1970s, the apartheid state examined the prospect of uniting the industrial relations system for black and white workers. The Wiehahn Commission recommended in 1979 to extend the definition of employee and the rights to belong to registered trade unions to black workers in order to incorporate and discipline them.[57] The new Labour Relations Act of 1981 that resulted unified the category of employee from its racial division under previous law, allowing black workers to join registered trade unions and to participate in industrial conciliation and bargaining. This prompted debate within the trade union movement as to whether the individual unions should indeed register and participate in apartheid industrial relations machinery (see Maree 1987). CCAWUSA decided to use its new status to push for recognition agreements with retailers, which led to a dramatic increase in membership in the 1980s (see Chap. 3).

At the moment when "employee" was (racially) unified in labour law, however, a subsequent amendment acknowledged a further split. A 1983 amendment attempted to regulate the use of "labour hire" under employment law. The specific term of "labour broking," as used in the amendment, referred to a firm which supplied labour to a client firm. Labour broking assisted employers to circumvent protections for wages and minimum conditions by using labour hire agencies, at the time when the state relaxed influx control over the supply of labour to urban areas (Benjamin 2013, see also 2014; Theron et al. 2005, 4–5). As a result, employers began to source labour through private employment agencies, rather than through state labour bureaus (or employing directly). The initial amendment was meant to reassert protection of employees in this relationship, and yet it also indicates, by virtue of attempt to regulate, that this form of employment was becoming more prevalent.

The 1983 clause required labour brokers to be registered with the Department of Labour, and defined them rather than the client firms as the employers of contract workers (Benjamin 2013, 292). It stipulated that a labour broker was an entity which "for reward provides a client with persons to render services to or performs work for the client or procures such persons for him, for which service or work such persons are remunerated by the labour broker" (quoted in Theron et al. 2005, 49n18).

Le Roux (2010, 149) suggests that the initial (racial) unification of the employment contract itself, emerging out of the Wiehahn reforms, may have in part led to processes of externalization of employment. This early splitting of the unified employment contract through regularizing labour broking – potentially for unskilled as well as skilled labour – then suggests that employers found new mechanisms through private contract to source labour at potentially lesser conditions. At the moment that "employee" came to apply to all workers, the subject of the employment contract divided, to reproduce a division between the norm of the standard employment contract and a secondary category marked by insecurity via the temporary labour contract. Still, little notice was taken until the 2000s when the use of labour broking had expanded.

Post-apartheid Labour Law Reform

In the post-apartheid period, labour law reform sought to codify gains won by the trade union movement in the 1980s (Adler and Webster 2000; Clarke 2004). One of the most important reforms to labour legislation was the further revision of the definition of employee. The first democratic Labour Relations Act of 1995 ensured a procedurally fair system that formalized unions' organizational rights and workers' right to strike and bargain collectively, and laid the basis for participation of all workers in the workplace (Clarke et al. 2003, 2). Coupled with the Basic Conditions of Employment Act of 1997, which gave all employees rights to basic leave and working hours protection, these laws broadened the definition of "employee" to include anyone who worked for an employer for more than 24 hours per month, and they brought in public service and domestic workers. Democratic labour law reform specifically sought, then, to extend rights to a broader subject "employee".

In so doing, legal reform made obsolete the very notion of "casual" labour as it had been used in retail. As a result, unions and employers in the retail sector embarked on drawn-out negotiations of a new (now renamed) "sectoral determination" to align regulation for the retail industry to these provisions. It was eight years later, in 2003, that the revised sectoral labour regulation was finally completed.[58] It removed the distinct sectoral category of "casual," bringing all retail workers under the same basic protections, a bottom line on which SACCAWU held firm. In return, however, several new statuses of part-time employment were added: those working less than 24 hours per week, those working less than 27 hours per week, and those working less than 40 hours per week. Workers employed as one or another part-time status could agree, by individual contract, to give up certain basic conditions of employment, most importantly for the sector, higher wages for unsocial working time, in exchange for time off. In the context of high unemployment, employees needed jobs and agreed to employers' "flexibilized" conditions. One consequence of the new regulation was, then, to make it incredibly complicated to assess what basic condition applied to which category of employment. In essence, reform designed to close the loophole of casual labour instead opened up new divisions in relation to the full-time, permanent employee.

More generally, regulatory reform in the retail sector retained the assumption that some form of non-standard employment was required in the industry. As in the past, it was defined on the basis of flexible working time, but now potentially foregoing overtime, Sunday and public holiday pay, all moves that retail employers had begun to push for decades earlier (see Lewis 2001). While part-time employment required an indefinite contract, and thus "casual" employees would have to be employed now on "permanent" contracts, the reform reproduced the notion that a time-flexible and cheapened workforce remained core to the sector.

Moreover, in the mid-2000s, labour broking spread. Employers increasingly used contract labour hired through labour brokers, or temporary employment services as the Labour Relations Act of 1995 termed them. While the 1983 amendment had designated the labour broker agency as the employer of contract workers, the 1995 post-apartheid reform sought to improve protections by tying the client firm into the risk of noncompliance of labour law. It introduced joint and several liability for breaches of the Basic Conditions of Employment, sectoral determinations, collective agreements, and arbitration awards, but there were rarely successful cases brought under this clause. Furthermore, a clause to make the client firm liable for unfair labour practices and unfair dismissals was taken out at in last minute negotiations, which made the longer term use of this type of labour easier. In addition, the provision that labour brokers register with the Department of Labour, as stipulated in the 1983 law, was removed, as was a clause that the client's premises be considered the place of work, both of which would have offered greater protections to workers (Benjamin 2013, 3).

Both the 1983 and the 1995 clauses, it seems, assumed that the temporary use of labour broking by client firms meant short-term work periods. They did not anticipate the indefinite use of employees placed through labour brokers. Yet since about 2000, this form of precarious labour has expanded in South Africa (Theron 2005), as well as in retailing. Indeed,

Ruth Ngobeni, whom we met in Chap. 1, was a cashier who had been outsourced from her job as a casual to a labour broker shortly after the new sectoral determination came into effect in 2003. While figures for labour broking are difficult to assess, economists have noted that there has been a "rapid growth" of temporary employment services in South Africa between 1995 and 2014; in particular, they find that 25% of all new jobs created in this period in the Finance and Business and Wholesale and Retail sectors have been in temporary employment services (Bhorat et al. 2016, 6). Labour broking is often used for low-skilled work, like cleaning, security, and packing across sectors. The continued use of temporary labour in de facto long-term arrangements produced greater insecurities for these workers who were easier to fire without notice, fair procedure, or compensation. Thus, over this period, "employee" as subject of labour law was again divided along lines that reproduced the association of "unskilled" labourer as having, by virtue of a differentiated contract, lesser rights.[59]

* * *

South African labour law reproduced a difference between a normative notion of "employee" and forms in variance to it. These fissures were marked by skill, race, gender, and age at different points in the history of retail work. In retailing, these divisions came to rely on employers having ongoing access to flexible and extended working hours through the use of part-time, casual, and contract labour in different ways.

From the foundation of labour legislation in South Africa, African workers provided the external split legitimating the category "employee." They were defined in a signifying chain as "servant/native/labourers" and regulated by different laws from white workers. In the 1980s, black workers had no interest in protecting part-time employment, as the NUDW had done earlier for white women, arguing that they were mothers with domestic responsibilities. Casual employment, too, marked a separate category of subordinate workers. Instead, the union fought for the rights of full-time, permanent employees. In the 1980s, workers and unions used this formulation of the subject of labour rights as the basis on which to begin to make decisive claims to citizenship rights. Workers' political consciousness, then, emerged in part because of how regulatory frameworks conditioned political subjecthood.

In the post-apartheid period, codified rights won by unions in the 1980s reaffirmed that the standard-bearer of these rights was the full-time employee, even as reforms sought to unify the category "employee" particularly by extending rights to all workers. Nevertheless, through the law, protection presupposed the comparative norm of the (full-time) permanent worker, such that neither casual nor contract workers were seen to hold the same status or provisions. Furthermore, in response to efforts to consolidate the category of "employee," labour broking then offered another moment of division by the 2000s. In this history, trade union and worker assumptions and claims influenced the boundaries of the legal forms, just as, as we will see in the rest of the book, these various employment categories with their legal foundations shaped the political subjectivity of workers.

In 2015, another round of labour law reforms introduced restrictions on the use of labour broking, in order to respond to abuses and to limit the indefinite use of contract labour, which offered important protections. In Chap. 8 we examine these reforms and consider how law once again affirmed the symbolic weight of a normative legal subject "employee."

Thus, as political subject, "worker" was not simply an abstract citizenship category, relying on incorporation through liberal democratic norm and modernist presumption (see Barchiesi 2011), but was constituted through a process which itself made the law, trade union action, and employer response. As Duncan Kennedy's words suggested at the start of the chapter, law is a language which works through positing categories through which we act in order to contest them. The legal subject "employee" was constituted within concrete social relations as symbolizing the liberal individual, and yet even for South African white workers it was mediated by differences, which gave it power. Black workers were alternately servant/native/labourer, and thus "employee" marked a terrain of political relationality – first of recognition by the state through rights to participate in a relationship of "equality," to recall the National Party's dismay at the end of Chap. 2, and second as meaningful engagement in the world, as adult being, claiming a "social life" as expressed by CCAWUSA. Black workers' demands for labour rights cannot be understood outside of this mapping of the division of "employee" by assumptions of skill, race, gender, and age. By examining the history of shifts and ambivalences within employment categories, this chapter has outlined the stakes of these legal terms, around which, as we will see in Chaps. 5 and 6, workers fought, as much with each other as with managements and the state. These legal categories surely disciplined and set limits to political claims, but in this history, we can see that those boundaries were constantly made anew even as they restructured orders of difference.

NOTES

1. "Part-time at Pages – A Monster to Workers," *CCAWUSA News*, Vol. 1, No. 8, July 1985, p. 1; IV (14); Karis-Gerhart Collection of South African Political Materials, 1964–1990 (A2675); Historical Papers Research Archive, University of the Witwatersrand (hereafter cited as A2675).
2. The Industrial Conciliation Act of 1924 formed the critical piece of legislation (see Lever 1978; Yudelman 1983, 40; Hirson 1990, 29). For the most thorough discussion of the Rand Revolt, see Krikler (2005). Antecedents to the Industrial Conciliation Act were the 1909 Industrial Disputes Prevention Act (Transvaal) and the Industrial Disputes and Trade Union Bill of 1914, which was withdrawn (see Lever 1978, 92; Chanock 2004b, 437).
3. An industrial council for a sector was composed of equal numbers of employers and employees. Councils passed agreements, which the minister of labour could make binding. The minister of labour could set up a conciliation board to hear disputes in sectors where there was not an industrial council. If a council or a board failed to come to agreement, the minister of labour could appoint an arbitrator (Duncan 1995, 156).
4. The Native Labour Regulation Act of 1911 regulated the supply of migrant labour to the mining industry and centralized state control over African workers to urban areas, including through a state labour bureau (Duncan 1995, 44–50; Chanock 2004b, 416, 435–38; Evans 1997). It also prohibited African workers from striking on mines (Duncan 1995, 209).
5. See Chanock (2004b, 425) for categories of white labour, including salesmen.
6. The Wage Board was composed of three permanent members and representatives of employers and employees. It heard evidence and made recommendations to the minister of labour on wages and conditions in a particular industry (Duncan 1995, 156). Hence, it was not a bargaining forum.
7. Herd (1974, 134) explained that the National Union of Distributive Workers (NUDW) was able successfully to conclude several Conciliation Board agreements which set wages and conditions under a sympathetic labour minister in the 1940s, but when the National Party came to power, the union was denied its further applications on the basis of insufficient representation in the sector. According to him, "Conciliation was preferable because it was possible to stretch a conciliation agreement over many issues with which the Wage Board refused to concern itself" (Herd 1974, 134).
8. Other examples of acts that did not apply narrowly to white workers include the Factories Acts of 1918 and 1941, and the Shops and Offices

Act of 1939 that established an inspectorate to monitor conditions. These acts initially maintained separation of workers and exclusions based on category of job (Duncan 1995, 55, 58).
9. Apartheid laws included the Native Labour (Settlement of Disputes) Act of 1953, the Industrial Conciliation Amendment Act of 1956, and the Native Laws Amendment Act of 1952 (see Evans 1997).
10. The cheap paid domestic labour of African women has been central to the making of South African modernity, and white women would have commonly relied on this hyper-exploited labour force to relieve them of domestic duties (Cock 1980). However, both union documentation and interviews have suggested that family responsibility and childcare remained central to white women's discourses of femininity (also see Chap. 2).
11. L.R. Dison, "Legal Opinion on Tea-Breaks for Part-Timers," October 23, 1963; Da 16.2; National Union of Distributive Workers (Head Office) Records, 1933–1980 (AH1494); Historical Papers Research Archive, University of the Witwatersrand (hereafter cited as AH1494). Letter from B. Robarts to The National Secretary, June 25, 1963; Da 16.2; AH1494. Letter from J.R. Altman to Branch Secretary, June 27, 1963; Da 16.2; AH1494.
12. Letter from Mrs. S.M. de Lange to NUDW, June 5, 1975; Ua 26.1; National Union of Distributive Workers (Witwatersrand Branch) Records 1939–1984 (AH1601); Historical Papers Research Archive, University of the Witwatersrand (hereafter cited as AH1601).
13. Letter from Mrs. S.M. de Lange to the NUDW, May 29, 1975; Ua 26.1; AH1601. See also letter from M. Kagan to Mr. E. Gosling, July 11, 1975; Ua 26.1; AH1601. Letter from M. Kagan to Mrs. J. Wheeler, October 23, 1975; Ua 26.2.c.; AH1601.
14. Letter from Mrs. H.C. Olsen, July 29, 1974; Ua 41.1.4; AH1601.
15. Letter from M. Kagan to the General Manager, Greatermans, August 14, 1974; Ua 41.1.4; AH1601. Letters from Mrs. H.C. Olsen to the NUDW, July 9 and 29, 1974; Ua 41.1.4; AH1601. See for other cases, letter from M. Kagan to M. Billson, October 30, 1974; Ua 26.2.c.; AH1601.
16. Letter from Mrs. H.C. Olsen, July 29, 1974; Ua 41.1.4; AH1601.
17. Case Record c27/73, 7/3/1973; Ua 41.1.4; AH1601.
18. "Shop Assistants Protest on Pay," *Cape Argus*, October 3, 1968; P.a1; AH1601.
19. Letter from Mr. D.G. Langenhoven to Mr. M. Kagan, December 18, 1969; Ua 41.2.5; AH1601.
20. Letter from M. Kagan to Mr. D.G. Langenhoven, February 4, 1970; Ua 41.2.5; AH1601.
21. Telegram from Langenhoven, Port Elizabeth, to Kagan, Johannesburg, September 2, 1969; UA 41.2.5; AH1601.

22. "Part-time at Pages – A Monster to Workers," *CCAWUSA News*, Vol. 1, No. 8, July 1985, p. 1; IV (14); A2675.
23. "Part-time at Pages – A Monster to Workers," *CCAWUSA News*, Vol. 1, No. 8, July 1985, p. 1; IV (14); A2675. The union contracted the Sociology of Work Unit to conduct research and offer an alternative to the company's proposal to cut hours.
24. Writing about Australia, Campbell and Burgess (2001b) discuss the relationship between temporary and casual employment. Temporary employment often means simply non-permanent, but it varies between a range of work, such as fixed-term contract, temporary agency, seasonal or irregular, and self-employed "disguised wage labour." Thus, it could be part-time or full-time; it could be short-term or long-term. In Australia, the commonplace notion of casual work revolves around the tentativeness and shortness of the employment contract (176). Because the contract of employment is assumed to be short, these employees are seen to lack any rights or entitlements of non-wage benefits or other protections.
25. In the 1968 Wage Determination (No. 302), the Wage Board added "but at least once per week," which seems to indicate longer or more common use of casual employees.
26. Morris Kagan, "Seasonal Labour in the Commercial Distributive Trade," *New Day*, January 1975, pp. 17–18; G1; National Union of Distributive Workers (Natal Branch) Records. 1937–1978 (AH1202). Historical Papers Research Archive, University of the Witwatersrand (hereafter cited as AH1202).
27. Letter from M. Kagan, to Mr. R. De Wet, July 2, 1970; Ua 43.2; AH1601. Morris Kagan, "Seasonal Labour in the Commercial Distributive Trade," *New Day*, January 1975, pp. 17–18; G1; AH1202.
28. "Casual loading" refers to paying a higher wage rate in compensation for the absence of paid leave, termination notices and benefits, and was the same in Australia as in South Africa (see Campbell and Burgess 2001a, b).
29. Unlike part-time employment, casual employment did not have a ratio applied to it to set its limit.
30. For instance, casual employment in off-school hours acted as an entry point for managers-in-training ("Head Start for Top Chain Store Manager was Checkout Porter's Job," *Supermarket & Retailer*, Vol. 27, No. 3, March 1980, pp. 11–12).
31. Morris Kagan, "Seasonal Labour in the Commercial Distributive Trade," *New Day*, January 1975, p. 17; G1; AH1202.
32. Letter from M. Kagan to Mr. D.A. Smith, December 15, 1972; Ua 41.2.7; AH1601.
33. For students as casuals, see "Super A – Only Casual Power (and sometimes Family) keeps this Store's Checkouts Ringing on Saturdays," *Supermarket &*

Retailer, Vol. 27, No. 3, March 1980, p. 9; "Casuals to Full-times Ratio – Measure of Store Labour Productivity for Chain-store Top Management," *Supermarket & Retailer*, Vol. 27, No. 3, March 1980, p. 10.
34. Mary Nkosi, interviewed by Bridget Kenny, Daveyton, August 26 and December 3, 1999, and September 7, 2000. For an example from US service workers of how young workers are perceived as temporary and a lower status to adult workers, see Tannock (2001).
35. For instance, Pamphlets, "Union members protest against longer shop hours," 1959; Qa. 1; AH1601. "NUDW Special meeting on shop hours, October 23, 1968; Qa.1; AH1601. "Changes in Shop Hours Act Urged," *Rand Daily Mail*, June 19, 1964; Da 2.4; AH1494. Muffy Turbeville, "Late Shopping: Which Way would your Vote Go?" *The Star*, January 26, 1977, p. 27; Ap 1.9.3; AH1494. "Saturday Afternoon Trading Christmas Success in Durban Demands Re-Look at the Question of Shop Hours," *Supermarket & Retailer*, Vol. 27, No. 1, January 1980, p. 4. "Checkers Trading Hours," *Supermarket & Retailer*, Vol. 29, No. 6, June 1982, p. 6.
36. Muffy Turbeville, "Late Shopping: Which Way would your Vote Go?" *The Star*, January 26, 1977, p. 27; Ap 1.9.3; AH1494.
37. "NUDW Shop Hours May be Extended!," July 29, 1952; Qa 3.4; AH1601. "Shops to Open 24 Hours a Day?," August 26, 1958; Qa 3.4; AH1601.
38. "Please don't shop after 5 p.m.!" (pamphlet), c. early 1960s; Qa.1; AH1601.
39. "Report of Interview between NUDW Representatives and OK Bazaars Personnel Manager Mr. H.B. Kampf," September 19, 1968; Ua 41.4; AH1601. "Report of Meeting between NUDW Representatives and OK Bazaars, Represented by Mr. Stanley Cohen, MD, and Mr. A.H. Fife, Personnel Director," November 4, 1968; Ua 41.3; AH1601.
40. Morris Kagan, "The Five Day Working Week," *New Day*, July/August 1971, pp. 8–10; G1; AH1202.
41. See, for example, "Further Representations to Transvaal Shop Hours Commission," *New Day*, May 1969, pp. 4–5; G1; AH1202. Morris Kagan, "Editorial: A Five-Day Working Week," *New Day*, December 1970, pp. 6–8; G1; AH1202. Letter from R.E. McMaster to M. Kagan, July 3, 1973; Ap 1.9.1; AH1494.
42. Casuals would be used particularly on Saturday mornings, see Morris Kagan, "The Five Day Working Week," *New Day*, July/August 1971, pp. 8–10; G1; AH1202.
43. Letter from R.E. McMaster to M. Kagan, July 3, 1973; Ap 1.9.1; AH1494.
44. Letter from J.R. Altman to M. Kagan, February 16, 1976; Ua 26.2c; AH1601.
45. "Joining the Swing to Extended Trading Hours?," *Supermarket and Retailer* Vol. 28, No. 4, April 1981, p. 33. The article reported that three major chains adopted these strategies.
46. "Flagmag," "Roving Report: A Look at Extended Shopping Hours," c. 1977, p. 2; Ua 26.2.c; AH1601.

47. "It's the Women who Man the Shops," *The Star*, March 8, 1972; Da 2.5; AH1494.
48. The National Union of Commercial and Allied Workers Union (NUCAW) became NUCCAW in this period.
49. Memo from Dulcie M. Hartwell to All Branch Secretaries and Officials, September 10, 1981; Ua 41.2.11; AH1601.
50. Minutes of a meeting held with officials of the NUDW and NUCCAW, February 7, 1979; Ua 41.3; AH1601.
51. Letter from Dulcie M. Hartwell to Mr. F.J. Yazbek, September 9, 1981; Ua 41.2.11; AH1601.
52. Jeremy Daphne, national organizer and negotiator for CCAWUSA and SACCAWU, interviewed by Bridget Kenny, Johannesburg, August 15, 2001.
53. Jeremy Daphne, interview.
54. See "Agreement, SACCAWU/ Shoprite Checkers Supermarkets/Meat Markets, Hyperama/Rainbow Finance," June 30, 1999; "Job Security Agreement, OK Bazaars/SACCAWU," February 26, 1996; "Agreement, Shoprite Checkers/ SACCAWU, Dealing with the Implementation of Flexi-time Work and the Conditions of Employment which Apply to Such Work," June 6, 1996. Copies of agreements in author's possession.
55. This pattern was similar to what happened in Australia (see Campbell and Burgess 2001a, b; Owens 2001).
56. The statistics did not differentiate between part-time and casual employment. After 1998, employment figures could not be disaggregated in this survey. See Lewis (2001) and Rees (1997) on the higher percentages of casual employment at shop floor and firm level.
57. Following labour and student unrest in the 1970s, the apartheid state set up the Wiehahn Commission to investigate labour law reform. In 1979, the commission recommended inclusion of black workers as employees and the recognition of black workers' trade unions as a means of incorporating and thereby disciplining workers (see Maree 1987, 138–153; Baskin 1991, 26). See Chap. 3 for more discussion.
58. Sectoral Determination 9: Wholesale and Retail Sector, 2002. For a discussion of the requirement of alignment of the previous Wage Determination (No. 478) to the Basic Conditions of Employment Act, see Lewis (2001, 127–31).
59. In 2015 further reforms to section 198 A to D of the Labour Relations Act set limits to employment through temporary employment services. This will be discussed in Chap. 8.

CHAPTER 5

Signifying Belonging: Restructuring and Workplace Relations

The 1980s had rendered the South African retail workplace a space of political contestation, a battleground of relationality, a specific material setting in which workers' action carried effect (see Chap. 3). The collective political subject, abasebenzi, was formed within these struggles and against regulatory reinscription and workers' own sense of how and in whom this standard-bearer bore likeness (see Chap. 4). This chapter turns to the period of the late 1990s when retail workplaces restructured in response to a rapidly changing economic and political environment. It examines experiences of workers at several Gauteng branches of Hyperama, a store in the "hypermarket" format that was introduced to South Africa as a model of innovation in the 1970s.

This new retailing format marketed modernity to a new "lifestyle" consumer. As discussed in the first section, these shops thus put forward an updated version of the nation that was based on delivering a "modern" experience of shopping to consumers through economies of scale and efficiencies of service, including self-service. The domesticated spaces of consumption of the 1960s, constituted through the aplomb of white women's labour (Chap. 2), were now replaced by fluorescent-lit realms in which a new black labour force appeared less consequential to consumption, even as workers were organizing therein (Chap. 3). Thus hypermarkets modelled a second moment of national belonging in retailing, in

© The Author(s) 2018
B. Kenny, *Retail Worker Politics, Race and Consumption in South Africa*, Rethinking International Development series,
https://doi.org/10.1007/978-3-319-69551-8_5

which the market offered a space of participation divorced from the affective relations of labour.

By the 1990s, these stores were exemplars of other changes wrought by retail restructuring more generally: capital consolidation, centralization of decision-making, supply chain reconfiguration, logistics technology innovation, and employment casualization and externalization. How workers understood, engaged with, and acted upon changes within these stores shows how these spaces were conjunctive "social sites" (Hall 1985, 99), in which relations, practices and modes of thought operated meaningfully, explaining labour politics. These stores symbolized South Africa's modernity (in proximity to the United States and Europe) in the 1970s, later democratic advance through near-inclusion, and then, by the late 1990s, neoliberal rationality and instrumentalism. Each discourse situated workers differently, in a "particular relation to the process" and thus "in relation to the account of the process" (Hall 1986, 39).

Restructuring in the latter period affected the three primary categories of workers now populating the labour market: permanent, casual, and contract workers. Each group expressed a sense of increasing control and surveillance being exercised over them, an incapacity to influence store-level decision-making or basic relationships, and a growing feeling of objectification within these workplaces. In short, these service sector workers explained their experiences of restructuring in terms of the incapacity to constitute relationships within the workplace. In their narratives, black workers became reinscribed as "labourers" marked by race (see Chap. 4). Thus, "relations in production" on the shop floor exposed workers to different forms of control and sets of conditions (Burawoy 1985, 13), but these criteria did not automatically explain how workers experienced them (Hall 1986; Scott 1991). As we will see, in the "subjectification" of workers, these new workplace relations articulated with concepts of labour, market, and nation in different ways than in the 1960s, reordering the markers of race, class, and gender (see Hall 1985). The meanings through which workers made sense of their experiences become critical to understanding their labour politics.

The Hypers: Revolutionizing Modern Retailing, 1975 to the 1990s

As black workers were brought into deskilled front-line service jobs in retailing from the 1970s (see Chap. 3), retailing itself was modernizing. The retail "revolution" of the 1970s and 1980s combined increasing store sizes with high volume turnover, lower prices, and greater market differentiation. The new "hypers" operated as decentralized business units, headed by white professional retail managers, and embraced new technology and merchandising systems that altered the labour process. These innovations were predicated on a model customer who was more informed, and a growing middle class looking for lifestyle shopping and entertainment. These changes toward "modernized" retailing transformed the meaning of service work, separating worker from consumer. This section gives a short portrait of the hypers of the 1970s and 1980s to be followed with examining the positions of workers within these stores in the 1990s. The "hype" of the hypers was in how they offered a new model of modernity and the nation to South Africa.

Internationally, the "hypermarket" emerged as a new retail format during the 1960s and 1970s after the development of supermarkets. These were larger stores, "one-stop shops," selling both food and non-food items,[1] which worked on price, larger volume sales, and product mix, including higher profit non-food items (Lucas et al. 1994, 39). Pick n Pay opened the first South African hypermarket in Boksburg on the East Rand in March 1975.[2] OK Bazaars followed with its first Hyperama opening in 1979, also on the East Rand. For retailers, the new format offered a way to innovate and to introduce exciting changes to keep customers returning and expand market share.

Pick n Pay's former chief executive officer Raymond Ackerman brought the format to South Africa after being inspired by France's *hypermarchés*.[3] On a visit there, he was apparently advised by the chairman of France's Carrefour that "all you need ... is 10% capital and 90% guts."[4] Ackerman reflected back on his decision to launch the hyper format in South Africa: "The guts proved the more difficult problem. 'Raymond, you're mad! You can't compare South Africa to Europe or America. We haven't got the population', was an often repeated chorus."[5] However, despite the "massive investment" required to start a hyper (Ackerman 2001, 121), the format took off in South Africa's retail market in the 1970s and 1980s, with such merchant-innovators leading the country into a future of First World standards.

The hyper format worked for retail capital. The market share of larger stores increased during the 1970s. According to surveys of the trade by marketing firm AC Nielsen, by 1979 larger stores ("hypers and majors") – all branches of corporate chains – accounted for 5% of the total number of stores but held 60% of South Africa's entire formal grocery market. This share represented a steady rise from 33% of the market in 1970.[6] In 1985, on the tenth anniversary of the opening of the first Pick n Pay Hypermarket, a trade journal celebrated the lasting appeal of these stores.[7] The success of this format – what the article called "the magic of Boksburg" – was determined by its location, promotions, decentralized management operations, and merchandising. Other companies had similar elements in their versions of hyper stores, like OK Bazaar's Hyperama. In no small apocryphal twist, Pick n Pay's Ackerman claims that "the late Sam Walton of Walmart resolved to build hypers in the USA after visiting us in South Africa and touring our stores" (Ackerman 2001, 121).[8]

For South African retailers and consumers, these new stores bred excitement. Above all, they were big. As one industry expert, a former Hyperama marketing manager, said of the Hyperamas: "We called them battleships." Hypers worked on high turnover: "For instance Roodepoort [Hyperama] in the summer had enormous turnover. Eight times a day, huge trucks would pull in to deliver stock, eight times per day! It was a revolution in the retail business."[9]

High volume sales meant that retailers could use economies of scale to sell cheaper products. Suppliers boycotted the Boksburg Hypermarket before it opened because of deep consumer discounts (thereby affecting supplier prices) which the retailer could insist on because it controlled distribution to this new market (Ackerman 2001, 126).[10] This kind of practice would become identified with Wal-Mart in sector literature (Lichtenstein 2009) (see Chap. 8), but we can see that already in the mid-1970s South African retailers were implementing contemporary versions of these techniques. During the 1970s and 1980s in general, price competition was a key factor to retail innovation (Humphrey 1998, 147). A former marketing manager explains: "The slogan became 'The Big Hyper with small prices'. It rested on large volumes. Everything was geared to large volumes. There was large size merchandise."[11] The hypers introduced South Africa to bulk buying. As one trade journal article reminded its readers: "Today [in 1985] everyone takes multi-packs of 15 toilet rolls for granted. Bulk packs such as 2 kg and 5 kg washing powder packs are now standard. Before Boksburg [Hypermarket], 1 kg packs were the biggest the consumer could buy."[12] The former marketing manager remembered: "Hyperama was geared … to buy in bulk, at the lowest prices. It really was very low: 25% margins, then down to 20% margins. At some point they were even selling at cost on some items."[13] Because of low margins and high turnover, retailers competed by providing different product mixes. While Pick n Pay used carefully calculated margins on food items to ensure profitability, OK Bazaars went for a higher proportion of greater-profit non-food products.

Marketers strategized about these mixes based on a new image of the consumer, one who was not just buying necessities (see Bowlby 2001; Humphrey 1998). One marketing team divided the merchandise into three categories: food, "fun, which was clothing," and "investments or ego" purchases, such as stereos or furniture. Whereas food was a necessary and regular purchase and the highest volume of sales, they took into account "research that talks about the British housewife who wants to shop as an entertainment. She doesn't want to buy her food for entertainment. She has to do that. It is a slog." As they experimented with the sizes of each of these categories, the mix "became more lifestyle driven."[14]

The "lifestyle" shopper (and see Bowlby 2001) helped retailers to adapt their accumulation strategies in the 1970s and 1980s. In the 1960s, retailers had expanded the number and location of chain branches (see Chap. 2). The hypers thus sought to out-compete these formats by offering something different by differentiating the market. They were located on stand-alone plots outside city centres, with their own parking and close to major traffic routes. They were tailored to upwardly mobile middle-class whites, who from the 1970s purchased their own cars and defined suburban growth, and thus had the means, time, and money to access these stores (Hyslop 2000; Beavon 2004).[15] In marketing the hypermarket format to these motor enthusiasts, retailers stressed the one-stop shopping at these mega-stores.[16] Further, while supermarkets were offering a wide variety of food products and sundry household items under one roof, hypermarkets added "lifestyle departments" that included gardening sections, do-it-yourself home improvement centres, "Outdoor Living" areas displaying camping and sports equipment, and furniture departments.[17] In 1981, advertisements for Pick n Pay's Hypermarket enticed customers with ice-cream eating competitions, country music bands, an ox braai [barbeque] lunch and oompah band, the East Rand Youth Choir, and Boksburg's St. Dominics drum majorettes. The "Hyper Women's Club" met regularly at the shop.[18] In a retailing environment of proliferating chain branches, the hypers sought competitive advantage through drawing customers into a new experience of shopping.

The hypers targeted the middle-class white housewife. A former Hyperama marketing manager noted: "It was the white market which was ideally suited for this type of store. The white market had great mobility." He continued:

> The people who travelled the most to Hyperama were the wealthy Sandton suburb ladies.[19] They would be the ones to go to Edenvale [20 km away] to buy in bulk. They would buy not just one [bag of] Epol for their dog, but 10 bags. They had the cars; they were well informed ... They were mobile and had enough wealth to buy in bulk.[20]

Hypers expanded their markets by tapping into a new consumer, one whom they portrayed as discerning. In order to consolidate customer loyalty, hypers developed new instruments to monitor customer needs. They reasoned that if they fulfilled these needs, customers were more likely to return to their chain. Pick n Pay, for example, used "consumer advisors, consumer panels, [the] hyper women's club, and staff" to tap into consumer desire.[21] In 1980 retailers predicted needing to use "much more scientific market research" to ascertain consumer habits and motivations.[22]

In Britain, the image of the shopper changed from the gendered "female dope" in the 1950s to the neutral smart shopper and modern individual by the 1970s (Bowlby 2001, 7). In South Africa, by contrast, this abstract ideal of smart shopper remained coded by gender and race. In TV advertisements, a new marketing medium that became available in South Africa only in 1976, Hyperama, for instance, pitched its house brand at young, upwardly mobile white women, represented in the character of (1975's Miss South Africa) Vera Sutherland "(nee Johns)," who has "just got married and is setting up home" and is value and quality conscious in her "new-found domesticity."[23] Retailers' use of house brands served to garner loyalty to particular store chains in an increasingly competitive environment.[24] And, in this effort, the trope of white women fulfilling their domestic duties, while radiating poise and beauty, continued to define this updated consumer.

Hypers worked on their branding in a bid to maintain customer loyalty. The Pick n Pay Hypermarkets were well branded because of their connection to the familiar Pick n Pay supermarket brand. The Hyperamas, introduced by OK Bazaars as a new brand, required a more intensively crafted distinction, as described by a former manager: "We did a lot of research on colour. We looked at the yellow of Checkers, the red of OK. The only colour that wasn't used was green and we went for it. We used to call it the "Mean Green Hypermachine."[25] Hyperama took on its own individual brand identity, separate from that of OK Bazaars, its owner and a very popular chain at the time, in order to emphasize its modern identity. The abstract, efficient rationality of the metaphor of Hyper-*machine* should not be missed. The stores were new, clean, and big, the pinnacle of modernity.

Modernizing management systems – rather than skilled shop assistants – became the gears of the machine, enabling quick turnover and special merchandising. The hypers used a combination of warehousing and direct supplier deliveries, which theoretically allowed quicker response times and cut the costs of storing stock. With direct deliveries, store-level management made buying decisions for their branches, especially sourcing perishables from local suppliers.

Computers helped hypers manage their merchandising, and they were some of the first stores in South Africa to install early versions of computerized stock control systems in the mid-1980s, including electronic point-of-sale technology.[26] Hyperama branches required point-of-sale information to monitor sales and merchandising in each of their large departments. These computerized systems would "ensure correct price and departmental registration, cashier productivity reports and sales reports by volume and by time-of-day and even departmental sales by time-of-day."[27] At the time, these were state-of-the-art systems, and very expensive to install.

In order to manage larger and quicker stock turnovers, hypers modernized other merchandising systems. Despite the perception that they offered customers wide choice of products, hypermarkets often had fewer product lines than most supermarkets.[28] To support the illusion of plenitude, the hypers made use of innovations in merchandising at the time, such as specialized display, use of "ends" (displays at the end of an aisle), in-store promotions, and new refrigeration technologies. While these innovations were considered widely across the industry, the hypers were able to incorporate them more immediately into the store layout and display as they were newly built.

These "scientific" tools fit the decentralized organizational model of hypers. For instance, in Pick n Pay, each Hypermarket was designed to run as a separate business unit and each department as its own profit centre. It decentralized buying where merchandise selection and negotiations were conducted by "each hyper's own buyers."[29] Similarly, each OK Hyperama had its own personnel manager and stores made staff hiring and firing decisions internally.[30]

During the 1970s and 1980s, store-level managers had extensive decision-making powers that coincided with their status of being "professional." Management training courses and practical experience were very much a part of retailing career paths for white men. A potential manager often entered at the bottom of the company's hierarchy and moved up through the ranks, sometimes beginning as a casual worker, as we saw in Chap. 4, learning every angle of the retailing business in the process. Not only did this practice train managers, but it also built a strong network of managers and contributed to maintaining the dominance of white men in these positions. Increasingly, however, managers were able to advance on the basis purely of training in professional retail management courses (see also Freathy and Sparks 1996). By the 1980s retail managers were professional men, adept in the science of selling: "Retailers became numbers men," versed in tracking bottom lines rather than the "gut feel" of salesmanship.[31]

Where sales in previous decades had been driven by the direct interaction between shop assistants and customers, as in the "battle of the wits" described with relish in Chap. 2, in this period managers orchestrated customers' "self-service" through floor planning and display (see Leidner 1993) which guided the selective consumer through the store. Similarly, computerized till technology left little to the cashier. Bowlby (2001) traces the "invention of modern shopping" to its pinnacle in the "haunted superstore," where customers wander alone in the aisles. This modernized space of desire relied on the use of "scientific" discourses of consumer psychology and marketing strategy.[32] It also functioned through the development of self-service, where the consumer could relish longer in the "dreamier delights" (Bowlby 2001, 3) of entertaining shopping without being brought back to reality with interpersonal interactions.

Yet, in South Africa real store relations rudely interrupted the picture of an idealized consumer and a rational bureaucracy that hyper management teams carefully tried to construct. The growth of hypers coincided with organized black workers militantly protesting against racist inequality, forcing engagement in a context of deskilling (see Chap. 3). Indeed, Hyperama staff participated in the bitter OK Bazaars strike of 1986/87 discussed in Chap. 3 (with shop steward Amos Tshabalala and worker Mary Nkosi both having worked there).[33] In South Africa, these retail fantasies sold progress and worldliness to white consumers precisely when the service workforce was changing. The hypers, then, represented an abstracted model of depersonalized employment and autonomous customer relations as another model of national belonging – in consumer markets (again made safe with white women's presence, now as consumers) – symbolically erasing the (black and troublesome) service worker.

By the late 1980s, an economic crisis introduced significantly altered conditions for retailers in South Africa (Gelb 1991). Large-scale investments in new stores that had epitomized the growth of the "hypermarket" format of the 1970s and 1980s now left retailers with "sunk capital" in giant branches (see Wrigley 1996). At the same time, retailers were confronted with demands for higher wages by organized and militant black workers in the sector. These developments posed dilemmas for South African retail accumulation which retailers addressed by increasing capital consolidation and concentration, deepening their power within supply chain relations, and making greater ordinary use of casual and contract labour, as we saw in Chap. 4. By the late 1990s, these changes altered the labour process and forms of control operating in these stores, as detailed in the remaining sections.

A "Culture of Threat": Changing Workplace Relations from the Late 1990s

In 1997 Shoprite/Checkers, one of South Africa's largest retailers, bought the giant OK Bazaars in a wave of sector consolidations in the 1990s, thus becoming the single largest food retailer in the country. OK Bazaars, a founder of South African retailing in 1929, had run itself into the ground. It faced massive losses despite the stable financial status of its Hyperama division. It had spent too much on a heavy bureaucracy, undermining efficient operations. In November 1997 parent company South African Breweries sold OK Bazaars and its divisions to the fast-moving expansion efforts of Shoprite for one rand plus debts. The consequences of this change in ownership offer an example of the wider developments in retail in the 1990s, with a shift to centralized management and logistical systems. A corollary was an increase in surveillance in the workplace. This section examines the implications of these changes through the specific example of Shoprite's acquisition of OK Bazaars.

Shoprite asserted a very different corporate culture, which altered concrete workplace relations (Schoenberger 1997) by cutting the top-heavy bureaucracy built up in the 1980s in order to professionalize retail management.[34] When Shoprite acquired OK Bazaars, it retrenched executive management and replaced them with a head who reported directly to Shoprite's executive team. As one retail sector representative explained: "Shoprite ... had success in their formula: highly centralized, few management, and very dictatorial. OK Bazaars had a heavy hierarchy. Shoprite went in and wiped it out through the rationalization of management."[35]

According to some, the takeover "has taken place smoothly. We knew about it three months before being sold. I didn't worry for my job. Everyone knew beforehand if they were staying or going."[36] Yet, from the perspective of those working in branches, the situation was more chaotic. Six "lower managers" left one manager's branch,[37] while at another 11 branch managers were retrenched or resigned.[38] Elizabeth Maseremule, a black female trainee manager at the time, described the situation:

> There were retrenchments from top to bottom, managers, buyers, supervisors at branch level ... We were told not to panic, that our jobs were still secured, but ... two weeks [later], those managers [who had informed us had] left ... Most resigned after Shoprite took over. [It is] only a few that is left.[39]

Restructuring the corporate hierarchy affected local workplace relations. Branch-level managers portrayed this moment of restructuring as one of a break with a past order built on best practice. As Johannes van Rooy, an Afrikaans-speaking white male line manager explained:

> Hyperama had training standards that were excellent ... after the Hyperama training, others would headhunt you ... We had very good relationships. We had human resources at the time, good standards. This was the time with the change to democracy. You'd do the courses, and then you'd do a practical in one of the flagship stores. You knew that something at the other end would happen.[40]

In Johannes' telling, Hyperama had rewarded merit consistently, and "people [had] felt wanted." He described the company's height of excellence as coinciding with South Africa's democratic transition, and he linked these training standards with broadening participation through career paths. Elizabeth, the former trainee manager, also emphasized a feeling of belonging: "They developed [their] own people. They recognized people."[41]

In Johannes' and Elizabeth's stories, this order of participation was reflected as having been deracialized, with black and white managers receiving equal attention. Before joining the trainee manager programme, Elizabeth, an ordinary worker at the time, was promoted to a supervisory position because "I used to act when my supervisor was not there. They saw that a person was capable, and can give her the position."[42] Indeed, her case marked a difference from Mrs. Marjorie Smith, wrongly dismissed for shoplifting (see Chap. 3), who performed supervisory work without being officially promoted in the 1960s. Johannes confirmed: "We had good affirmative action for the time, well before other retailers."[43] Thus, Hyperama's rules of inclusion worked to reward merit. These managers framed their firm-based "strategic imagination" (Schoenberger 1997, 142) within South Africa's democratic transition. They avowed the values of a "non-racial" workplace, where rights of participation were based on individual effort, in a clearly defined procedural order of expectations operating through store relationships.

In discussing restructuring, then, line managers recalled a specific past where valuing staff was central. Johannes explained his managerial philosophy at the time: "You must work with your staff and be available. They are assets to the company."[44] Frederick Smith, a coloured male line manager, remembered how his store manager epitomized this period:

> He was a darling of a man. When he left, everything changed ... If you go to him and ask him for a raise, he will look over the budget and look over your record and if you are doing well and deserve it, he will give you now. Other managers don't even find out what the budget is; if he doesn't like your face, you are down.[45]

Frederick's store manager represented all that was good in Hyperama. The fundamental break occurred for him with the replacement of this "darling of a man" with a nameless unreceptive manager. A personalized order where the store manager increased wages based on a fair and kind assessment of worth, and where he had authority to make these decisions, was superseded by arbitrary and individualized prejudice, associated with Shoprite. Managers who stayed on explicitly compared the two firms' cultures:

> With the take-over by Shoprite a lot changed. I think that the draw card to work for Hyperama [the old order][46] was its vision, its focus on people. You can say it had a moral purpose. It was not just operating for profit. Shoprite took over, and it is very profit orientated. Not caring about people.[47]

Shoprite restructured with the intention of centralizing key functions, such as personnel management, as well as limiting the powers of store managers.[48] Management-worker relations, previously defined at the branch, were sundered, and many managers with whom workers had built relationships over years of confrontation and engagement left. Under Shoprite, Elizabeth, the black former trainee manager, was retrenched and rehired as a casual wage clerk. She felt betrayed by the company that seemed to operate out of pure self-interest with no regard for loyal and productive staff:

> On the retrenchment letter they sa[id] that the position was being made redundant, seek for alternative jobs. After two weeks, they paid me out. In two months time, they advertised positions again. That is where I felt bad. With children to look after ...[49]

A second aspect of the new corporate culture that Shoprite introduced was a punitive regime. In a former department manager's language, Shoprite "infiltrated the company ... They wanted to find things wrong that people were doing. Find them doing something wrong and punish them."[50] Johannes reported there were "disciplinary actions for everything ... In my last two years with the company, there were more hearings than ever I had in my entire career with the company."[51] These actions resulted in dismissals of the affected staff. A former human resource manager who worked for three major food retailers over the course of his career explained how a new focus on profitability informed this conduct: "If it smacks of a loss, they dismiss their people. [We] can't talk about fairness. It is a culture of threat."[52]

Under Shoprite, control shifted from positive buy-in by staff to proceduralized punishment against them, where the company made tactical use of post-apartheid labour law (see Chap. 4). Theft became a headline issue in 2000 when Shoprite disclosed to stockholders that it had incurred losses of R100 million due to "shrinkage" (Klein 2000, 20). Shoprite's management team emphasized its proactive uprooting of all theft, from the distribution channel to opportunistic stealing by workers on the shop floor.

Consolidation of retail capital coupled with aggressive strategies to squeeze profit from the relatively small domestic market thus set the company on a path of "profits before people." In the early 1990s, for line managers the former Hyperama – that clean, bright, and fully modern retailer – represented the pinnacle of democratic, participatory organization, a model of new nationhood. With Shoprite's buy-out, new centralization of power away from the branches meant that there were limited branch-level channels for workers to engage management around key areas affecting their work lives, the focus of the next section.

A Disordered Present: The Past "Moral Economy" of the Workplace

Permanent workers explained the effects of restructuring in terms of how these changes eroded their capacity to maintain workplace relations in ways that could be constructed as mutual, even if they were not. When Shoprite took over, it ended a number of institutionalized procedures for dealing with staff, breaking the existing balance of power between management and shop floor workers. Shoprite reportedly stopped its training programme for permanent workers, leaving many feeling that they no longer had opportunities for promotion. According to workers, it substantially shortened compassionate leave. It cut death benefits for workers' family members. It refused to pay overtime for stocktake and Sunday hours, instead altering permanents' ordinary working hours or hiring casuals, following trends we saw in Chap. 4. It no longer allowed workers to take advances or staff loans against their salaries. It downgraded canteen services and eliminated subsidized lunches. It ended the weekly visits of a nurse who provided free remedial health services to workers.[53]

Kethiwe Dlomo, a bakery assistant, described her experiences: "We are no longer working overtime. [Shoprite] said that they do not pay overtime. They do not pay public holidays. When they pay, it's paid as normal hours." Instead Shoprite used casual workers, whom it paid less, to work these hours. She explained the effect this had on workers: "We used to work on Sundays. I was never home because I wanted to make sure that my family get[s] food. So I used to go to work, because I knew that when I knock-off, I get paid. But with Shoprite they totally stopped that thing and they used casuals [*amacasual*]." Shoprite ended other informal shop floor practices that assisted permanent workers to survive. Kethiwe described: "We used to have markdowns, like in bakery, fruit and vegetables, perishables. We survived with that. They completely closed it down. [The food] must be thrown away and counted as wastage."[54] Able to demand refunds from suppliers for "wastage," Shoprite's shrewd cost accounting took precedence over shop floor traditions for the workers.

These changes brought Hyperama employees in line with Shoprite's general standards of employment, and made clear to workers that the company's priority was cost reduction. Because the South African Commercial, Catering and Allied Workers Union (SACCAWU) had brokered these "benefits" of employment in the early 1990s, removing them became highly symbolic and deeply resented by permanent workers. They explained:

> The management that we started with in 1991 was agreeable on certain issues and not agreeable on certain issues. And that's where the union got involved and the management came to understand [*iyazwanyana*, began to hear]. But now, from 1998 up to now, 1999, it's bad.[55]

These workers said that Shoprite also halted workers' ability to leverage their jobs to obtain bank loans, and ended job benefits, such as family bursaries and company loans, which the union had put into place. Permanent workers had used these methods to finance their children's education, to build up financial security, and to meet their social obligations.[56] Kethiwe's description above shows how Shoprite's austerity broke with Hyperama's practices that had enabled workers actively to construct their social worlds.[57]

This discourse reverberates with the concept of "moral economy" in which workers asserted claims of (past) obligations to push back against dislocations caused by capitalism (Thompson 1971).[58] In his study of mineworkers in South Africa, Dunbar Moodie (Moodie and Ndatshe 1994) applies moral economy to describe the agreed-upon rules of engagement between workers and management that predict expectations of obligation from management and tolerance of certain forms of worker resistance.[59] His use of moral economy stresses the interactive (and instrumental) negotiations between workers and managers explained in part by workers' subordinate position. Instead, in thinking about retail workers' narratives, I follow William Roseberry (1989, 57) to focus on how relations described in terms of a "moral economy" are "*perceived* [to be] in the past from the perspective of a disordered present."[60] Thus, recourse to a discourse of *past relations*, represented under the sign of "Hyperama," where obligations were met and abided by, signifies not so much the authenticity of that prior reciprocity, nor the terms of brokered relationships, nor even the ability to instantiate these rules of obligation, but rather the crux of what is experienced as most egregious in the present. As Hall (1985) might put it, it becomes necessary to explain the conjuncture, the appeal – in our case of a language of relationship, which insists on a version of workers as political subjects, where they have effect – at this moment of change. Thus, the language used to describe the phenomenon of "restructuring" discloses discursive framings, conditioning forms of action and thus processes of subjectification.

These retail workers employed a language of reciprocal obligation with managers when their "disordered present" made a union-backed order securing communication and respect increasingly ineffectual (see also Collins 2003, 102). In short their discourse of "moral economy" did not hark back to authentic historical and cultural relations of trust per se, but pointed to a moment when this possibility was altered. Permanent retail workers' claim to a moral economy denoted a betrayal, posed in terms of a notion of national belonging in post-apartheid South Africa and in terms of the ability to have effect on their concrete relations. The "union" was a shorthand for the possibility of maintaining an active engagement in a set of relations which coalesced around the political subject of "workers."

It was management that subverted these relations in these narratives. Kethiwe and many other permanent workers used the imagery of predation to describe how Shoprite was "eating" [*adliwe wuye* in isiZulu] their benefits.[61] The metaphor of "eating" denotes the absorption of an individual's autonomy and power through political, economic, and ritual means. A person who is "eaten" by political rivals loses self-determination, no longer able to construct ties of interdependence (Comaroff and Comaroff 1992, 164). In this discourse, Shoprite's changes removed black permanent workers' capacity to be engaged participants in the workplace order, to be constitutive subjects, and to leverage their jobs to resource other ties, as we will see in more detail in Chap. 7. As Kethiwe expressed it: permanent workers "are not progressing with Shoprite; we are just standing in one place."[62] Zama Ntuli, a permanent cashier for the store since 1988, remembered, "We were used to them [managers], they were treating us well."[63] The phrase "used to" implied that managers and workers had built up a relationship over time and had worked out understandings. In contrast,

> Shoprite does not want [discussion]. At Hyperama we would call the manager and the management would come ... the shop stewards would ask him that he should see us individually because we've got individual problems. So he is requested to make sufficient time ... Shoprite does not even want to discuss with a black employee as we are sitting like this ... They do not care. They don't want to know.[64]

This refusal to meet workers (and the reinscription of workers as an undifferentiated group) led to growing hostility between Shoprite managers and permanent workers and their union. Often this conflict came to be marked by race.

By the late 1990s, Shoprite's measures had destroyed the premise on which agreements and rules could be negotiated. In workers' language, they were "sitting," stuck and unable to act,[65] and the company was immoral. Sara Dlamini, a canteen supervisor, said the company did not "care for the staff, they only care for the customers, that is all, because they bring money."[66] Others said that Shoprite's profit motive made it dishonest even to customers: "Even when [Shoprite was] trying to bring back the Heydays [sale], customers were very aware that it's still the normal prices ... [Customers said,] 'They think we don't see'."[67]

Proving its lack of commitment to quality service, according to workers, Shoprite undid measures that had been introduced at the Hyperamas at the suggestion of shop floor workers, such as staggered tea breaks that had been introduced to provide uninterrupted service to customers: "We were thinking that we were sacrificing for the company so that there should not be [long queues of customers] by having tea in our department. We negotiated that thing [the staggered tea breaks] from 1991 when [the store] was opened."[68] Kethiwe expressed her grievance in particular against Shoprite's betrayal of a negotiated practice that had led to better store operations. She summarized: "We even call Shoprite Shop*wrong* because everything is wrong, there is nothing right."[69] Under

Shoprite ownership, workers felt increasingly acted upon, with less capacity to affect relations. Yet this change in relationship between management and workers impinged on casual and contract workers even more forcefully, as detailed in the following section.

Subjectification of Workers: Outsider, Criminal, Labourer

Within their daily activities, workers experienced forms of control – such as surveillance technology, customer service monitoring, weekly scheduling, and direct supervision – as making them into outsiders in their workplaces. While all workers expressed these feelings, casual and contract workers described forms of subjectification brought about through these shop floor relations which made them particularly invisible at work.

In 1998 Shoprite upgraded the stores' computer systems with a fully integrated till point-of-sale computer technology, including bar coding of products. This equipment enabled the retailer to manage stock supply and consumer profiling even more efficiently than before. Critically, it also enabled increased surveillance of employees. In February 2000, Shoprite installed closed circuit television (CCTV), assuring stockholders that this would halt major losses through theft. It insisted on branch accountability for theft and increased the importance of branch shrinkage ratios in store evaluations. Managers met regularly with workers to report on changing shrinkage ratios. Graphs were posted at staff entrances to chart the rise and fall of these figures. Workers were concerned to see these numbers fall, because behind them was a threat of job losses or store closure. Shoprite contracted private security firms to monitor customers' and workers' activities.[70] The company negotiated an agreement with the union by which workers were encouraged to turn in colleagues they suspected of stealing. Picturing skull-and-cross-bones, menacing warnings papered canteen walls: "Shrinkage has no friends," "Shrinkage is no jobs," "Shrinkage is dishonesty," "Shrinkage is concealing stock," "Shrinkage is not paying for own uses." Notices provided telephone numbers of managers and shop stewards to report evidence, offering a reward upon conviction (Photo 5.1).

Most union members ignored these appeals for information and relied on the fact that the union would represent them if they were ever charged.

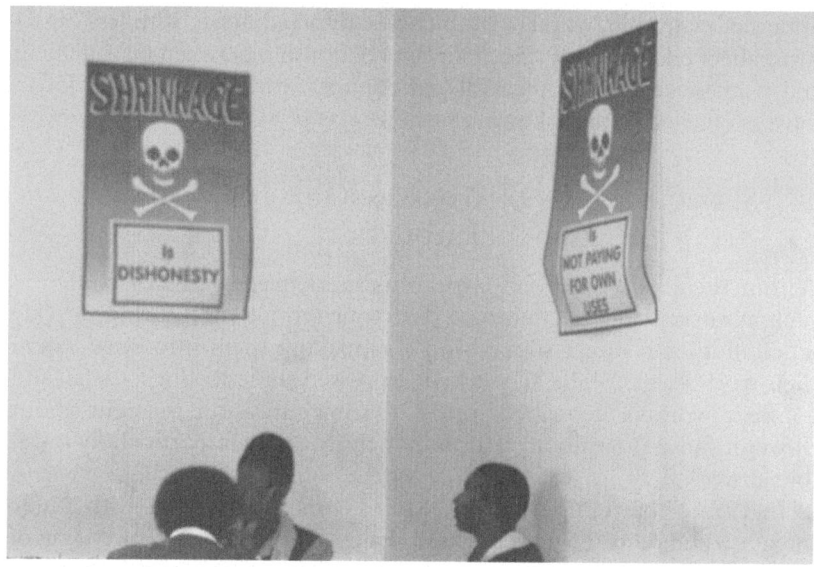

Photo 5.1 Warnings against "Shrinkage," c. 2000 (Image by Bridget Kenny. Edits by Simon Gush)

Yet, according to shop stewards, an unprecedented number of employees were subjected to hearings or dismissed on charges of theft in these years.[71] In several instances, groups of permanent workers were fired for alleged theft.[72] These workers stood as an example to others. One shop steward recalled pleading with the union members, "okay guys, now the times are different. If you steal now, you could lose your jobs."[73] Yet many permanent workers saw in these technologies a different danger: "This is a management strategy to eliminate us and employ more casuals because they misuse and threaten them."[74]

Casual cashiers and bag packers at the tills, in turn, felt particularly watched by CCTV cameras pointed at their workstations. Unathi Shabalala, a casual cashier, was accused of theft when she bent down to pick up a tissue that had fallen from her shirtsleeve. In an instant, several security guards surrounded her and she was taken to the manager's office: "They said that [they could see on CCTV] I had taken a twenty rand [note] from the till. And they did this in front of my customer and the staff. I was frightened. I thought they were going to hit me, or chase me then and there."[75] Her story has a hyperbolic quality to it, if only for the unusual immediacy of the security response. More often, management charged casual workers with theft months after the alleged event which often meant that workers had no means of disproving the accusation. In her story, Unathi described the attention focused on her, the visibility (to security, to fellow workers, and to customers) which shone upon her, and ultimately the objectification and humiliation she felt by being accused.

"Merchandisers," or what roughly used to be called "distributive workers" (see Chaps. 2 and 3), who operated in the aisles and the storerooms of branches moving and packing stock, are the third category of worker under consideration. In the mid-1990s, the Hyperama contracted many of them out to be employed by labour brokers to pack product lines. They too were well aware of the cameras installed to monitor theft, as Vuyo Nokabu explained: "Now they put cameras all over the shop."[76] Security managers would threaten merchandisers that "'I am going to call the police ... I am going to call the manager so that he can come and see you on the TV', because they['ve] got the cameras."[77] All three groups of workers – permanent, casual, and contract – identified the new surveillance systems as a mechanism to control them. Initially signalling modern retailing and national status, this technology turned to discipline over the labour force. Workers felt they were being interpellated as potential criminals, as outsiders to the store rather than as active members of the workplace.

Such discourses of punishment pervaded the shops, with customer service coming to be seen not as an autonomous skill by service workers, as in earlier decades, but as another mechanism to control them. Cheryl Issacs, a permanent worker, worried: "They said because we don't serve our customers right, with smiles and 100%, so we are not going to make money, and they are gonna start retrenching, or we are going to work like three days in a week, permanents."[78] Management linked poor service ratings to the issue of declines in branch sales turnover figures. Cheryl was a supply clerk and knew first hand that there were regular delivery inefficiencies, which left shelves under-stocked and customers complaining: instead of addressing these issues, she argued, managers blamed poor service for branch failings. Because branches now competed with each other on their numbers, managers put more pressure on workers, at times threatening them with dismissal.

Casual workers also felt the punitive effect of customers whom they directly served as cashiers and bag packers. Customer service was stressed before they even entered employment in formulaic manner. In order to get a (casual) job, applicants had to take a basic exam which centred on the golden rule that "The customer is always right." The potential employee was handed a packet containing company rules and procedures, given half an hour to read the information, and then asked a series of rote questions dealing almost exclusively with conduct relating to customers, such as "Fill in the blank. The customer is always _____."[79] Despite this rather cursory screening process, and little to no training after being hired, customer service could have a serious impact.

Complaints from a customer about small mistakes by a worker, for instance not packing a customer's groceries well, could lead to formal warnings.[80] In many cases it meant that both customers and managers blamed workers. As one worker said: "We are not happy with their slogan, 'The customer is always right'. What must I do when the customer is in line and the machine is off-line?"[81] Yet, as this worker knew, she would be criticized from both sides for a malfunctioning system for which she was not responsible.

The "white customer" still held a heavy social weight over black workers, particularly front-line casual workers. In discussing the job application form mentioned above, casual workers joked with me by insisting that they filled in their application, "The customer is always WHITE" and that management did not notice the difference (between "right" and "white") and hired them. Whereas most workers said that black customers rarely complained about service or products, in disagreements with white complainants, management would support the customer and threaten to dismiss casuals for "causing" a scene.[82] Casual workers had to bear the humiliation of the interaction: "We are supposed to treat them with care, irrespective whether they swear or what."[83] Female cashiers risked being assaulted by customers. When, in one case, an irate, Afrikaans-speaking white man hit a black casual cashier in the chest with a polony, insisting that the price was wrong, the white male manager shouted at her for not providing adequate service to the customer.[84] Several workers experienced blunt racism when white customers refused to touch their hands when exchanging money.[85]

The racial divide with white customers was less about adequate service, which had become devalued as the labour process changed with self-service and deskilling, than about quelling anxieties around democracy in these interactive spaces by reinforcing ongoing expectations of privilege and distinction of whites in these service encounters.[86] Management's implicit acceptance of racist behaviour by customers through its customer service approach, and the concomitant undermining of black workers, suggests that management positioned black workers as low-skilled labourers. The one-time skill and pride that white women workers asserted in their service (see Chap. 2) was replaced with customer service as a mechanism of discipline.

Such processes of subjectification of workers – as re-racialized outsider and other – were replicated in other mechanisms. For casual workers experiences included encounters with a disembodied authority in regular occurrences when they were underpaid their wages. Casual worker Tsakane Baloi described what she did in such a situation:

> You see, we query at customer service … You write [down] the days you worked, and how much you got. We don't speak to anyone, we just write it down. Then they take that book to the office. We don't actually know who addresses those problems. We just find the book signed. If the book is signed it means that it is fixed, but even if you don't get it [the backpay], it has been "fixed."[87]

Similarly, casuals learned of their work schedules for a certain week from a roster posted on the preceding Friday, a system which many felt was opaque: "Every Friday you find your name on the notice board, and the days on which you will be working. But we still don't know how they come to make these decisions."[88]

These impersonal management techniques removed casual workers from a relationship with those who paid them and scheduled their hours. In addition, much to the frustration of the casual workers, the schedule was frequently wrong, so that workers found themselves down incorrectly not to work, or turned back when clocking-in because of an error on the plan. When workers complained, they were told that "computers" had made the mistakes, marking the depersonalized nature of their employment relationship that workers resented:

> I came to check the list and my name was there but the days on which I am supposed to work were not there. I went to ask them, and they said that they noticed the problem but that the computer didn't show all the information. But I thought to myself that the computer is controlled by people. They then said to me that this means that I will stay the whole week without working.[89]

Casual workers were thus caught in the effects of the centralization of personnel administration at regional offices, where schedules were determined (and see Chap. 6). No longer having power over such decisions, branch management blamed the remote force of the computer for mistakes. Yet casual workers experienced this as a fetishization of the schedule, uprooted from the social relations of work. The number of days they worked was critical to them since more hours meant more income (see Chaps. 4 and 7). This daily depersonalization of authority reinforced their own sense of powerlessness and also made them feel like bulk labour, not a member of staff.

Finally, forms of direct supervision from other black workers fortified the punitive order, which subjugated casual workers. Cashiers and bag packers were supervised by till controllers, often (black) permanent workers and union members who dealt with cheque and credit card payments, but also monitored workers' speed and customer service at the tills. Till controllers reported to the cash bank manager, located within the administrative department. These managers were white or Indian women in these stores at this time, and most casuals rarely interacted with them. Sfiso Shenge, a young casual worker, described the relationship between casual workers and till supervisors as fraught. One day he and a colleague were instructed to return unpurchased items left at the tills to their shelves, a task called "back-shopping," when his colleague was called to do something different:

> There were many trolleys full of groceries, and I alone had to shelve all the items in them. The till controller, a black guy, came to me and said that if I haven't completed this task before the shop closes, I should not come to work forever. I started working harder, and at about 3:30 I was helped by other workers. But when the shop closed at six, I still had not completed the work.[90]

Sfiso thought he would be fired, but the next day no one said anything to him. The authority exercised over him was not by the proverbial white manager, but by a "black guy," who threatened him with dismissal. Unlike permanent workers who could rely on union assistance if threatened with dismissal, casual workers like Sfiso had little room to manoeuvre daily relations with their superiors (see Chap. 6), so that such relationships could be filled with risk for them. Supervision from permanent workers constituted another line along which casual workers' subordination became reproduced.

Labour brokers, by contrast, rarely directly supervised contract merchandisers.[91] Rather, product representatives ("reps"), also employed by the labour brokers, periodically visited stores to assess merchandisers' performance: "[Reps] are coming in, like now on Fridays, to check me; they just come to check how is my [stock], how is the store, and he goes again."[92] Themba Nyembe, a contract merchandiser employed by a labour broker regularly to stock several lines of products in one branch, explained his daily work (Photo 5.2):

Photo 5.2 Worker checking stock in warehouse, c. 2000 (Image by Bridget Kenny)

When I get to the store, no one tells me what to do. After signing, I go to the floor and check how the shelves are ... I go to the warehouse. I take a trolley and draw stock ... After doing my work, I get the [retail] manager to sign my form with the store name, and then I go to another store.[93]

While supervision of merchandisers' work was uncommon, retail managers in charge of merchandising, security, and food and non-food departments closely monitored the contract workers in their sections. These relationships were often described by contract workers as aggressively penalizing: "Merchandisers are seen as dogs, like a jackal [*inja yase sgangeni*] by both [retail] management and security personnel. Security has a negative attitude towards merchandisers. They see them as thieves."[94]

A relationship that was particularly tense for contract merchandisers was with the store security managers who controlled the branch security systems and the guards. While managers were relieved of many branch-level responsibilities at Shoprite's takeover, security became an elevated branch-level task. Branch security managers were often Afrikaans-speaking white men, and contract merchandisers, who were mostly African men, experienced the relationship as racially hostile, often complaining of "those racist *boere*."[95]

Managers approached contract merchandisers with an aggressive masculinity not shown toward other workers. I witnessed several such antagonistic interactions. When on one occasion a black male merchandiser approached an Afrikaans-speaking male security manager to ask him a question, the manager looked past him, and acted as if he did not hear the question. When the merchandiser repeated his question, the manager physically shoved him aside and walked past him. Another time, as I was entering the staff entrance, the branch's security manager stood, boots planted, hands on hips and belly jutting out, and bellowed at a merchandiser to leave the store.[96] Security managers' treatment marked these contract workers as criminals and outsiders. Hyperama managers expected merchandisers to obey unilateral orders in "their stores" at the risk of dismissal:

> You have to listen to [the Hyperama manager]. If he tells you something and you try to discuss with him, he tells you that "if you do not want to listen to me, you must go out of my store." He does not waste time.[97]

These rules focused less on the substance of merchandisers' work and more on controlling their entry, exit, and movement within stores. When contract merchandisers entered and exited a store at the staff entrance, they had to sign in and out via a "guest register" at the security counter to record their hours of work, regardless of the fact that most worked at the store eight hours a day, six days a week. This was just one of several clocking-in and clocking-out procedures they had to fulfil:

> You do not just go and work. You go to the security, and they give you a card. You leave your [personal identity document], and they give you their own card. You then go to the buyer [order clerk], and you give him a form, which he signs that you've clocked-in. After clocking-in you go to get your stock and pack it. After packing that stock you then put stickers on the items ... When you're finished you get the buyer to sign for you. [Then] ... you get the receiving manager to sign. [Then] ... you get the store manager to sign, and then you leave.[98]

Contract merchandisers experienced these elaborate procedures as a well-rehearsed exercise of control. They applied only to them, not to direct employees of the retailer. Infringement of these rules was one of the most cited reasons for action against contract merchandisers: "If you did not go to them first [to get signatures], they chase you away from the store."[99] Contract workers often discussed stories of merchandisers who were thrown out of the store for returning late, even though they had started a break late in order to finish unpacking busy stock deliveries.[100]

Despite the fact that legislation provides for mandatory regular break times in the working day, store managers tried to prevent merchandisers from taking them:

> We used to smoke before in the warehouse, [but] he said, no, I mustn't smoke in the warehouse ... Okay, fine. You stand outside; you are smoking. [He comes and says,] "This is my time. Why are you smoking in my time?" If you go to the toilets upstairs, [he says] "Where are you from?" "I'm from the toilet." Then he starts, "This is your working time. You mustn't just walk around," which means you must go and explain to him, "May I go to toilet?"[101]

These petty regulations drew merchandisers' ire: "When they say do this, you must do it. You are always standing up. You never sit down. When you are in the shop, you always have to be standing up [active] until you knock-off."[102] The merchandisers experienced their relations within stores through these forms of control which portrayed them as criminals, outsiders, and manual labourers, akin to the "servants" and "natives" of latter years (see Chap. 4), requiring them to subjugate their every movement to managerial check and to ask permission for every action.

In general, workers experienced retail workplaces in the late 1990s in these hypermarkets as a site of subjugation, where they were racialized. Moreover, all three groups of workers spoke of these relations as turning them into non-workers. As Kethiwe commented: "It's just like we are not working [*sifana nokuthi a si sebenzi*]. We are just like the ones who are loitering in the location [*abajika*, moving around, *nelokishi*]."[103] Casual worker Zanele Mathebula explained that her manager no longer saw casuals as "workers": "[T]hey always hire new people everyday. So if there are new people around, the manager stops considering us as workers [abasebenzi] and begins to treat us badly because now there are new people."[104] Contract merchandisers, too, explained: "We are just working."[105] "Just working" and being a "worker" were not the same thing, removed from social relationships of the workplace.

* * *

In the 1980s and 1990s, globally retailers adopted a variety of innovations to further their goals of accumulation. Bent on lowering operating costs and increasing turnover to increase profits, they expanded the numbers and sizes of chain stores and concentrated capital through mergers and acquisitions, deepening market dominance through price competition and economies of scale and operation (Bowlby 2001; Freathy and Sparks 1996, 179; Humphrey 1998). Hypermarkets paved the way for these trends in South Africa. These modern superstores changed workplace culture. As managers became increasingly professionalized, self-service lifestyle shopping, particularly exaggerated in the huge hyper formatting, gave the impression of requiring less from workers. These formats leeched the service content out of front-line jobs. By eliding the difficult labour relations of these workplaces at the time, these retail spaces offered a discourse of a modern, indeed "First World" country, positing national belonging in consumption.

By the 1990s, when retail restructuring was at full pace, a new "culture of threat," demonstrated in this chapter through the Hyperama example, emphasized cost cutting and centralized managerial control. Employees discursively contrasted their reorganized stores with a past order of democratic participation and recognition. Yet by the late 1990s, workers in different employment categories experienced intense surveillance and control over them in these spaces. Resenting the lack of relational engagement, workers told stories of how they became seen as criminals or outsiders; they were objectified as a mass of low-skilled labourers; and they were racialized through customer service and management practice. These processes of subjectification, importantly, challenged their belonging in the workplace and claims to being abasebenzi. The workplace itself constituted an emotive space where articulations of race, class, and gender established a terrain of relationship. Thus, practices common in retailing across the world, which describe changes within the sector in South Africa, must be understood as occurring in and through specific sites (Hall 1985). In the next chapter, we see how the political subject abasebenzi was reconfigured.

Notes

1. A supermarket had a selling area of between 4,306 and 26,910 square feet (Humphrey 1998, 213n3), whereas a hypermarket had at least 53,820 square feet (Humphrey 1998, 237n12).
2. It had a trading area of 7,300 square metres (78,577 square feet) and non-food items made up more than 30% of its trading (see "Pressure on food space behind Boksburg's R12m expansion," *Supermarket and Retailer* Vol. 32, No. 4, April 1985, p. 52).
3. France pioneered the first *hypermarché* in 1963 near Paris (Humphrey 1998, 77; Lucas et al. 1994, 39). American and British retailers also borrowed its format innovations after seeing them in France (Humphrey 1998, 77).
4. "Boksburg: 10 Years of Hyper Magic," *Supermarket and Retailer* Vol. 32, No. 4, April 1985, p. 50. This phrase is ubiquitous in retailers' tales of their merchant entrepreneurialism, sometimes with more "balls" than "guts" (Raymond Ackerman, interviewed by Bridget Kenny, Sandton, August 16, 2001). See Ackerman (2001, 120) for discussion of the visit to France.
5. "Boksburg: 10 Years of Hyper Magic," *Supermarket and Retailer* Vol. 32, No. 4, April 1985, p. 50.
6. In 1979, AC Nielsen added a new survey classification, "hyper and major" to account for these larger stores. The "major" stores included the supermarket branches of corporate retailers ("How Do You Measure Up in the

Retail Grocery Market?," *Supermarket and Retailer* Vol. 27, No. 9, September 1980, pp. 29–30).
7. "Boksburg: 10 Years of Hyper Magic," *Supermarket and Retailer* Vol. 32, No. 4, April 1985, p. 50.
8. See Moreton (2009) for the history of Wal-Mart. She locates Walton's inspiration in 1950s discounters in the Northeast United States. The first Wal-Mart store opened in 1962 (27–28).
9. Former marketing manager, interviewed by Bridget Kenny, Johannesburg, July 18, 2000.
10. The suppliers' tactic was eventually deemed a contravention of the Monopolies Act (Ackerman 2001, 127), but this scuffle between retailers and suppliers points to the increasing power that retailers gained in the value chain through the hyper formats.
11. Former marketing manager, interview.
12. "Boksburg: 10 Years of Hyper Magic," *Supermarket and Retailer* Vol. 32, No. 4, April 1985, p. 55.
13. Former marketing manager, interview.
14. Former marketing manager, interview.
15. At the same time, retailers' market differentiation began to capture lower-income consumers, and a growing black consumer base in town and increasingly closer to black residential areas (see Chap. 3).
16. "New Hyperama Housebrands Follow Hyper Ranging and Feature Multi-Packs of Related Non-Food Items," *Supermarket and Retailer* Vol. 27, No. 4, April 1980, p. 16.
17. Advertisement for Pick n Pay Hypermarket Boksburg in *Benoni City Times*, February 20, 1981, p. 2; "Imagine, More Room to Move at Hypermarket," *Benoni City Times*, April 3, 1981, p. 1.
18. Advertisement for Pick n Pay Hypermarket Boksburg in *Benoni City Times*, February 20, 1981, p. 2; Advertisement for Pick n Pay Hypermarket Boksburg in *Benoni City Times*, March 27, 1981, p. 3; and see "Boksburg: 10 Years of Hyper Magic," *Supermarket and Retailer* Vol. 32, No. 4, April 1985, p. 55.
19. Sandton is a wealthy neighbourhood in the north of Johannesburg that since 1994 has become the business centre of the city.
20. Former marketing manager, interview. Epol refers to a brand of dog food.
21. "Boksburg: 10 Years of Hyper Magic," *Supermarket and Retailer* Vol. 32, No. 4, April 1985, p. 55.
22. "What's In-Store For You in the 80's: Part II," *Supermarket and Retailer* Vol. 27, No. 2, February 1980, p. 15.
23. "New Hyperama Housebrands Follow Hyper Ranging and Feature Multi-Packs of Related Non-Food Items," *Supermarket and Retailer* Vol. 27, No. 4, April 1980, pp. 15–16.

24. Own-label brands also serve to increase the power of retailers over suppliers in the value chain (Doel 1996; Hughes 1996).
25. Former marketing manager, interview.
26. "Boksburg: 10 Years of Hyper Magic," *Supermarket and Retailer* Vol. 32, No. 4, April 1985, p. 54; "Checkouts and Terminals at the OK: A Different Point of View," *Supermarket and Retailer* Vol. 28, No. 5, May 1981, p. 32.
27. "Checkouts and Terminals at the OK: A Different Point of View," *Supermarket and Retailer* Vol. 28, No. 5, May 1981, p. 39.
28. "Boksburg: 10 Years of Hyper Magic," *Supermarket and Retailer* Vol. 32, No. 4, April 1985, p. 56.
29. "Boksburg: 10 Years of Hyper Magic," *Supermarket and Retailer* Vol. 32, No. 4, April 1985, p. 54.
30. John Stephanopoulis, former unit manager, interviewed by Bridget Kenny, Ekurhuleni, May 10, 2001.
31. Former marketing manager, interview.
32. Leach (1993) called the original department stores a "land of desire."
33. Amos Tshabalala, former shop steward, interviewed by Bridget Kenny by telephone, Tembisa, August 11, 2000; Mary Nkosi, interviewed by Bridget Kenny, Daveyton, August 26, December 3, 1999, and September 7, 2000.
34. Erica Schoenberger (1997, 120) argues that firm culture is a set of "material practices, social relations and ways of thinking" in specific places. It helps to explain the direction of strategic restructuring occurring in specific companies. Specifically, she re-evaluates corporate strategy within localized power relations involving meaningful conflicts between managers.
35. Lindsay Mentor, Director-Human Resources at JDG Trading, interviewed by Bridget Kenny, Johannesburg, July 1, 1999; and Retail consultant, interviewed by Bridget Kenny, Johannesburg, March 28 and June 26, 2000.
36. Martinus Bezuidenhout, unit administration manager, interviewed by Bridget Kenny, Ekurhuleni, June 23, 1998.
37. Martinus Bezuidenhout, interview.
38. Annelie Pieters, interviewed by Bridget Kenny, Ekurhuleni, March 25, 2000.
39. Elizabeth Maseremule, former trainee manager, interviewed by Bridget Kenny, Ekurhuleni, October 24, 2000.
40. Johannes van Rooy, former department manager, interviewed by Bridget Kenny, Vereeniging, October 13, 2000.

41. Elizabeth Maseremule, interview.
42. Elizabeth Maseremule, interview.
43. Johannes van Rooy, interview.
44. Johannes van Rooy, interview.
45. Frederick Smith, former department manager, interviewed by Bridget Kenny, Johannesburg, November 7, 2000.
46. At this time the stores were still branded as Hyperama. Shoprite later rebranded them as Checkers-Hypers.
47. Johannes van Rooy, interview.
48. Research on superstores in other markets suggests that with restructuring in the 1990s, firms often transferred responsibility from store-level management to head office (e.g., Broadbridge 1999, 138; Christopherson 1996, 171; Freathy and Sparks 1996, 192).
49. Elizabeth Maseremule, interview.
50. Johannes van Rooy, interview. Indeed, a survey from the time noted that retailers were the largest category of employers taking dismissals to the Commission for Conciliation, Mediation and Arbitration (CCMA) (De Villiers 1999).
51. Johannes van Rooy, interview.
52. Retail consultant, interview.
53. Focus group interviews with permanent workers by Bridget Kenny, Ekurhuleni, February 7 and 29, and March 2, 2000.
54. Kethiwe Dlomo, interviewed by Bridget Kenny, Daveyton, August 1 and 8, 1999.
55. Kethiwe Dlomo, interview.
56. This will be discussed in greater detail in Chap. 7 (see also Moodie and Ndatshe 1994).
57. Leveraging less-than-formal relations to assist in other realms outside of work has been identified as central to bargaining strategies of domestic workers (Ally 2009).
58. E.P. Thompson (1971) used the concept of "moral economy" to signal how resistance to the emergence of capitalist relations of production in England was formulated out of people's lived experiences, embedded as they were in cultural relations of trust, reciprocity, and communality. The claim to a moral economy by new proletarian subjects resisted disembedded capitalist relations by asserting the social character of labour (see also Thompson 1967; Nash 1979; Taussig 1980). Multiple critiques were raised with the concept, while still appreciating its insights (e.g., Roseberry 1989, 200; Kelley 1996, 19–20; Austin 1993, 92–94).
59. Moodie's argument does not refer back to pre-capitalist values, but is the "mutually acceptable rules for resistance within systems of domination and

appropriation" (Moodie and Ndatshe 1994, 86). For him, moral economy describes the rules which can be "taken for granted" by both sides.
60. Italics in original. Roseberry draws on Raymond Williams (1973) to critique the use of moral economy to signify a break from the past. Instead he emphasizes how this language and associated practices offer insight into "consciousness" in the present (see also Portelli 1997). See also Austin (1993, 94) for the usefulness of "moral economy" in marking "understandings of capitalism" in specific "conditions of access to material resources."
61. Kethiwe Dlomo, interview.
62. Kethiwe Dlomo, interview.
63. Zama Ntuli, interviewed by Bridget Kenny, Daveyton, January 12, 1999.
64. Kethiwe Dlomo, interview.
65. See Chap. 7 for an extended discussion of the metaphor of "sitting."
66. Sara Dlamini, interviewed by Bridget Kenny, Soweto, June 19, 1999.
67. Kethiwe Dlomo, interview. Similar sentiments were expressed in focus group interviews with permanent workers by Bridget Kenny, Ekurhuleni, June 4, 1998, May 18, 1999, and February 2, 2000.
68. Kethiwe Dlomo, interview.
69. Kethiwe Dlomo, interview.
70. For the importance of surveillance more broadly in service work, see Tolich (1993), and Macdonald and Sirianni (1996).
71. Mzwandile Mkwanazi, shop steward, interviewed by Bridget Kenny, Ekurhuleni, April 17, July 20, and August 30, 1999, and Johannesburg, September 18, 2000; Paul Mahlangu, shop steward, interviewed by Bridget Kenny, Ekurhuleni, March 25 and 27, June 3 and 26, August 5 and 29, 2000; Thomas Guto, shop steward, interviewed by Bridget Kenny, Ekurhuleni, February 16, 2000.
72. In two branches, there were incidents of between 12 and 20 permanent unionized workers fired *en masse* (Buhle Bhengu, interviewed by Bridget Kenny, Daveyton, August 27, 1999; Vuyiswa Xaba, interviewed by Bridget Kenny, Daveyton, August 27, 1999; Zama Ntuli, interview).
73. Mzwandile Mkwanazi, interview.
74. Focus group interview with permanent workers by Bridget Kenny, Ekurhuleni, February 7, 2000.
75. Unathi Shabalala, interviewed by Bridget Kenny, Daveyton, August 21, 1999.
76. Vuyo Nokabu, interviewed by Bridget Kenny, Daveyton, May 6, 2000.
77. Khenzani Nkuna, interviewed by Bridget Kenny, Daveyton, June 12, 1999, and May 14, 2000.
78. Cheryl Isaacs, interviewed by Bridget Kenny, Ekurhuleni, May 25 and 27, 1999.

79. This was from an informal discussion I had in the canteen with a group of job applicants.
80. Nozipho Khunyedi, interviewed by Bridget Kenny, Tembisa, August 11, 1999.
81. Focus group interview with casual workers by Bridget Kenny, Ekurhuleni, June 5, 1998.
82. Thandile Ziyane, interviewed by Bridget Kenny, Daveyton, February 22, 2000.
83. Unathi Shabalala, interview. I once observed an older white man yelling at the cashier to stop "throwing his food around." He was referring to a 10 kilogram [22 pound] bag of potatoes that the cashier, sitting at the till, had to lift and pass over the scanner.
84. Focus group interview with casual workers by Bridget Kenny, Ekurhuleni, June 5, 1998.
85. Focus group interview with casual workers by Bridget Kenny, Ekurhuleni, June 5, 1998.
86. For a comparison of class distinctions, see Sherman (2007).
87. Tsakane Baloi, interviewed by Bridget Kenny, Ekurhuleni, August 3, 1999.
88. Sarah Mahlangu, interviewed by Bridget Kenny, Ekurhuleni, July 27, 1999.
89. Palesa Bogasu, interviewed by Bridget Kenny, Ekurhuleni, July 30, 1999.
90. Sfiso Shenge, interviewed by Bridget Kenny, Germiston, July 28, 1999.
91. Often they did not even know who their employers were or where their offices were located. Many only had a cell phone number (focus group interviews with contract merchandisers by Bridget Kenny, Ekurhuleni, June 2, 1998, and February 7 and 28, 2000).
92. Vuyo Nokabu, interview.
93. Themba Nyembe, interviewed by Bridget Kenny, Daveyton, August 14, 1999.
94. Focus group interview with contract merchandisers by Bridget Kenny, Ekurhuleni, February 7, 2000.
95. *Boere* is Afrikaans for farmers. It was a term appropriated to symbolize racist Afrikaner men, as in the pre-1994 ANC youth slogan "Kill the farmer, kill the *boer*."
96. I found out later that the infringement was being late for his shift.
97. Themba Nyembe, interview.
98. Themba Nyembe, interview.
99. Themba Nyembe, interview.
100. Vuyo Nokabu, interview.
101. Thabo Phasha, interviewed by Bridget Kenny, Daveyton, March 28, 1999.

102. Joseph Hlangwani, interviewed by Bridget Kenny, Daveyton, August 15, 1999, and May 9, 2000.
103. Kethiwe Dlomo, interview.
104. Zanele Mathebula, interviewed by Bridget Kenny, Ekurhuleni, May 27, 1999.
105. Themba Nyembe, interview.

CHAPTER 6

"Tools Down, Everybody Out to the Canteen!": Wildcats and Go-Slows, Political Subjects Reconfigured

Leaning forward and with staunch assurance, permanent worker and unionist Sara Dlamini explained her branch to me: "And they like strikes [*laughs*]." She said that suddenly workers would stop what they were doing, flushed and shaking their heads, a call would go out: "*Uyazi khona- manje nje bazothi hayi sesihlala phansi* [They will say, right now, we must sit down]. Tools down, everybody out to the canteen! Nobody must go on working." Raucous cries of "*Phansi emanager* [Down with the man- ager]" would sweep a stream of workers off the trading floor and up the stairs to the canteen where they would strategize. Any permanent workers remaining behind would be strongly chastised: "If he can go and work, a *klap* [smack]."[1]

In the late 1990s and early 2000s, there were many informal, "unproce- dural" wildcat actions held at hyper branches, some of which will be exam- ined in this chapter.[2] Often taking the form of sit-ins in the canteen above the shop, permanent workers would refuse to go to work until managers addressed their demands. Casual workers also tried this tactic, with less success. Contract merchandisers, limited in the actions they could address to the retail client firm (see Theron 2005), embarked on go-slows.

This moment in the early 2000s marks a critical conjuncture in the story of retail workers in South Africa. It was a period of global signifi- cance for the transformation of retailing, described by the specific effects of neoliberalism in the sector. Between 1990 and the mid-2000s, the

© The Author(s) 2018
B. Kenny, *Retail Worker Politics, Race and Consumption in South Africa*, Rethinking International Development series,
https://doi.org/10.1007/978-3-319-69551-8_6

world's major retailers showed an unprecedented growth of 550% (Baum and Durand 2012, 245). Consolidating trends already underway in the 1970s (see Chap. 5), this was the beginning of an innovation "revolution," led by supply chain management, global sourcing and the multinationalization of retail capital (Lichtenstein 2009; Weatherspoon and Reardon 2003; Wrigley and Lowe 1996; Baum and Durand 2012) (and see Chap. 8). These dynamics contributed to retail firms cutting costs, particularly labour costs (Baum and Durand 2012).

For retail workers around the world, the consequence of these changes was an increased use of temporary and part-time labour (Bernhardt 1999; Perrons 2000; Carré et al. 2010b; Luce 2013; Coulter 2014, 25–27; Grugulis and Bozkurt 2011). But, as we saw in Chap. 4, the particular mechanisms by which these labour practices emerged and operated in South Africa need to be understood in a longer local history of state regulation; articulations of gender, age, race, and skill meanings; and union and worker politics. Furthermore, workers experienced these changes through the concrete conjuncture of meaningful relations – those many "determinations" (Hall 1985, 92) that we have been tracking (see Chap. 5). Workers in all three categories felt a new management constructed them as outsiders, criminals, inputs, a bulk of (black) labourers in the context of changes to the labour regime, as we saw. The stories in Chap. 5 show how black workers confronted a basic antagonism: restructuring and a market rationale which justified casual and contract labour at the same time that a rights-based regime promised a participatory order in the work space where they would be truly consulted on matters affecting them.[3] In this chapter, we examine how those workers acted in these moments, and how their struggles shifted relations and categories (Hall 1985, 112).

In our case, workers reasserted themselves as abasebenzi, but with consequences. The subject abasebenzi continued to describe a political relation and in so doing remained affectively potent. At the same time, this collective category became internally divided, as each employment group claimed its status and organized to distinguish itself from the others. By the early 2000s, then, workers identified in terms of particular categories of workers – *amapermanents* (permanent workers), *amacasuals* (casual workers), and *amamerchandisers* (contract merchandisers). Each of these groups claimed the identity of abasebenzi for itself and thus activated an existing subject through new conditions where legal parameters, workplace power, and notions of belonging in nation had changed. Second, workers' actions became localized to branches – indeed, as the title of the chapter suggests, taking many of their protests into the canteen, away from a public audience. The abasebenzi were thereby reconstituted.

Global sector developments thus were instituted through specifically local relations that directly reflected in labour politics (see Hart 2002). This chapter considers retail workers' politics in this critical moment. Something unusual, then, was taking place in terms of retail worker politics in South Africa at this time. In other contexts, confronted with poor conditions, retail workers became individuated, isolated within labour relations, or exiting and contributing to high labour turnover (Wharton 1996; Erickson and Wharton 1997; Carré et al. 2010a; Coulter 2014). Where trade unions organized retail workers, relative power in bargaining followed institutional leverage in specific national contexts (Tilly and Galván 2006; Askenazy et al. 2012, 596; Coulter 2014; Ikeler 2011; Mrozowicki et al. 2013; Lynch et al. 2011; Bailey et al. 2015). In South Africa workers were not atomized, as this chapter shows; still, while having a national sectoral union representing them, clearly an important factor, nevertheless the union did not solely explain worker politics and outcomes. The contradictions of labour law reform with a political subject that claimed a stake in determining social relations enforced retail worker politics, but in ways that simultaneously reproduced collective militancy and inscribed limits to that politics. To understand these contradictions, we also have to see how articulations of race, class, and gender constituted this moment in different ways than they did either in the 1960s or in the 1970s/1980s.

"We Are Grown-Ups": Permanent Workers as Adult Decision-Makers

In 2000 permanent workers in one Hyperama conducted a sit-down action in response to additional security measures introduced by a new floor manager: workers had to submit to an additional search after they had already undergone a regular search and had clocked out for the day. For this the manager locked the outside doors. Because staff had already clocked out, the time they had to wait in line until they were searched – more than an hour – happened off the clock. Permanent workers caucused the matter over two days, and then decided in a meeting that they would not "go to work until management explained and until management gave a consistent decision."[4]

Branch management had indeed tried once before to introduce such a second search, according to the shop steward. When permanent staff argued that they could only accept a second search if the time was part of their working hours, management had backed down. But, as the shop steward explained, "one manager had decided that day to do it on his own. Then he had the doors locked, when staff refused to be searched. So Wednesday morning, I sent word to [the branch manager], we are not going to work until a final decision was made about it."[5] The permanent workers thus protested the manager's breach of their agreement (and see Chap. 5).

The branch manager called in the regional office that held authority over personnel matters, and everyone waited for a regional office representative to come to the branch. In the absence of the permanent workers, casual workers and the managers worked the floor, as did contract merchandisers in their normal capacity. The branch manager later reported to the shop steward that when he went out to his car to get something, "people out there wouldn't let him out of his car and pushed on his windows." The shop steward stepped in to calm tempers: "I just said [to him], 'Look, don't use those tactics, face us, what do you say? Let's resolve this.'" The branch manager thereupon agreed to stop the second search. Staff accepted his promise and by 10:30 a.m. were back on the floor; the branch manager told the regional office representative not to come. The shop steward recounted, "People like [the manager] would rather resolve the issue because of his name in the company. He would rather not have problems."[6] Similarly, the reaction of the shop steward showed that he too did not want to escalate the disagreement to a "fight," in his words. He preferred finding an agreement by talking. Since security remained a responsibility of branches, the manager was able to work out an informal agreement between himself and the shop steward.

In this example, the permanent workers were not only aggrieved by the loss of pay, but also by the breach of a standing agreement with their managers and the humiliation of the distrust implied by additional searches. In fact, the manager's act of locking them in was illegal and the workers could have chosen to lodge a formal grievance. Instead, they asserted their authority and argued for a branch-level resolution through the existing informal relations with the branch manager brokered by the shop steward. The fact that casual and contract workers continued to work was irrelevant to their struggle, as permanent workers were confident they could win their demand. As the shop steward described, whenever there was a sit-in, managers as well as some regional office managers would ask, "'Okay, what do you want?' They seem willing to try to resolve an issue, rather than for [them] to look bad to the big bosses."[7] Ironically, permanent workers had room to negotiate an informal arrangement because of the centralization of power away from branches. Branch managers themselves used the contradiction to find openings to resolve problems, both to assure themselves of their power within branches and to protect their own reputations in relation to regional managers in a context of increased monitoring in Shoprite (see Price 2016; Grugulis et al. 2011; also see Chap. 5).[8]

Permanent workers effectively used wildcat actions to maintain relationships with branch managers (see von Holdt 2003). Through the actions they reasserted their position within the long-standing relationships with branch managers and reaffirmed their role in in-store communication and decision-making regarding issues that affected them directly.[9] In this way, they maintained solidarity through the union: while they were critical of the regional and national structures of the South African Commercial, Catering and Allied Workers Union (SACCAWU) (see Ndala 2000), they remained loyal to their union branches and shop stewards. Many had joined the union in the early and mid-1980s when it was first organizing, and nearly all of the permanent workers I interviewed were union members. The shop stewards called for weekly branch meetings before work started, which normally drew between 10 and 20 workers. The shop stewards were respected and worked hard to engage branch member grievances.

Shop stewards proudly saw the many spontaneous, wildcat actions called by branch membership as evidence of SACCAWU's militant tradition (see Chap. 3). In fact, national SACCAWU officials now had to come to tell their branches "to stop these wildcat strikes,"[10] because they were unprocedural under democratic labour dispensation and could result in workers getting fired, a comment that signalled to this shop steward that branches remained militant in contrast to the national office. As one worker explained, it was almost as if "they were two separate unions," one in the branch and the other at national level.[11] At this time, wildcat strikes in other sectors garnered attention for how workers critiqued the perceived timidity of their unions, how unions stood against their members to discipline them, and how striking workers had to face the consequence of dismissals (Rachleff 2001; Buhlungu 2010). Wildcat actions were part of a militant tradition in South African "independent" unions (Seidman

1994), entwined now with workers' frustrations with the effects of restructuring, national African National Congress (ANC) alliance politics that contained trade unions, and the constraints of democratic labour law that hindered spontaneous protest (Buhlungu 2010; von Holdt 2003). The wildcat actions signalled a critique by members of the shift that unions had undergone from representing workers' issues to becoming bargaining partners with management in restructuring efforts.

These permanent retail workers focused their attention on in-store relations and on influencing their own managements rather than critiquing their union. The very call "out to the canteen" was a summons to leave the public space of the shop floor and to move into an arena which workers held as their space, where they met for tea and meetings. In these cases, the collective subject of abasebenzi worked to push back against managers, to correct procedures and actions that had upset the careful balance. The call was directed at other permanent workers and, sometimes, at casual workers, although permanents accepted the limited capacity of casual and contract workers to "down tools."

The historical collective category abasebenzi became divided. Permanent workers demanded participation in workplace relations, especially the capacity to make decisions there, which was disrupted by restructuring (see Chap. 5). Being able to impact on decisions confirmed their adult status, on which they insisted when engaging with managers. This status, "adult" – a main affective lineament of the collective political subject abasebenzi (see Chaps. 3 and 4) – worked in their stories to ascribe an identity specifically to permanent workers, in contrast particularly to casual workers. In trying to grapple with their growing insecurity in these shops, permanent workers emphasized their distinct status over casual workers, always placing the latter in the separate *amacasual* category in comparison to their own *amapermanent*. Permanent workers naturalized this difference through metaphors of age and generation (see Bhengu 2010), where casual workers were infantilized. This metaphor was reinforced by the fact that casual workers were often younger than permanents, sometimes younger relatives or students taking these positions (see Chap. 4). Yet, similar to permanent workers, many casuals were adults with family responsibilities.[12] Instead of reflecting a real demographic difference, this discourse rather served the purpose of affirming permanent workers' higher status.

Many permanent workers regarded casual jobs as exploitative, and sympathized with workers in these positions. The canteen supervisor Sara said,

"I hate this business of being casual. They should be taken as permanent staff ... How can you work for a place seven to eight years being a casual? That is not right."[13] At the same time, permanent workers carefully maintained the status difference between casual workers and themselves. This divide was marked by presumptions about their seniority. For instance, despite agreeing that casual staff should get permanent employment contracts, permanent workers held firm that they should have priority for promotions, even if it meant casuals remained insecure:

> I don't know what [casuals] want because when you are casual, they can't promote you at the same time. If there is a position [open], they take, say, from the permanents, and then you [the casual] will be next ... They can't promote casuals and leave people who are experienced. It goes step-by-step, you see.[14]

Permanent workers also articulated a clear sense of workplace hierarchy in which they characterized casual workers as dependent on them: "They listen to us. They know nothing. They can't do anything without us, even the manager listens to us."[15] Despite recognizing the casuals' extensive tenure in stores, permanent workers saw them as reliant on others. This portrayal of dependency related directly to permanents' own rhetorical constitution as active adults. This is very visible in the manner in which Kethiwe Dlomo described a situation when permanent workers were not given salary slips at her branch. In her discussion she positioned permanent workers in relation to their managers in the store hierarchy, but authenticated their very expectation of engagement with managers by drawing a comparison to casual workers:

> Right now our pay slips are gone, the shop stewards are saying that shit flies [*ku ya nyiwa*] up there, those people's faces are red [*babovu*], get ready for anytime. We are going to stay up there and fight for [*lwela*] the pay slips and want to know where that money is ... We are grown-ups [*sibantu abadala*] here; we are not school children [*asisi bantwana besikolo*]. Even those ones [casuals] are school children but they also have their own responsibilities that they have to meet with this money.[16]

Kethiwe viewed permanent workers as a collective "we," unified by their just "fight." Here she used the word *lwela* (to fight for), the meaning of which is closer to arguing or contending with than engaging in a physical fight. Kethiwe thus indicated that active and assertive negotiation with managers would resolve their problem.[17] She defined a meaningful opposition between managers and them partly in terms of race, as with white managers' faces turning "red" with anger or embarrassment. Adulthood denoted the status to engage managers through meaningful communication. The certitude of permanent workers' position rested in being "grown-ups" [*sibantu abadala*], contrasted explicitly with casual workers. By implication she placed casual workers outside relations of negotiation, because they were "school children," even where they too had reproductive responsibilities.[18]

This discourse of speaking for casual workers was prevalent among permanents: "These casuals are exploited. We'll just speak for them. They do not know how much they're supposed to earn. Management forgets how much these children [*abantwana*] spend on transport."[19] The assertion of difference marked by generation in relation to casual workers was even more explicit in discussions of the union. On one hand, permanent workers understood that uniting workers would strengthen SACCAWU. Permanent workers attempted to bring the casual workers into the union, "to be one with us."[20] They expressed that "if the casuals ... have a problem, we will support them"; "an injury to one is an injury to all"; "we are under this umbrella together. We want them to be like us."[21] On the other hand, however, this apparently strong articulation of solidarity held an assumption of status difference. Permanent workers assumed the right to command casual workers:

> when we ask them to sit-in upstairs, they must leave the tills ... If we fight for them, they should see that. Like at home, if you ask a child to do this or that, a child would do that because s/he can see that you are also doing it.[22]

While permanent workers expressed a genuine concern for casual workers as workers, potentially to be unified with them, they also revealed their assumptions that permanent workers occupied a more privileged position in the relationship, as knowing, experienced, and responsible adults.

The power of oratory to convince and thus to control terms of the debate was seen historically as an important component of a man's repertoire to build interdependent social relations to ensure personhood, with this very skill signifying adulthood and political prowess (Comaroff and Roberts 1981). Historically, women and children were dependents, represented by men. In this way, dependency was implicitly feminized (see also Comaroff and Comaroff 1992; Comaroff 1987).

In a group discussion, a permanent worker explained that permanent and casual workers "get along well. There is no classification. We are from the same situation and shelters, and they have responsibilities."[23] Permanents also remarked sympathetically that, "Some of them [casuals] are mothers of homes [*abu mama bemizi*]. They have children. They have certain responsibilities. They need to get a better place, but they do go there [to work] because there is nothing they can do."[24] It is thus possible to argue that, by permanent workers' own logic, having "their own responsibilities" meant that casuals should be recognized as "adults." The representations seem to be drawing on common experiences of precariousness to construct collective identities encompassing both permanent and casual workers. Instead, permanent workers' language often called up the figure of casuals as tenuous reproducers to pity them, rather than to denote a commonality with them. And, as shown above, they were clear that casuals were incapable of engaging, negotiating, communicating, and participating in decision-making with managers.

Thus, instead of acknowledging casuals as adults, referencing them as providers highlighted their vulnerability and feminized them as a category. Kethiwe outlined, "Our casuals are too excessively oppressed, we feel pity [*si ya wa hlabekela*] for them. Even if you are casuals you must be permanent casuals," an oxymoronic colloquialism in retailing (not a legal category) indicating an informal commitment to employ long term as a "casual" (see Owens 2001; and see Chap. 4). She continued poetically, "But you are nowhere. You are just casuals, like washing blown by wind on a washing line."[25] This poignant image captured the fundamental difference with which permanent workers marked casual workers. The specific form of dependency which characterized casuals was that of not being able to speak for themselves and not being able *to effect* relations, but instead being acted upon.

While all workers expressed difficulties with survival (see Chap. 7), only for casual workers did this predicament become attached as a characteristic of their employment category. Permanent workers' discourse stamped casuals categorically as fragile reproducers, gendered female. The domestic metaphor of powerlessness – washing blown by wind on a washing line – located casual workers within the physical place of home and at the mercy of external forces in order to characterize their structural vulnerability. For permanent workers, by contrast, claims for worker identity rested on traditional adult masculine competencies of disputation and communication, as when they forced managers to face them.

"I Must Make a Sale": Contract Workers as Skilled Men

Unlike permanent workers, contract workers did not embark on wildcat actions but used other tactics to force retail managers to address their complaints. In one instance, for example, contract merchandisers conducted a go-slow of customer service to demand the reinstatement of a contract merchandiser who had been "dismissed." Merchandisers spent much of their days in supermarket aisles, unloading and packing goods onto the shelves. Customers assumed that they were employed by the stores and often asked them questions about prices, products and where something was located. The merchandisers were often more available to assist than permanent workers who were positioned at stations away from the self-service shop floors. In this situation, infuriated by yet another retail manager throwing a contract worker out of the store (see Chap. 5), merchandisers strategized a campaign to slow down and halt customer service:

> There is that guy that was chased, so we decided not to do customer service. A customer came in and maybe asked, "Where is a firelighter?," and merchandisers would say, "I don't work for Hyperama" and a customer would go away not buying. That created problems 'cause they lost a lot of money.[26]

Well aware that they could not refuse to pack shelves, contract workers instead focused on boycotting a service that technically was not in their job descriptions. As customers' irritation filtered back to branch managers, they were forced to acknowledge the critical role played by merchandisers in a context where deskilling left most service workers with little product knowledge or incentive to conduct meaningful customer service (see Chap. 2 for comparison). Yet it took a full two months of the workers' go-slow before managers agreed to the return of the expelled merchandiser. Nevertheless, contract workers considered this an important victory.

Like permanent workers, contract merchandisers sought to influence managers through informal relations, in this case through a service relied on but unrecognized by retailers, to force their demand. They did not resort to a legal solution to bring back their colleague. Knowing that labour rights around dismissal made it difficult at the time to pin liability on Hyperama, the client firm (see Chap. 5; Theron 2005), contract workers instead chose to put informal pressure on branch-level managers. Like permanent workers, this tactical decision paid off sometimes.

Contract workers generally had negative experiences with SACCAWU and felt the union was not interested in organizing them: "Every Thursday they've got that union meeting ... [W]e don't attend their meeting. They don't invite us; they don't invite us."[27] Contract merchandisers realistically assessed that SACCAWU could not effectively represent them because they were not employees of the retailer:

> I hear about the union when [Hyperama staff] are standing [around]; they are talking about the union ... I am not interested in joining them. Because they are Hyperama staff and I'm working for Fastpack ... So how are they going to contact my company? ... [W]e are merchandisers; we have to have our own union.[28]

Yet they realized that forming their own union would be difficult because they worked for different employers, and many of the labour brokers reportedly expressed strong anti-union sentiment. While contract workers generally knew that they had a right to join a union, they also understood that doing so might in practice lead to being fired.[29] Instead, contract merchandisers formed branch committees to protect themselves against abuses by retail managers (Photo 6.1).

Merchandisers met weekly in the shop to discuss problems that had come up, and then a representative elected within the structure raised the issues with store managers. The formal purpose of the store committees was "to make sure there is a good working relationship between merchandisers and [retail] management." Labour brokers, however, were not to know about the committees, or "some workers might lose their jobs as this committee might appear as a threat to these companies."[30] The organization thus did not aim to tackle employment conditions, but to protect workers within in-store relations, which were immediately important to contract workers, as we saw in Chap. 5: "No security is supposed to arrest a worker within the premises of Hyperama ... Another thing that was resolved is that no management was to talk badly to employees, merchandisers and vice versa."[31] Workers mobilized their committees around the "chasing" (dismissal) of contract workers. They also negotiated with management to establish and clarify rules around tea breaks and their mobility in the stores,[32] issues at the heart of contract workers' experiences (see Chap. 5). These committees began to make some headway with branch

Photo 6.1 Contract merchandisers playing cards, c. 2000 (Image by Bridget Kenny. Edits by Simon Gush)

managers, with them willing to listen to contract workers' concerns. Unable to call on a union, which would have to represent workers to an employer, contract workers established their own store-based organizations that cross-cut the many different labour brokers (i.e., employers) operating in each branch to negotiate around common concerns with the retailer.

Material to their collective identification was a view of themselves as skilled workers. They claimed to hold "professional" skill.[33] After being retrenched by one labour broker, Vuyo Nokabu was rehired by another because of his expert product knowledge: "Now they have taken me," he emphasized, "because I know all the products."[34] Critically, merchandisers needed to know which products moved fast, so that they could restock shelves before lines ran out. Describing his job, Vuyo explained:

> You must … know your products; which one is the faster [selling product] line, which one is the slow line … [The fast lines] you must know; if you order them, they must go straight to the floor [once they are delivered]. As long as you know when you are going to order [from the supplier] [that is

the most important issue]. You are going to order stock that goes straight to the floor. The ones that are fast you can have a back-up stock.[35]

Merchandisers kept track of which product lines sold well and which did not, although this part of merchandising was formally the responsibility of "reps," representatives of suppliers' lines, who were also employed by the labour brokers and whose job was to visit each store to check stock and to place new orders. Merchandisers claimed their skill in relation to reps, who often supervised them. They argued that reps were inclined to overstock products because they earned commission on what they sold: "[The rep] can order the lines that are slow. While we've got seven boxes, [he'll] order another six boxes. Where are you going to put those boxes?"[36] The merchandisers said they often had to correct the order forms when extravagant orders from reps could leave stock to become damaged. Thus retail managers approved (or could alter) these order suggestions, but the day-to-day work of keeping track of stock was in the hands of labour broker employees.[37] Retailers did not pay for stock upfront. They bought it on credit, which could be repaid 30 or even up to 60 or 90 days later. Spoiled or damaged stock could be returned in some cases to suppliers at their cost (Mather and Kenny 2005, 187), but retailers wanted stock supply to be efficiently maintained in order to turn over stock.

Contract merchandisers argued that they knew more than many store managers. Thabo Phasho said, shaking his head:

> You give [the store manager] a catalogue; he doesn't understand what is going on in that catalogue. He just puts in his signature. When the stock arrives in the store, maybe it's more than three pallets for that supplier. He starts moaning, "Who signed this order?" ... You tell him, you must understand what is going on.[38]

Merchandisers also took credit for being salesmen: "We are merchandising. We do sales in stores."[39] In retailing, good "shelf management" is commonly acknowledged as contributing to higher sales (Bowlby 2001). While shelf placement was a matter of negotiation between the retailer and suppliers, merchandisers claimed to finesse the positioning, the aesthetics, and cleanliness of presentation as part of generating greater sales; they also answered customer queries about products.[40]

These contract merchandisers bypassed their immediate employers (their labour brokers) and built narratives around the centrality of their skills to the retailers themselves. As Vuyo argued, their superior product knowledge was a benefit to the stores' customers:

> [L]ike you see those machines for Baracuda [automatic pool cleaners].[41] I don't know nothing about that machine, how is it doing the pools. I don't have a pool. I must make sure those things are selling, *I must make a sale* ... Ja, I must teach myself. Which means I must learn all those things ... I must teach myself, read the instructions, what is it doing. Because you [as a customer] cannot come and buy [a product] without explanation. I must explain to you what is the use of this thing, what it does to the pool.[42]

Vuyo claimed the skill of a merchant. In this case, he conveyed the breadth of his expertise, learning about a product – stereotypical of suburban white South African living – with which he would normally have had no intimate knowledge.

In effect, these contract merchandisers enabled just-in-time stockkeeping to increase retailer profit-making. They protected the interests of both the labour brokers and the store: "returns" could incur costs or cancelled contracts for their employers, and warehousing stock tied up retailer capital (Mather and Kenny 2005; Lichtenstein 2009). Through their own product and market knowledge, technically not part of the job, merchandisers claimed to bring about efficient sales.

In contrast, according to contract merchandisers, labour brokers viewed their employees as unskilled labour. Themba explained that he was not supposed to spend time and use his skill to provide a better service, for instance by correcting pricing mistakes.[43] The labour brokers considered these workers as only "shelf packers" and paid them low wages to do what they saw as a menial set of tasks. Themba commented on what he perceived to be his lower status: "The agents [labour brokers] have many names. Some agents are called Merchandising Tool. I mean, as people who are thinking, how come a company is called a Merchandising *Tool?*"[44] Merchandisers rejected the attribution of being manual labourers, that historical positioning of black male distributive workers (see Chaps. 2 and 4).

Contract workers were well aware, too, that permanent workers perpetuated the association of contract workers with this inferior status: "The permanent staff don't regard the merchandisers as people, they are just regarded as filling the shelf, you are not using your reasoning capacity."[45] Jabu Mbambisa argued that if a contract worker made a suggestion to permanent workers, they did not listen: "They shut us down. They don't let us have a say ... You are just a merchandiser, you just go there 9:00 and 5:00 go home."[46] Being "just a merchandiser" meant that they were considered to enter and exit the store, but not to contribute to it in any substantive way. Jabu summarized by explaining that when permanent workers wanted solidarity for their actions, they "tell us" to strike "without asking."[47]

Contract merchandisers did not join together with casual workers either. Like permanent workers, they saw casual workers as individualized and vulnerable: "Should anything happen to you [as a casual] in the store, they take you like anyone walking in the street. It's just a piece-job. It's just for you not to stay at home and do something."[48] While merchandisers were sensitive to casuals' plight – some merchandisers had initially been casuals for the retailer[49] – rather than jointly taking up mutual concerns such as easy dismissals or poor conditions, they drew a line of difference between themselves and casuals. Merchandisers often spoke of how casual workers were non-unionized and unable to protest[50]; they saw them as fragmented, metaphorically working for "piece rates," and barely able to escape total marginalization in townships. Thus, while contract workers might have sympathized with casual workers, they considered them vulnerable and unable to act.

In the protest action described above, which they engaged in without the support of permanent workers, contract workers boycotted precisely what they perceived as the skilled labour of sales, the work that in the past was actually central to the job of shop assistant, as we saw with white women advising customers with products (see Chap. 2). In emphasizing their skill, contract merchandisers collectively rejected being manual labour, with its long history of association with colonial and apartheid despotism (Chap. 4). They asserted belonging in the stores when they negotiated with management to contest being treated as interlopers. By professing their skill, they insisted on their authority to act and to organize, in contrast to how they viewed casual workers, despite commonalities between the two categories.

"[WE] BRING MORE MONEY": CASUAL WORKERS AS EXPLOITED LABOUR

Casual workers also tried the tactic of wildcat sit-ins to pressure managers. At two branches, they sat-in to demand that a newly introduced four-hour shift be cancelled and their regular seven-hour shift be reinstated, thus picking up the core issue of working time in retailing. When Shoprite took over the Hyperama stores, it introduced a new shift for casual workers running from 2:00 p.m. to 6:00 p.m. Casual workers hated this new arrangement because the four-hour shift meant that their daily wage for four hours, at the time R24, was barely enough to cover their transportation costs, which averaged between R10 to R15 per day. Already aggravated by Shoprite reducing their weekly hours to less than 24, casual workers decided to act.[51] They voted to hold sit-ins modelled after permanent workers' successful actions. They remained in the canteen, not answering calls by their supervisors to return to the floor. Neither permanent nor contract workers joined them in their action, yet in two branches casual workers asked a shop steward to speak to management for them.

In one branch, the shop steward succeeded at securing a meeting between the casual workers and the regional personnel manager responsible for the work schedule.[52] At the meeting the manager argued that, by law, casual workers were only allowed to work for three days per week, misrepresenting the statute at this time that regulated that casual staff could be employed for no *more* than 24 hours per week and eight hours per day.[53] However, the regulation did not stipulate a minimum number of hours per week (or per day), and employers had the right to vary casual workers' weekly shifts as they wanted.[54] The workers countered that this did not prevent the company from allocating more than four hours a day per worker, their basic demand. The first response by the company was to offer longer hours to some workers, but not all. Casual workers "rejected this, saying that they wanted to have some consistency [among them]."[55] In the end, the regional office refused to agree to the demand, and within a few weeks the four-hour shift had made its way back into the work schedules. At the other branch, the casual workers were defeated immediately, unable to secure a meeting with the regional manager: "We tried striking and many [workers] were chased away." The shop steward told them that "there is nothing that [the union] could do" to change their shifts.[56] While some casual workers were union members, many were not, but the shop steward still tried to represent them.[57] Because the computer at regional office generated casual workers' schedules (see Chap. 5), the shop steward had little room to negotiate informal arrangements with branch management.

In another example, casual workers demanded the same uniform as permanent workers: "We wear black and white. Permanents wear green and white."[58] Casual workers had to provide their own clothes, black pants or skirts, and white shirts, while permanent workers received a company uniform – green pants or skirts, with white shirts and green jerseys carrying the company logo. Casual workers not only resented the extra expense of having to buy clothes to specification, but contested the symbolism that visibly marked their subordinate status with customers and fellow workers: "We want to have the same uniform, green and white! ... [Permanents] say if you are wearing a green [Hyperama] skirt, they ask 'What do you think you are!' as you are just a casual." The difference in uniforms also reinforced permanent workers' view of them as children, due to the fact that this outfit resembled public school uniforms: "We are tired of wearing black and white. They make us look like school children." Casual workers demanded green and white uniforms and requested the shop stewards to represent them.[59] Management rejected their effort, despite the fact that the law dictated that employers had to provide uniforms or a clothing allowance.[60] Instead, the casual workers were told that they could wear the green and white company uniform, but only if they purchased it second-hand from permanent workers at their own expense. An entire uniform might cost R120, a high amount considering weekly wages of approximately R140 at the time. In practice, casual workers often settled for buying one item, such as the jersey, and wearing it over the black and white outfit. But the agreement did not address the primary complaint, that those who earned less had to pay for the symbolism of being employees. While they had "won the right" to wear uniforms, it still reinforced their lower status in the store.

Casual workers tried to contest the ascription of their secondary, dependent status. Instead they identified as (super-)exploited labour, which in their rendering connoted agency: they were the true workers. In discussing their work and their actions, casual workers indicated that they wished to be acknowledged as proper workers rather than as "cheap labour."[61] Casual workers compared their low pay directly to the money that they brought into the stores daily, as front-line workers at the tills. Sfiso Shenge contrasted his wages to the amount he took in regularly: "I handle a lot of money a day. I make about fifteen or twenty thousand [rands]. And you only get R120 of that money."⁶² In Sfiso's understanding, he "made" the money for the store: because he received the money from customers everyday, Sfiso thought of his role as materializing the retailer's profits. In that role, casual cashiers compared their role to permanent workers who, as Thembi Skhosana explained, "are not aware of how much profit the casual workers earn the store ... because we are working even on holidays."⁶³ Sfiso argued:

> [T]he casuals are the ones who bring more money into the store. [Permanents] do not bring in even a cent ... From the first till to the last one, it's all casuals. And the tills in that store start from [number] one up to number forty-seven.⁶⁴

In these discussions, permanent workers did not "bring in" money because they did not operate the tills. Nor did they work the busy weekends and public holidays, those unsocial hours which full-time workers resisted taking on (see Chap. 4).

Working at the till was demanding labour. Thando Shabalala, a 31-year-old casual packer, said of her job: "I do not like it. It's a difficult job, your body is always tired, and on top of that they do not pay us well."⁶⁵ In addition, they had to take over tasks which they considered as properly belonging to permanent workers, for instance, working the tills in the evenings and doing the hated task of back-shopping⁶⁶ when permanent workers had already clocked out. Permanent workers would give casuals tedious tasks to do, such as finding prices, while they chatted with friends,⁶⁷ to such an extent that casuals felt that they "are permanent workers' slaves."⁶⁸ Yet rather than experiencing themselves as dependent on permanent workers, casual workers defined their own status as "workers" – the ones who physically laboured and generated profit – in contrast to permanent workers' idleness.

Casual workers further differentiated themselves from permanent workers by rejecting what they perceived to be paternalistic relationships they entertained with management. Casual workers often repeated that they were not considered for promotions and blamed this on the operation of personal networks from which they felt excluded. Sarah Mahlangu, who had worked as a casual for five years, explained that "We are still at the tills even though we started long time ago. They only promote people they know." She argued that even higher levels of education did not offer an advantage, given that casual workers with degrees were not promoted: "There are many people who brought certificates [of degrees, diplomas,

Photo 6.2 "Nobody is born to be a casual for life," c. 2000 (Image by Bridget Kenny. Edits by Simon Gush)

courses], not *a* certificate, *certificates*, but they have never been promoted. Which means they don't look at education"[69] (Photo 6.2).

In the discourse around paternalism, casual workers were particularly miffed about a group they called "white casuals." In their stories, these new appointees were quickly selected to more secure casual positions, entailing better jobs doing clerical work and regular or longer working hours: "What surprises us is that the white casuals are hired and then after a month, the following month they work Monday to Friday."[70] These "promotions" happened without clear reasons and over the heads of those who had already worked as casuals for years: "How come they take white casuals and put them in switchboards or whatever? People who just came in during December! We who have been here for long, why can't we get opportunities, but some people do."[71] According to the regular casual workers, the only explanation could be that the manager "still has apartheid. He likes white people more."[72] In their opinions, racialized patronage overrode the casual workers' expectations. Although promoted only to better casual jobs, in these narratives, "white casuals'" quick advancement strengthened workers' arguments that personal networks operated against them.[73]

Casual workers invoked a collective identity not around their precariousness then, but in terms of the substantive contribution they made as a black proletariat, exploited and embroiled in a system where personal relationships reproduced racist privilege, while they laboured to produce employer profit. Thus, their protests, in these examples for longer daily shifts and for company uniforms, cited critical signs of belonging within these shops. Yet, like with other groups, their claims to being abasebenzi also reinforced divisions among workers.

JOINT ACTIONS: RACE AND RIGHTS

In this period, two actions that might be viewed as cross-cutting categories of workers can be used to compare efforts and effects. The first is a wildcat protest in one of the Hyperama branches, which united some workers over racist practices by managers, and the second is a national SACCAWU strike in 2003 against Shoprite over the conditions of casual workers, in which the union demanded the company implement new sectoral legislation.

In early 2001, a wildcat action at one Hyperama branch, initiated by permanent workers and supported by some casual workers, brought branch managers and workers to a head, and carried the potential to unite workers at that branch. The issue that sparked the protest was a series of interactions with abusive and racist managers. It should be noted that at the time, managers were white or Indian in these stores and shop floor workers were mostly African (see Fig. 6.1 for occupational division by gender and race in the sector as a whole during this time).

A range of issues led up to the action, but one of the final events that led casual workers to join was an egregious strip-searching of two casual women cashiers on a Saturday afternoon, ordered by one of the managers, Mr. Pretorius[74]:

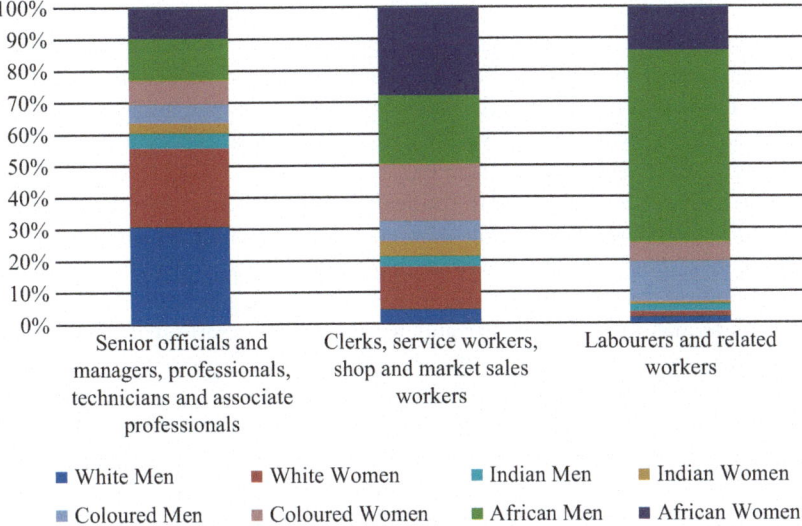

Fig. 6.1 Selected occupational categories in wholesale and retail trade by gender and race, 2000. Source: Adapted from Wholesale and Retail Sector Education and Training Authority (2001, 96 Table 6.2). This presents only the most relevant occupational groups

> These ladies wanted to go to the loo. They were working at the tills for long hours. Because there were no queues, they asked the till controller if they could go. This lady could not lock the till. The women went to the loo [anyhow] … at the end of the sale … When they came back from the loo, the security guard [accused] them that they didn't put the money [from the last sale] there in the till. They phoned Botha and Pretorius. [The managers] took the ladies to the change office, next to the front tills. Then they said that a security lady was to strip search them. [The women] said they didn't take the money. They took off their clothes. They were crying. [The security guard] found nothing.[75]

This interaction happened on a Saturday afternoon after "most of the permanent staff left."[76] In the week afterward, the branch union and the permanent workers held a sit-in to protest against it and the union took the case to the Commission for Conciliation, Mediation and Arbitration (CCMA).[77] The union demanded and won an apology from the managers to the women.

Nevertheless, staff were appalled that the (white male) manager would order something as humiliating as a strip-search of two women and were especially angered that this occurred after permanent workers had left the store. The women's gendered vulnerability was palpable, and it made the discrimination worse in the eyes of the permanent workers (both women and men) not there to protect them.

This incident compounded multiple daily abuses from several managers – shouting, being rude, bringing workers up on disciplinary charges over petty issues. The permanent workers moved to demand that the worst of the offending managers be fired and that other managers be disciplined for their rude and racist behaviour and for lodging indiscriminate and arbitrary charges against workers. The workers embarked on an extraordinary wildcat protest. Permanent and some casual workers prepared bibs on which they wrote slogans that highlighted their complaints about three managers: "'Mr. Pretorius said I was a lazy black'; 'Franklin Reddy must leave. He's a monster'; 'Pieter Pretorius must go'; 'Hein Botha must go.'"[78] Over a lunch hour, they taped the signs to their fronts and returned to the floor like that. Their embodied resistance conveyed to customers the unpleasant reality of their work relations. Management balked and called in the regional managers. The action resulted in a high-powered meeting involving the shop steward, "three regional personnel managers" and a SACCAWU official "to discuss our problems and come up with a way forward." The main topic for negotiation was the "attitude of management." As one worker explained, "there were grievances right around the store. All the managers were giving out warning letters" (and see Chap. 5). The meeting agreed that all pending cases against staff would be suspended or withdrawn with immediate effect and the regional manager reprimanded the branch managers for their excessive use of punishment. According to the shop steward, this manager said, "You have pushed these guys too far. You have to come back."[79]

Ostensibly, this action was a major victory for the unified protest of permanent and casual workers, although contract workers did not join in despite having common experiences. Regional management and the union together appeared to restore viable workplace relationships and to restrain racist practices. Yet, during the protest store managers "came with video machines" and recorded the employees who wore bibs and participated in the action. Within a few days, workers received "personal letters" from regional managers:

We got letters saying if you do it again within a twelve-month period – any stay-away or picketing – you will be fired. These letters came from regional office. They said that even if a Hyperama manager does something wrong, we will force people to surrender ... Some casuals were participating. Casuals were given [written] warnings. But permanents were given letters clipped on their pay slips.[80]

Regional managers thus turned the letter of the law into discipline to impede future wildcat protest after this one had raised grievances around race to the public, potentially embarrassing the company. Worker action in the early 2000s had very different effect to the 1980s when public exposure of wrongful management practice served to support organizing workers. Under democratic labour law, managers could legitimately restrict wildcat actions.

Furthermore, before a second meeting could happen to consolidate the concessions that workers won with respect to disciplining the managers, allegedly the grocery manager, Mr. Reddy, fabricated a situation through which to fire several contract merchandisers for insubordination: as a shop steward recounted, he asked them to clean shelving in the warehouse which they refused to do because it was not part of their job. When the merchandisers tried to arrange a mediator to assist with solving the disagreement, he suspended them and threw them out of the store on the grounds of "refusing orders from a superior."[81] Thus, while workers had won acknowledgment from regional managers that this particular manager be chastised for his punitive approach, the manager continued acting in the same manner, leading to the dismissal of more workers, in the period before he was formally dealt with.

Finally, the distrust and ill feeling within this branch erupted when a permanent worker assaulted one of the other managers who was to be disciplined after the bib action. When the manager screamed at the worker and called him incompetent and stupid, the worker snapped and starting hitting him. For a few minutes, the staff stood shocked, slow to step in as "everyone hated Botha. He was rude and intolerant."[82] The display of physical aggression by a permanent worker was unusual. Yet, according to workers, the physical punishment he inflicted on the racist manager seemed acceptable to them in that instance given the manager's history. Nevertheless, the union member was brought up on assault charges and fired. Only after this case did the company transfer Mr. Botha out of the store.[83] These actions brought workers' victory within their branch relations, as ultimately the offending managers were removed from their workplace, but at a high price: increased disciplinary clampdown on wildcat actions and the incontrovertible dismissal of a long-standing union member as well as several contract workers.

Permanent workers focused securely on branch-level relationships, particularly when racist managers transgressed relationships to the point of unravelling them. The workers were relatively successful with actions around matters that did not directly threaten the branch managers and that fell within their scope of resolution. Matters that went beyond branch managers' competency, however, required the involvement of regional authorities who asserted their own power over both the branch managers and workers.

Race became a means to protest the unsustainable breach of shop floor relationships. It also served to bring some casuals into the action with permanent workers, but contract merchandisers still did not participate, and permanent workers pursued the protest against managers partly by inscribing casual workers as gendered and as dependent.

In October 2003, SACCAWU organized a national strike at Shoprite, the first of its kind around the conditions of casual workers ("Shoprite strike" 2003). It followed several months of engagement with the company about how to implement the new sectoral determination that redefined casual workers as permanent part-time workers (see Chap. 4). SACCAWU's deputy general secretary, Mduduzi Mbongwe, said that Shoprite had "been undermining gains for workers by drastically reducing the hours of work and therefore the income of non-fulltime workers" ("Shoprite strike" 2003). The union demanded a minimum of 27 hours per week for part-time employees, the scrapping of a normal rate of pay for Sunday hours, and the provision of uniforms, among other issues ("Union threatens" 2003). The strike specifically addressed issues which these casual workers had been raising, then, and which the new sectoral determination would partly resolve. In striking, the union upheld the company's duty to comply with the intent of the new legislation and used the moment to raise issues around casual workers' conditions that had been building for years on shop floors.[84]

SACCAWU won a number of provisions for casual workers, including, importantly, a minimum of 100 hours per month as well as employer-provided uniforms. It was the first SACCAWU strike that explicitly represented casual workers' grievances and that brought casual and permanent workers together, and won important gains for casual workers (Masondo 2008; Forrest 2005). And yet, to a large extent the strike secured rights for casual workers that were due to them on the basis of the newly promulgated sectoral determination (although a guaranteed minimum number of hours per month was not stipulated in the determination). And, the union lost on Sunday pay. The strike signifies the shift in power between organized workers and retailers, where the union was forced to contest each variation in conditions enabled by an ideology of "flexibility." Moreover, it portended the next iteration of the regularizing of a bulk labour supply in the sector (see Chap. 8).

Despite shop-level worker critique of national structures, during this time SACCAWU tried to counter the precariousness of casual workers and to raise the difficult issue of division between permanent and casual workers in congress after congress (Forrest 2005). It introduced casual shop stewards to be elected specifically to represent casual workers in stores, and it made efforts to recruit casual members. It also introduced new ideas like organizing through mall committees to bring workers in a geographic centre together, in order to recruit more casuals (Kenny 2011). Still, what was sedimented in practice, against its best efforts, was the institutionalization of a subordinate category of employment (casual/now flextime or part-time), which could be used to work on public holidays, in the evenings and on Sundays. And, even as casuals were gaining security through conversion to indefinite employment contracts, in the stores studied, workers recorded how Shoprite contracted out cashiers and bag packers to labour brokers, the fate of Ruth Ngobeni who we met in the ATM alcove in Chap. 1.

Thus, when workers managed to come together in joint actions to contest either common grievances or to support those, like casual workers, who were the most vulnerable, retail worker politics became often more localized to branch dynamics; or, as with the national strike, the politics reinforced the significance of the difference from the ever more esteemed, full-time, standard-shift "employee."

* * *

The call "everybody out to the canteen!" was symbolic of the changes to workers' actions in the post-apartheid moment. With it, workers marched off the shop floor to sit-in in the canteen to wait for managers' replies.

Leaving the public space of the store and the street, workers tactically engaged their colleagues to change relations at the retailer.

Permanent workers organized through the branch union structures and embarked on informal, wildcat actions. These sit-ins were sparked by management infringements of the relations that established permanent workers' status as adult decision-makers in the workplace. With wildcat actions, permanent workers affirmed two things. They asserted a collective identity bounded by branch union relations, if not always formal structures. By focusing on reconstituting their position within branch relationships with managers, permanent workers localized their politics to their particular branch. Contract merchandisers used their own collective organization to negotiate within the workplace for rules protecting them from arbitrary, personalized, often despotic interactions with managers. Unlike permanent workers, the merchandisers did not instigate dramatic sit-ins, but worked through calling formal meetings with branch managers to air their concerns, rather than negotiate with their employers, the labour brokers. At other times, merchandisers collectively embarked on go-slows or boycotts of auxiliary services, consistent with their weaker position within shop relations (see Kelley 1996, 18). Casual workers, in turn, attempted to contest reduced shifts, which barely allowed them to cover their costs, and to change their visible status within the stores by demanding uniforms. Their struggles show contests over the definition of employee within the workplace that aimed at positioning themselves as abasebenzi. Still, at the point when they might have won these demands through labour law reform (pushed by the union strike), many of their jobs were subcontracted out and the workers themselves re-employed by labour brokers.

In the post-apartheid context, the workplace remained a formative site of subjugation. The protests by workers in the late 1990s and early 2000s show that they rejected the worst infringements of racist relations, often mobilizing around and formulating subjectivities in terms of race. In comparison, gender as a coded set of meanings came to define the terms of difference between workers (see Scott 1988). Permanent workers built a language that at the same time as protecting vulnerable workers, subordinated casual workers' grievances and feminized them. Contract workers too separated themselves from casual workers' precariousness, something which they shared, by identifying as skilled men. This mapping contradicted the vulnerability that permanent and contract workers felt as changes to the labour market affected their sense of adult gendered selves beyond the workplace, as we will see in the next chapter.

And, yet, workers still collectively responded. Two important facets of the constitutive subject abasebenzi endured: its relationality and its collectivity, both of which can be seen in workers' shop floor actions. Their claims and protests were a form of obdurate endurance (cf Povinelli 2011), in which retail worker politics defined not only engagement in workplace relations but also that this was a site of the constitution of political relations and on changing terrains of national belonging. Each category acted as "workers," and thus claimed ways of being-related-to. Even as abasebenzi was reproduced as a political subject, however, it divided along categories separated by labour process and by law, and localized worker politics by branch. Furthermore, the enduring affective attachment to this subjectivity linked to the urgency with which jobs became resources for other parts of life, as we will see in the next chapter, making all the more complex the relationship between precariousness and abasebenzi.

Notes

1. Sara Dlamini, interviewed by Bridget Kenny, Soweto, June 19, 1999.
2. South African democratic labour law stipulates conditions which must be met by workers embarking on collective action. Wildcat actions per definition did not meet these conditions and were thus unprocedural. In such a case, workers could be disciplined or even dismissed.
3. Adler and Webster (1995) suggested what this new order of labour relations should look like under democracy.
4. Paul Mahlangu, SACCAWU shop steward, interviewed by Bridget Kenny, Ekurhuleni, March 25 and 27, June 3 and 26, August 5 and 29, 2000.
5. Paul Mahlangu, interview.
6. Paul Mahlangu, interview.
7. Paul Mahlangu, interview.
8. Others have written about the pressures put on store managers in other contexts as retailing centralized firm control and rationalized staff (Broadbridge 2002; Smith and Elliott 2012).
9. The branch manager reportedly joked with the shop steward about joining a union because of disaffection with Shoprite: "We need a union for managers now!" (Paul Mahlangu, interview).
10. Paul Mahlangu, interview.
11. Daniel Madonsela, interviewed by Bridget Kenny, Ekurhuleni, May 13, 1999.

12. In the survey I conducted in 2000, the average age of casual workers was approximately five years younger than that of permanent workers (see Kenny 2007, 490).
13. Sara Dlamini, interview.
14. Focus group interview with permanent workers by Bridget Kenny, Ekurhuleni, May 18, 1999.
15. Focus group interview with permanent workers by Bridget Kenny, Ekurhuleni, May 18, 1999.
16. Kethiwe Dlomo, interviewed by Bridget Kenny, Daveyton, August 1 and 8, 1999. Phineas Riba translated this passage from isiZulu, in detailed discussion with me.
17. The assertive language used here stands in marked contrast to the passive manner in which casual workers were required to address payment problems (see Chap. 5).
18. See Clive Glaser (2000) for a discussion of "youth" in the South African context, with particular reference to experiences in urban townships: "For all its vagueness ... the concept of youth coheres around the notion of transition between childhood and *responsible* adulthood" (4, italics added).
19. Focus group interview with permanent workers by Bridget Kenny, Ekurhuleni, March 2, 2000.
20. Thandile Ziyane, interviewed by Bridget Kenny, Daveyton, February 22, 2000.
21. Kethiwe Dlomo, interview.
22. Kethiwe Dlomo, interview.
23. Focus group interview with permanent workers by Bridget Kenny, Ekurhuleni, February 7, 2000.
24. Kethiwe Dlomo, interview.
25. Kethiwe Dlomo, interview.
26. Focus group interview with contract merchandisers by Bridget Kenny, Ekurhuleni, February 7, 2000.
27. Vuyo Nokabu, interviewed by Bridget Kenny, Daveyton, May 6, 2000.
28. Stembiso Vilakazi, interviewed by Bridget Kenny, Daveyton, December 2, 1999.
29. Thabo Phasha, interviewed by Bridget Kenny, Daveyton, March 28, 1999; Jabu Mbambisa, interviewed by Bridget Kenny, Daveyton, June 20, 1999, and August 31, 2000; Thabang Maloka, interviewed by Bridget Kenny, Daveyton, August 13, 1999; Themba Nyembe, interviewed by Bridget Kenny, Daveyton, August 14, 1999.
30. Focus group interview with contract merchandisers by Bridget Kenny, Ekurhuleni, February 7, 2000.
31. Focus group interview with contract merchandisers by Bridget Kenny, Ekurhuleni, February 7, 2000.

32. Focus group interview with contract merchandisers by Bridget Kenny, Ekurhuleni, February 7, 2000.
33. "Skill" itself is deeply gendered (see Cockburn 1983; Crompton and Jones 1984; Kaye 1994; Salzinger 2003), and in claiming the skill of product knowledge these merchandisers, mostly men, called on a masculine identity of merchant, not service worker. For a discussion of changing skill in front-line retail work, see Ikeler (2016b).
34. Vuyo Nokabu, interview.
35. Vuyo Nokabu, interview.
36. Vuyo Nokabu, interview.
37. A few of the large suppliers had their own employees merchandising their products in branches.
38. Thabo Phasha, interview.
39. Themba Nyembe, interview.
40. Where a product is placed on the shelf relative to eye level has become a "science." How store space is constructed – the size of aisles, the design of shelves and refrigerated display, et cetera – to present products is important (see Bowlby 2001). Merchandisers assisted with keeping shelves well tended, not only in terms of quantity of products but also keeping them neat and clean. They were responsible for moving older-dated items to the front of the shelf and packing newer ones at the back, so customers would first buy the older stock. They claimed that this work lowered stock returns.
41. The popular name for such a pool cleaner is "kreepy-krauly."
42. Vuyo Nokabu, interview.
43. While bar coding had been introduced in the stores in 1998, sometimes the computer systems listed incorrect prices.
44. Themba Nyembe, interview.
45. Jabu Mbambisa, interview.
46. Jabu Mbambisa, interview.
47. Jabu Mbambisa, interview. I did not encounter any actual examples of merchandisers striking with permanent workers.
48. Themba Nyembe, interview.
49. For example, Thabo Phasha, interview; Vuyo Nokabu, interview; Zodwa Zondi, interviewed by Bridget Kenny, Daveyton, May 7, 2000.
50. Thabo Phasha, interview; Anele Ndlovu, interviewed by Bridget Kenny, Daveyton, June 15, 1999; Vuyo Nokabu, interview.
51. In a survey I conducted in 2000 in these stores, casual workers' average weekly hours were 19.7 (see Kenny 2001, 95).
52. Thomas Guto, SACCAWU shop steward, interviewed by Bridget Kenny, Benoni, February 16, 2000; focus group interviews with casual workers by Bridget Kenny, Ekurhuleni, February 8 and 28, 2000.
53. Wage Determination 478 for the Wholesale and Retail Trade.

54. This became an issue in the SACCAWU strike in October of 2003, as we will see below.
55. Paul Mahlangu, interview; Ayanda Nkosi, interviewed by Bridget Kenny, Daveyton, August 8, 1999; see also Nandipha Dlomo, interviewed by Bridget Kenny, Daveyton, July 31, 1999.
56. Focus group interview with casual workers by Bridget Kenny, Ekurhuleni, February 10, 2000.
57. Some casual workers had joined the union, but many left again after not feeling represented (Focus group interviews with casual workers by Bridget Kenny, Ekurhuleni, May 25, 1999, February 8, 10, 28, and 29, 2000).
58. Focus group interview with casual workers by Bridget Kenny, Ekurhuleni, June 5, 1998.
59. Focus group interview with casual workers by Bridget Kenny, Ekurhuleni, June 5, 1998.
60. Basic Conditions of Employment Act, 1997.
61. Focus group interview with casual workers by Bridget Kenny, Ekurhuleni, May 25, 1999.
62. Sfiso Shenge, interviewed by Bridget Kenny, Germiston, July 28, 1999.
63. Thembi Skhosana, interviewed by Bridget Kenny, Daveyton, August 18, 1999; see also Unathi Shabalala, interviewed by Bridget Kenny, Daveyton, August 21, 1999.
64. Sfiso Shenge, interview.
65. Thando Shabalala, interviewed by Bridget Kenny, Daveyton, October 12, 1999.
66. Phindi Masango, interviewed by Bridget Kenny, Daveyton, July 29, 1999. Back-shopping means returning items that customers left at the tills to the shelves.
67. Tsakane Baloi, interviewed by Bridget Kenny, Ekurhuleni, August 3, 1999.
68. Mandla Moyo, interviewed by Bridget Kenny, Daveyton, June 21, 1999, August 17, 24, and 31, September 7 and 14, 2000; Sfiso Shenge, interview; focus group interview with casual workers by Bridget Kenny, Ekurhuleni, May 25, 1999.
69. Sarah Mahlangu, interviewed by Bridget Kenny, Kempton Park, July 27, 1999.
70. Palesa Bogasu, interviewed by Bridget Kenny, Ekurhuleni, July 30, 1999; see also Mbali Gumede, interviewed by Bridget Kenny, Daveyton, June 12, 1999; Phindi Masango, interview; Nandipha Dlomo, interview.
71. Thendeka Menzi, interviewed by Bridget Kenny, Ekurhuleni, August 5, 1999.
72. Zanele Mathebula, interviewed by Bridget Kenny, Ekurhuleni, May 27, 1999.

73. There were very small numbers of white workers who worked as casuals, but their employment under better conditions was highly symbolic to the regular casual workers.
74. All names are pseudonyms.
75. Mandla Moyo, interview.
76. Mandla Moyo, interview.
77. This statutory body deals with various disputes in sectors without bargaining councils, such as retail.
78. All names are pseudonyms.
79. Mandla Moyo, interview.
80. Mandla Moyo, interview.
81. Mandla Moyo, interview.
82. Mandla Moyo interview.
83. Mr. Pretorius had resigned after the previous event.
84. In the stores that I studied, some permanent workers reportedly did strike with casual workers. By this time, however, the company had subcontracted out many of the former casual jobs, which were now filled by contract workers employed by labour brokers (Ruth Ngobeni, interviewed by Bridget Kenny, Daveyton, July 10, 2005).

CHAPTER 7

"To Sit at Home and Do Nothing": Gender and the Constitutive Meaning of Work

Shoulders pressed against other workers, silently rocked by the shaking of the taxi, Thando Shabalala returns home in the evening. Disembarking at the taxi rank in Daveyton, she walks down Eiselen Street to catch a local taxi to bring her nearer to her home. She feels the tiredness deep in the heels of her feet. The casual retail worker walks the remaining blocks to her mother's four-roomed house, buying a packet of tomatoes on the way from the hawker on the corner. She needs to cook for her child, her sister's sons, her father, and her unemployed brother. Levering the lash up and aside, she opens the metal gate to her small yard. She walks up the path to an open backdoor. Her five-year-old daughter runs to hug her mother's legs. She smiles down at the little girl, and then enters the kitchen. The glare of the late afternoon sun throws deep shadows. The small kitchen is tidy. She will start a pot to boil. First she moves quietly through the house. Her brother sleeps in one of the bedrooms and her father dozes in front of the television. Despite the waves of sound pulsing from the set, the house seems still. The air is humid and stuffy. She returns to sit for a moment at the kitchen table. She settles into the seat, the heaviness hangs on her shoulders like an overgrown child demanding to be carried. She turns to me and says, "I do not want to sit at home and do nothing."[1]

Thando used a common expression for being unemployed, "sitting at home." This chapter examines this metaphor in order to understand the meaning of work for retail workers. There are two parts to the expression.

The first is the spatial marker "home," divided off as private; the second is its association with inactivity, "sitting" and "doing nothing." Thando's invocation seems to affirm a separation of private space and inaction from public space and action that on first blush seems rather Arendtian: "A man who lived only a private life, who like the slave was not permitted to enter the public realm, or like the barbarian had chosen not to enter the public realm, was not fully human" (Arendt 1958, 38; Pitkin 1998). Yet, the spatial metaphor offers an alternate reading of the meaning of "work"/ wage labour that subverts the binary of public/private, and offers an understanding of the political relevance of "work" to building personhood, social relations and future (political) community.

While the heaviness of Thando's burden seems to confirm a kind of binary division in which inaction overlaps with priorities of survival, her physical traversal conjoins the hushed private space of home with the bustle of city street and workplace. While Thando Shabalala only releases her shoulders and sighs at home, her movement from workplace to home, back to the workplace becomes a metaphor for her own activation as a person in the world, stretched out across space, and indeed time (White 2013a), as we shall see, particularly when it is intimately tied into establishing children's futures.

The metaphor for unemployment, "sitting at home," offers a substantive meaning of wage labour that involves the constitution of relations between people. "Work" directly effects (brings about) the ongoing becoming of persons; in southern Africa, personhood is itself public and political, creative, generative, and constitutive of social relations (Comaroff and Comaroff 2001). What makes a person is fundamentally the same thing as what makes a public world. Personhood is about activating social relationships to bring through others. Thus, "No living self could be static. Stasis meant social death" (Comaroff and Comaroff 2001, 271). The wage becomes a conduit for this activity and hence for the building of social relations.

In this chapter I explore how retail workers understood employment and wage labour to sustain (although tenuously) these political gestures. None of them aspired to work in low-paid, low-skilled jobs. Yet "working" was necessary in order to enable one's ability to activate one's desires – for material possessions, maybe for a more rewarding job in the future, but, most importantly, for a good life for their children. Working was thus a future-orientated activity, a pursuit that ensured the circulation of resources and enabled mobility: physical, as in the movement between spaces, and (sometimes) economic, but more often the movement of people toward something to come. As Hylton White (2004, 2010) has explained so beautifully, for the unemployed a job is a future achievement that would enable a posterior affirmation of self within a lineage. Historically, wage labour disrupted the making of persons and life worlds (Comaroff and Comaroff 1987), and yet in post-apartheid South Africa, *un*employment now stutters these connections (White 2004, 2012, 2013b).

While a new "politics of distribution" may very well be emerging within South Africa in which, in the context of declining wage labour, people affirm networks of dependency, for instance with the state (through grants) (Ferguson 2015), this chapter looks at the enduring mundane attachment to "the job" and reflects it back through workers' narratives, which tie employment to making (political) community. As White writes, it is not whether people depend on people, "but what kind of thing dependency is within a form of life" (White 2013a, 256–57). For these retail workers, working remained a counter pole to what was generalized as the inoperativity of "sitting at home." The job was set against the always-present possibility of losing employment and of becoming one who could "do nothing." The job allowed one to bring others into being, which in turn affirmed adulthood in specifically gendered ways. As we saw in Chap. 6, permanent workers feminized mere survival in the category of "casuals," marking an inability to act.[2] In this chapter, I examine how all workers, including permanent, contract, and casual workers like Thando, tied working to bringing others into being and hence acting. These processes were articulated through notions of motherhood and of masculinity. While households were places of much activity, the negotiations over resources and the affective economies they signalled reflected back on the meaning of "work," as that which enabled action. The work of providing – what I call here the "praxis of providing" – reproduced deep gendered anxieties among parents that, I suggest, informed the political subject abasebenzi among precarious retail workers. Part of the political semiotics of work resided, then, in how it constituted social relations, forms of affinity, and orders of participation. Not to have a job meant "to sit at home and do nothing."

"Sitting": Statis as Social Death

The common expression that people used for being unemployed was *ngiya hlele ekhaya* ("sitting at home" in isiZulu).[3] It was used in different ways to explain a range of positions in which retail workers found themselves. Anna Zwane, a casual worker, explained that she liked working because "It's not like sitting at home ... I do not want to stay at home." When asked why, she said that "there is nothing that you can do when you are at home."[4] Gcwabaza Nomhle explained that she would rather cope with poor conditions in the store than be unemployed because "what will you say because you've got no job. You must work. I will do anything rather than sitting at home."[5] Dismissed for theft in 1997, former full-time, permanent worker Zama Ntuli was "just sitting."[6] She did not engage in the informal economy, for example, selling fruit or vegetables from a small stand in the street, for fear of being robbed.[7] She represented her life without a job as confined to the isolation of her house and her yard: "I wake up and clean and then after cleaning I sleep. There is nothing else I can do." Her solution to this malaise: "I am looking for a job."[8] Using the related idiom "staying in the location,"[9] contract merchandiser Thabo Phasa explained that, while he did not like the type of work he had, "I work because I cannot do anything [else], because I cannot stay in the location until I find the right job."[10] Another contract worker, Vuyo Nokabu, said, "Now I am not used to staying in the location, that's why I just go to work."[11]

In examining the meaning of employment through its limit in this ubiquitous metaphor for unemployment "to sit at home and do nothing," I am not saying that there is no "work" being done at home, nor am I saying that there is not a vibrant affective and political life being created in spaces outside of wage labour. I am exploring this metaphor to try to understand the meaning of "work" and its significance for labour politics. These low-paid service workers did not have the resources – neither enough monthly earnings nor a retrenchment package waiting for them – to plan to leave wage labour (see Barchiesi 2011; Scully 2016). While their precarious wage was quite low, they confirmed the centrality of the meaning of the job to relations outside of the workplace, as we shall see.[12]

The spatial metaphor of "sitting at home" or "staying in the location" marked the physical distance between segregated residential areas and jobs in previously "white" towns. It signified the chasm between destitution and survival, but it also coded a clear distinction between inactivity and social personhood.[13] The parataxis of the sentence, in which "sitting at home" was coeval with "doing nothing," bound these two meanings together when workers spoke of wage labour. Money activated social relations. Only through earning money could one claim to be "doing anything." "Work" enabled earners to provide for themselves and their extended families and most importantly their children. "Providing for" meant building a life.

Karl Marx (1976, 162–63) observed the magic of the fetish of the commodity under capitalism, which required the abstract standard of money to circulate as a medium of commensurability, of exchange. Money acted as a symbolic repository of value, which abstracted social relations in the market (Simmel 2004). But, as anthropologists have noted, money came to hold for many a symbolic power to affect social beings and relations; rather than signalling a disembedded cash nexus, its circulation mapped relationships of obligation (Taussig 1980; Nash 1979; Guyer 2004; Appadurai 1986).[14] Service workers knew that "Life changes when you are working because you've got money; you can do everything that you want to do,"[15] to be engaged in a social world. As casual packer Gcwabaza said: "But the life here [in the township] is not easy. Because we depend on money. Everything is money, money. If you don't have money, you can't live here,"[16] within a set of relations that require active support.

Having money meant being able to contribute to building relations with other people. Permanent worker Cheryl Isaacs referenced her daughter when she explained the import of her job: "I'm growing her now. She's eleven, Standard 4 [Grade 6], and at least I'm still young and I can look after her ... She is great. She just needs the money to take her somewhere."[17] While Cheryl actively "grew" her child, "the money" would act to elevate her daughter elsewhere.

This notion of actively building social relations defined the sense of personhood of seTswana men in colonial times, as well as in the 1970s (Comaroff and Comaroff 2001). This sensibility implied that no person existed as an isolated individual and that "identity ... was forged, cumulatively, by an infinite ongoing series of practical activities" (Comaroff and Comaroff 2001, 268). It was a matter of becoming through one's ongoing accumulation of "wealth in people" (Comaroff and Comaroff 1987; Guyer 1993, 1995). This constructive activity was "work" (*tiro*), associated with the word for "to make" or "to do" (*go dira*), and it was differentiated from wage labour (*bereko*, derived from the Afrikaans word *werk*), which was seen as the opposite, destructive, and anti-social (Comaroff and Comaroff 1987, 1992, 162–64; 2001, 272; see also Moodie and Ndatshe 1994). Thus to be an adult, active person in the world, one constituted relations with others; one built oneself by bringing others into being. If something halted this constitutive activity, it meant "social death" and indicated some untoward intervention, such as witchcraft, or was definitive of the status of a dependent minor (Comaroff and Comaroff 2001, 272). This notion thereby explained some of the panic associated with post-apartheid rural unemployment, interpreted through a rising incidence of reports of "zombies," the ultimate anti-social beings who, rather than building up, consumed others (Comaroff and Comaroff 1999).[18]

For retail workers, their jobs enabled the capacity to constitute themselves and others around them. The wage can be seen here not as simply destructive, as in older renderings, but in fact as incorporated into this active sense of personhood (see Moodie and Ndatshe 1994; and see my discussion of the linguistic shift from *izisebenzi* to abasebenzi in Chap. 1). Not working – or "sitting at home" – would arrest action because it would halt the capacity to move across space as well as to enact relations.

The Praxis of Providing

Retail workers whom I interviewed in the late 1990s and early 2000s lived in townships that had been racially segregated during the apartheid period, removed from the centres of employment, but closely tied into the local labour market of the region. Most grew up in these urban communities with mothers, fathers, and extended networks of people who had worked in the East Rand's manufacturing economy in the 1950s to the 1980s. By the 1990s, the average number of wage earners had gradually declined so that each wage earner was supporting increasingly larger extended households. The corporatization of social service provisioning and shift to cost recovery, beginning in this period, placed an additional burden on urban township residents. Pre-paid electricity metres, for instance, ensured revenue collection by making citizens responsible for regulating (and disciplining) their own electricity consumption (Naidoo 2007; von Schnitzler 2016). Social welfare had an ameliorating effect through old age, disability, and the newly introduced child support grants, although many retail workers earned above the threshold that would have qualified them to receive child support grants then.[19] In these contexts, the retail wage was certainly important, but grossly undercompensated household needs. While the economic difficulties of households and inequalities engendered therein certainly echoed through workers' stories,[20] this section highlights the energy and affect that pervaded this constant praxis of providing (see also Povinelli 2011).

Many experienced precariousness in terms of anxieties over their prolonged and reliable ability to provide for partners and extended families, and especially for children, to be explored in the next section. This section examines how workers spoke of their household contributions, as a measure of the embodied labour going into supporting specific resources. It then examines the work of making and keeping housing. Providing meant enabling households to survive and was tied into these complex social relationships.

The commodities which workers contributed were spoken of as discrete use values, rather than registering as abstract quantities (see Zelizer 1994); furthermore, household members embodied each household resource. Gcwabaza lived in her father's house in Daveyton with her sister and her daughter. As was common, she described her contribution to the household in terms of the concrete items that she paid for: "Me and my sister must pay the rent [municipal services]. Me, I'm casual. I must buy food, pay the rent, everything." Housing, education, transport, "rent," and food materialized in terms of the person who provided each (also see Hunter 2010).

Workers explained that they were "responsible for the electricity" or "the rent" or, if they earned a smaller amount, they "helped with food."[21] Thirty-seven-year-old casual worker Lerato Kgasago lived with her siblings and her 13-year-old son in her parents' house in Daveyton. There were six adults living in their household, but only she and her brother were employed. Her brother had a stable permanent, full-time job as a prison warder nearby, which enabled him to be the main breadwinner: "He buys food, he pays electricity." Lerato herself "sometimes [buys] food, but I am mostly paying the society."[22] A "society" was an informal savings association in which some workers participated as a form of enforced savings against future expenses, such as funerals but also other expenses (James 2015).

Workers' income went to providing basic costs of living, but behind these tallies lay the worry of the responsibility for others. Long-time permanent worker Sara Dlamini had lost her husband, another earner, and on her own supported her two unemployed sons and a grandchild who was still at school. While she had a relatively large house, which she and her husband had extended over time, since her husband's death she worried about basic needs: "I am trying but I can't … I've got to pay rent. I've got to pay electricity and buy. Another thing [is that] you can't keep eating [the same food]. Like David [her son] is cooking pap [maize porridge] and cabbage every day or maybe pap and chicken everyday. You've got to change."[23]

Palesa Bogasu, a casual worker, lived in her aunt's house in Tembisa. As a single parent, she sent her children to live with her mother in Limpopo province, a common strategy to deal with child-minding challenges in the context where paid childcare was an added cost and her schedule meant she had to be available to work changing shifts (see Chap. 5). She visited them only when she saved enough money to travel there. Her mother conducted subsistence farming if there was enough rain, but in other years survived by getting "credit from the shops." She was unable to offer much to her mother financially for food, but paid for her children's school uniforms.[24] She also contributed food to her aunt's household, but often was short when it came to paying for her own keep. Palesa tied her wages to specific material needs, for instance to enable a child to remain in school, against other choices, a balancing in which all workers engaged (and see Hunter 2015). And like other workers, she said that her financial problems stemmed from her low-paying job: "Right now I am the only one in the house who is doing everything. It's just too many things. Mainly it's job problems … because I am the only one [earning]."[25] Thus, while her aunt gave her a place to stay and her mother cared for her children, Palesa contributed the only wage income between the households.

Housing, then, was another critical yet tenuous economic resource for many of these workers (see Cooper 1983; Hansen 1997; Martin 1992; Bank 2011; and see Peck 1996 for the importance of housing in local labour markets). Often obtaining security of housing was an ongoing practice for which workers activated a wide range of social ties to sustain. From the late 1980s, the economic situation in South Africa meant that workers were confronted with a declining stability of residential tenure. Their parents' history of securing their own housing often defined options for workers later as adults, and discussions of where they lived converged around stories of access, holding onto, and contesting housing options.

In order to achieve a measure of independence, workers often preferred to move out of their parents' houses to rent a room or shack in the yard.[26] This usually meant that the worker separated his or her own income from those of the parents. Thabo, who lived in a room behind his father's house, explained that this enabled him to come and go as he wanted and to bring his girlfriends home without disturbing the rest of the family.[27] Staking this claim to his independence was a large part of his decision to leave the parental house and pay rent to his family for a room in the yard.

In the context of a severe housing shortage in the large urban agglomerations of South Africa, some workers rented a plot of land in an informal settlement and erected their own *mkhukhu*, or shack, built out of corrugated iron sheets (see Hunter and Posel 2012). On the East Rand, informal settlements began to expand on the edges of black townships and in unoccupied farmlands in the late 1980s (Malinga 2000). Generally, workers considered a home in an informal settlement the most precarious form of housing. At the time, many of these informal settlements commonly received no municipal services, such as garbage removal, sewerage, or electricity. Sometimes violent landlord factions exploited residents either for political control or basic usury. Contract merchandiser Khenzani Nkuna and her husband decided to move from her mother's house in Daveyton to the Chris Hani informal settlement near Daveyton in 1996 on rumours that the African National Congress (ANC) was going to provide houses for people. They rented a piece of land and built a shack. It was a dangerous time with political factions operating within the boundaries of the informal settlement. Often they would force men to participate in patrolling duties at night, putting their lives at risk: "Guys came during the night [to] wake up our husbands, says let's go look for the Inkatha people, let's go and patrol, the whole night. And then sometimes in the morning we find that they have shot some other guys, some of them are dead you see."[28] Because of this risk, Khenzani and her husband decided to sell their shack and return to her mother's house.

Many workers interviewed for this study lived in the house a parent had first rented in Daveyton in the 1950s under long-term leases from the municipality.[29] With democracy, these leases were converted to titles, transferring ownership to the parent, often the mother.[30] The houses ranged from older four-roomed houses to newer houses that workers' families had extended over time (Photo 7.1).[31] A house in the township proper was a real resource. With the privatization of municipal services and the state's policy shift to cost recovery, however, many residents of secure housing felt increasingly under threat of water or electricity cut-offs or even repossession.[32]

Some workers lived in a "family house" after the death of the parents. This option was both an advantage and a liability (see James 2015, 176–77, 182–92). While it provided workers with a scarce relatively stable residence,

Photo 7.1 Street scene in Daveyton, c. 2000 (Image by Bridget Kenny. Edits by Simon Gush)

it also exposed them to claims to the house by other family members. Disputes were common, and distant relatives claimed properties as a strategy to find a base in urban areas.[33] Jabu Mbambisa, a contract merchandiser, grew up in his grandmother's house in Daveyton, not seeing much of his mother who was rarely home, and not knowing his father. He continued to live there after his grandmother's death, but worried that his mother could return to claim the house: "This is not my house. It's a family house. My mother can decide to come back home and I have no right to refuse her."[34] Vuyo, also a contract worker, had problems with his sister challenging his wife's presence in the family house: "I want my own house because this one is a family house. Sometimes my sister comes and shouts [at] my wife ... and my wife is crying, 'Your sister was here, talking this, talking this, telling this'. [She] says, 'It's [your] father's house. It's not your house, you mustn't do like this.'"[35]

Several permanent workers had obtained a "bond house" in the early 1990s, bought with bank loans when township housing markets were deregulated (Bond 2000). The houses were also located in the townships but in areas that were newly developed. The bank loans were granted to couples where both partners were in full-time, formal employment.[36] Thus, Mary Nkosi's and her husband's full-time retail jobs qualified them for a mortgage in the early 1990s with which they bought a house in the newly developed area of Etwatwa, next to Daveyton (Malinga 2000). When Mary lost her permanent job in 1999, she worried whether her husband's income was sufficient to cover the monthly bond payments.[37] At the time of interviewing them, they were "boycotting payments" because large cracks in the plaster walls had opened up, and she had lodged a claim with the bank against the developer.[38]

A few workers qualified for a government-subsidized "RDP" house, named after the ANC's "Reconstruction and Development Programme" that formed the basis of its 1994 election platform.[39] Zanele Mathebula, a casual worker, had managed to get one of these two-roomed houses in Tembisa, and lived there with her three young children. She and her children survived on her casual wage, as well as on the rent she received for three shacks she had built in her yard.[40]

A fragmented context of tenure security cut across workers in different employment categories, as well as women and men. Housing was definitive for household security, and workers spent much time and energy worrying about this resource. In most situations, housing depended upon a wider network of social connections. Regardless, to become an adult, in standard practice one was meant to establish one's own (patrilineal) household. Thus, many of the men who were contract merchandisers stayed in informal settlements or *mkhukhus* in order to build their own place, while many female casual workers lived in family houses; nevertheless, as we have seen, many workers regardless of gender continued to live with parents or in parents' houses, thereby signalling the disruption of the norms of becoming "adults" (see Hunter 2010).

With the increasing difficulty of finding affordable housing from the late 1990s, and as labour market options changed, household composition began to change (see Beittel 1992; Smith and Wallerstein 1992).[41] Even workers in more stable households felt an increasing sense of precariousness. Stable earners often supported multiple unemployed adult dependents. Frequently extended kin members moved into these "stable" households, putting increased pressure on existing income earners (see May 1998; Mosoetsa 2011). Research on households in southern Africa shows consistently that most working-class and poor people rely on household members for support even if these relations are conflict-laden and that household residents include a wide variety of family, non-family, and extended kin (Mosoetsa 2011; Beittel 1992; May 1998; Murray 1987; Sharp and Spiegel 1985).[42]

Wage earners, then, often supported several unemployed co-residents. Kethiwe Dlomo – the permanent worker who described casual workers categorically as vulnerable, as clothes being blown by the wind on a washing line (see Chap. 6) – lived in a home in an informal settlement with her two unemployed adult children and one grandchild.[43] Cheryl, also a permanent worker, lived in a room built in the yard of her parents' house in Tembisa with her unemployed boyfriend and her 11-year-old child from a previous relationship. She commented that "I took him [her boyfriend] to come and stay with me. In their culture [isiZulu] it's not right [for the man to live with the woman's family]. But, I mean, we are *sukkeling* [suffering]. So where will he go to? Go and sleep on the *stoep* [front porch] by his place? No ways."[44] Economic vulnerability meant that the couple lived with her family.

Twenty-seven-year-old casual bag packer Ayanda Nkosi lived with her partner and their five-year-old daughter in a shack in the yard of her parents' house. Her boyfriend was also unemployed, but sold "sweets and beers" from the yard: "It's not a good business ... I can't say we make sufficient money. Sometimes it's going well, but sometimes no." The combination of her part-time casual job with the unevenness of his income meant it was difficult to meet basic household expenses: "[S]ometimes at Hyperama I work only two days, and you'd find that in that two days I have to buy mealie-meal [maize meal] and rice, food for the house. And you'd find that he had to buy meat for the whole week; the child needs clothes. I want clothes; he wants clothes. So that money cannot satisfy [those things]." Both she and her boyfriend also helped their parental families when they could: "And no one works at his home. So when they need something they come to us to ask for something ... There is no one who works in that house, all of them are just like people in my home." Five adults and four grandchildren lived in the boyfriend's parental home with his mother's state pension as the only income. In her own extended family, few people were employed so that she assisted there too: "When my sisters need something, they tell me and I try something. They are not working."[45]

Workers felt the responsibility of having to provide for their extended families. Often family members had very clear expectations of them as earners, as Zodwa Zondi, a female contract worker, explained:

> You know the most painful thing is when it comes toward December, neh, everybody is happy. "I've got a bonus, I've got a bonus". You've got nothing. With R800, you separate it, and how much grocery are you going to buy? Then what about accounts [store credit cards]? Then there is nothing with a bonus. [Family members] even say you are a liar [when you say], "I've got no bonus". I mean the way it sounds you can say that you are a liar, neh? They say you are lying. It's impossible, you don't have a bonus! How?! You have a job.[46]

Expectations of earners added to pressures on them as providers.

All workers in this study, across categories of employment including full-time unionized jobs, faced conditions of economic household insecurity. Their wages contributed critically to the survival of their households, but all worried about their ability to support their households' basic expenses sufficiently. The social security system introduced in South Africa after 1994 improved the level and provision of old age pensions and introduced child grants, so that households were increasingly able to rely on a wider range of income than only wages (May 1998; Ferguson 2015; Barchiesi 2011; Vally 2016; Scully 2016; Seekings and Nattrass 2005, 2015). Yet, because of their jobs, retail workers assumed the status and the burden of being providers for wider networks.[47]

Within wide-spread precariousness, workers' wages circulated to support households and social relationships in ways not traced by those describing the declining import of wages to livelihoods (Seekings and Nattrass 2005; Ferguson 2015).[48] Thus, in the context of declining wages, precarious earnings stretched thinner and also affected the relationships of those earners to families. Beyond the quantitative level of support, then, the meaning and circuit of the wage for earners involved affective content: compulsion, responsibility, anxiety, negotiations of gender and generation (see Hunter 2010). The wage, then, was a conduit to building and maintaining ties and relations of obligation, including fraught and bitter binds. Retail workers embodied specific provisions; put into circulation specific networks with mothers, siblings, children, and grandchildren; and actively laboured to fulfil the relations of providing. This praxis suggests how "work" carried meaning beyond the quantitative contribution of the wage.

Gendered Anxieties: Working for Children, Working for the Future

The meaning of work in the context of acknowledged precariousness in South Africa has most frequently been discussed in terms of social dislocation and its specific form of the disruption of gendered identities, and has been linked to a gendered analysis of shifting relations among men and women and within households (see, for instance, Hunter 2010; Mosoetsa 2011; Khunou 2012).

Both men and women retail workers integrated the necessity to provide for household members into core gender identities. Yet the changing local labour market and the vulnerability of households threatened workers' ability to provide. Men articulated their anxieties around their declining ability to take care of their families in terms of their manhood. Women expressed their concerns by worrying about their incapacity to build up resources to facilitate their children's access to a better life. While expressed in terms of gendered identities, these formulations suggest an orientation to a future set of relations that required active constitution in the present, and through which these workers' own place in the family and the lineage would be secured (White 2004).

As has been widely documented, men expressed masculinity partly in terms of their ability to provide for women and children (see Hunter 2010; Waetjen 2004; Morrell 1998, 2001; Ramphele and Boonzaier 1988; Richter and Morrell 2006; Moodie and Ndatshe 1994; Gibbs et al. 2014).[49] Manhood has historically been associated with work in southern African cultures, shifting to wage labour particularly as migrant mining labour integrated into a man's life cycle marking the end of youth (McAllister 1980; Moodie and Ndatshe 1994; Morrell 1998; Breckenridge 1998; Hunter 2010). Thus Vuyo took a job when he learnt in initiation school[50] that "you must be a man, you must provide now," suggesting that to be a proper man he should have his own household and family.[51]

Defining masculinity through forming one's independent household and providing meant that the loss of work could impact severely on a worker's sense of manhood.[52] After Jabu lost his job as a contract merchandiser, his younger sister supported him and his son. The fact that he no longer provided an income to the household was at the core of his sense of undermined masculinity: "Because according to my tradition, you must not every time beg for it from the woman. How can you ... I mean you are a man, that you must try to see, ok, what must I do in order to survive."[53]

Gendered divisions of household labour were deeply entrenched among workers interviewed. Jabu did the unpaid household labour, while his sister worked, but he clearly felt tensions in doing so:

> So, it's like I'm still surviving, although I'm not that much happy ... I had to do some of the things which I'm not allowed to do. Like, I mean, doing the household cooking ... I don't have any choice, I had to do it. I mean sweeping. I mean, okay, if I like to do that, okay, I can do it. But not now in that situation where I am forced to do it, you see. I mean my sister, she comes here late, I have to help. Okay, I'm prepared to do it, but now the thing is that I don't have *a-n-y choice!* Whether I like it or not, I don't have any choice. Because at the end of the day, I need to eat. I need to have a plate in front of my face in the evening, and I need to have a plate in front of my kid. You see, but I'm trying my utmost best to get another job.[54]

Jabu's explanation shows the ambivalence he felt at doing the housework. In the context of losing his job, he adapted, but he experienced this change directly in terms of masculinity. Jabu told me confidently how close he had been to his girlfriend when I interviewed him a year earlier when he was still working, and how he was planning to marry her in the future. Yet, since having lost his job, his girlfriend had been less than enthusiastic about their relationship: "Like I said, it's like if you're not working ... Even your girlfriend doesn't care about you!" About his plans for marriage, he explained:

> Yeah, I was speaking of that. I was about to do something like that. But now I took it like a man ... because I always have that room for disappointment. We still speak ... but the thing is whenever she must come and visit me, she is now telling me different stories. She cannot come and visit me because she

doesn't have money, or she cannot come and visit me because of this. So ... I said to myself... I must adopt the attitude of just wait and see, and just try to get a decent job or get a job and then get on with life.[55]

Mark Hunter (2010, 153–77) describes how work and labour market shifts can complicate relationships. New class hierarchies among men, increasing inability to pay bridewealth to marry women, changing ideas around multiple sexual partners and women's sexuality and status, and changes to men's ability to provide for children have affected men's sense of themselves as men and of having power to act in the world. Jabu's answer to his relationship problems was to find another job. Where other analysts have picked up signs of new forms of sociality developing in South Africa in which state protection and ethnic identity replace older work-centred structures, offering a new basis for the formation of masculinity (see, e.g., White 2012), for Jabu working (still) defined his ability to reclaim his masculinity and reorder his social relations.

Women's gendered identity has been tied up with motherhood and providing for children (Walker 1995; Hellmann 1935; Hunter 1936; Ramphele and Boonzaier 1988; Comaroff 1985; Walker 1990).[56] With urbanization and wage labour in the later twentieth century, women became less likely to marry and form households with men, yet they continued to have children, considered a strong status symbol of womanhood (Preston-Whyte 1993). Motherhood was rooted in the capacity of women to support their children economically (Bozzoli and Nkotsoe 1991; Izzard 1985; Preston-Whyte 1993; Walker 1995). Women historically contributed income to households either through wage work or informal activities like beer brewing (Bonner 1990a; see also Berger 1992; Cock 1980; James 1999; Bozzoli and Nkotsoe 1991). For urban women in the retail sector, working became integrally bound up with a notion of capable motherhood (see discussion in Chap. 4 on black women's rejection of part-time work in the 1980s).[57]

Mothers in particular were concerned to provide enough support to educate their children to give them better opportunities for later. In the context of changes to state education and to labour markets in the 1960s, urban black women increasingly invested in a "bond of education" (Hunter 2014) by which they tied their contribution to their children's education to the children's later obligation of support (and see Hunter 2015). Zanele worked "for her children" and worried whether her casual job would support her children when they grew bigger and the costs of schooling increased.[58] Thandile Ziyane, another casual worker, proudly supported her son on her own even though it was financially difficult. The father of her child did not contribute to her child's upbringing after their divorce:

> I didn't bother myself to go to the maintenance [court], you see. I told myself that if I am working, I will take care of my child … If he is serious about his child he would knock at the door, visit the child, give the child some money, take the child and buy something in town, you see. So he doesn't do that. I am raising my child on my own. My child is doing matric [Grade 12] now! He is big.[59]

Thandile's words demonstrate how women took responsibility for their children (see Khunou 2012).[60] She was proud that her son had advanced to matric and drew her strength as mother from the success of her child at school.[61]

Not all women managed to support their children on their own, however. Casual worker Busi Sithole struggled to take care of her 18-year-old son on her wage. Her son had been attending a vocational school to get a diploma, but had to abandon his studies because of money problems. When she discussed with him the option of getting help from the priest of his church,

> He says to me, if there is no food in the house, I must not ask the next-door neighbours or my friends for food because people will talk about our poverty. He also doesn't want help from the church. When I said I would go and talk to the priest [to see] if he can help him pay for his [school] fees, he told me, "Don't ever do that, how can the priest know everything about us?" He doesn't even want me to invite his priest to the house because he says, "What or where will the priest sit? We have no chairs."[62]

She despaired over her inability to provide for her son's education and thus be a good mother, while her son felt shame at mobilizing resources that would invoke dependency.

Permanent workers also worried about their ability to provide for their children's education and future. Kethiwe said, "I wish to help [my children] study further, and also to build them a home, because in our time now, you do not know what would happen. They need to have a home. At least if they have a home."[63] Women often emphasized educating children not as an end in itself, but as a resource to facilitate their children's access to economic stability in the future. However, as Kethiwe's words suggest, working for children fundamentally meant building up a "home." This implied not only a physical space for living but also and critically a set of social relations that would ensure their place in the world. Kethiwe compared her children's situation to that of a co-worker whose parents left her a resource upon which to construct an independent life: "Anna has been left [behind] by older people [when they passed away] to look after the home. Even where they are resting [in death], they know that their children are not suffering, they have a home. Some [of Anna's siblings] are married and they stay with their wives in their own place." In Kethiwe's understanding, parents would be secure of their position within their lineage when they passed on because they had produced children able to forge independent households, which would stand in tribute to the parent. As John L. Comaroff and Jean Comaroff (2001, 272) put it, adults "realized themselves as parents, spouses, citizens of substance, ancestors-in-the-making; by these means they insinuated, objectified, and embodied themselves in their offspring. And ensured their perpetuity as persons." Yet, as Kethiwe critically concluded the discussion, "But we cannot do it because of the company we work for."[64] For her, the retailer obstructed her ability to set up her own children's future, and yet it was the job that continued to focus her attachment on this possibility.

Time and yearning are palpable in Kethiwe's words, and those of many other workers. In an analysis of migrant workers who laboured in Johannesburg but returned to rural homes, White (2010, 509) describes a "necroculture" where the rewards of work were considered to come in some future time, indeed in death, when, the migrant worker would be affirmed as part of kin and community: "the temporal structure of working life made culture a delayed form of life acquired only in death" (White 2010, 511). A worker worked to constitute future relationships in order to ensure a place in the past, as ancestor (White 2004). White suggests that as work became more precarious, these binds and promises became less sure and more troubling. With access to jobs, these urban retail workers were engaged in an ever-present praxis of providing as the wage circulated, constituting men and women, mothers and fathers, and the future lives of children. Similarly, the changes in employment affected retail workers' sense of ability to continue to provide in this manner into the future. Povinelli (2011, 128) describes such feared and real difficulties as "enduring" (in exhaustion) such "economies of abandonment" which in itself becomes a holding on for a future yet to come. In the case of these retail workers, the landscape of "enduring" included ongoing attachments to work, reproducing these affective circuits.

*   *   *

Retail workers (still) laboured within the circuits of capitalist valorization (see White 2013a), with perhaps the praxis of providing holding greater meaning precisely because of precariousness. Many writers have emphasized the displacement of relations resulting from sharply rising unemployment. They suggest that a thinning affect of work and wage labour has meant turns to other relationships: of state dependency (Ferguson 2015), of authoritarian populism (White 2012), and of melancholia (Barchiesi 2011). Yet White (2004, 2013a) recognizes that the semiotics of capitalist valorization abide in wage labour even for those unemployed. What about those employed in the very jobs that have expanded as those in mining and manufacturing have contracted? These retail workers, many of whom are women, suggest that work enabled them to support people's futures, most critically, children in an attempt to establish their own place in their worlds as adult and active subjects, even if these efforts were precarious and constantly renegotiated.

Vulnerabilities within workers' households and communities produced anxieties among women and men over whether they could meet gendered expectations as family providers. Workers succeeded if they could leverage their wages to resource relations in other realms. In the common phrase "to sit at home and do nothing," we can come to understand the meaning of work as a site of politics, for now as even a frayed connection, it enabled activation. A discourse of unemployment as inactivity and powerlessness reinforced workers' experiences of work as conduit to agency. Workers did not simply earn income, they physically bound together the separated spaces of work and home in their movement between and in the meanings of home as a place of the constitution of people through work. In these precarious retail workers, we see not so much the arresting of futures as the doubling down of energy of devotion to them, and the enduring appeal of the route to get there. As Thando Shabalala and her co-workers' phrasing "to sit and home and do nothing" implied: mere survival was equivalent to social death; it meant being not "fully human," as in the Arendt quote at the start of the chapter.

These workers suggested that work represented not simply economic interest, but a historically embedded set of relations imbricated into forms of sociality and political community. Abasebenzi as political subject was co-constituted through workers' relational production of future political ties, marked most clearly by how children function in these circuits of meaning. In fact, dependencies explained the enduring affective attachment to work as a site of action. The space of constitutive relationship lies between these separated "spheres."

If we apply this significance to those who remain, if tentatively, attached to the circuits of capital through wage labour, then the meaning of work cannot be reduced only to a source of income or to a past value, a ghostly residue, especially for these service workers who bring to life a national economy of consumption, credit, and desire. Forms of personhood and constitutive relational life become defined through and in these enduring circulations. The wage remains an embodied capacity to make others, to enliven future worlds, and so to ensure one's adult being. The simple but ubiquitous metaphor "to sit at home and do nothing" conveys the sense of activation of the circuits tied to the job. It counters abstract relations with a persistent energy of "work" that, as we will consider in more detail in the last chapter, both reproduces and suppresses such gendered anxieties. The concluding chapter explores the political consequences of these circuits today and the significance of their tenuousness demonstrated in the contradictions condensed within the political subject abasebenzi (see Hall 1985).

Notes

1. From fieldnotes; Thando Shabalala, interviewed by Bridget Kenny, Daveyton, October 12, 1999.
2. Arendt (1958, 83–85) uses the word "necessity" for labour that is cyclical, unending, and directed toward survival.
3. Mabena (2017, 44) explains that the word *mahlalela* for someone who is unemployed derives from the isiZulu word *uk'hlala* which means both to sit and to live.
4. Anna Zwane, interviewed by Bridget Kenny, Ekurhuleni, August 12, 1999.
5. Gcwabaza Nomhle, interviewed by Bridget Kenny, Daveyton, June 8, 2000.
6. Zama Ntuli, interviewed by Bridget Kenny, Daveyton, December 1, 1999.
7. Female services sector workers who lost their jobs stood in marked difference to male manufacturing workers in the same position, who tended to engage in the informal economy with resources leveraged from employment (e.g., Barchiesi 2011).

8. Zama Ntuli, interview.
9. "Township" or "location" colloquially refers to residential areas that were legally segregated for blacks under apartheid.
10. Thabo Phasha, interviewed by Bridget Kenny, Daveyton, March 28, 1999.
11. Vuyo Nokabu, interviewed by Bridget Kenny, Daveyton, May 6, 2000.
12. In 2000 in a survey I conducted, permanent workers reported earning on average R10.45 per hour (R1898 per month); casual workers R7.17 per hour (R575 per month); and contract merchandisers, R7.19 per hour (R1276 per month) (Kenny 2001, 95).
13. See, for comparison, Stewart (1996).
14. See also sociologist Zelizer (1994). For South Africa, see James (2015), Ferguson (2015), Neves and du Toit (2012), Hunter (2010), Comaroff and Comaroff (1992), and White (2013b).
15. Maserame Khumalo, interviewed by Bridget Kenny, Daveyton, December 3, 1999.
16. Gcwabaza Nomhle, interview.
17. Cheryl Isaacs, interviewed by Bridget Kenny, Ekurhuleni, May 25 and 27, 1999.
18. My emphasis in this notion of personhood differs from James Ferguson (2015). He highlights the activity which people assert in order to be imbricated into relationships of dependency, especially in times of increasing precariousness. Following Jean and John Comaroff, I am emphasizing the generative capacity – bringing others into being. It was not only the accumulation of people, but it was also the ability to bring others into being that I am highlighting. This ability determined "adulthood."
19. The child support grant was introduced in 1998. In these years, the earning threshold for urban dwellers was R9,600 per year for an individual caregiver (see Beukes et al. 2016, 4).
20. There is an extensive body of research demonstrating the effects of gross inequality on South African households. For the post-apartheid period, see, for example, Mosoetsa (2011), Fakier and Cock (2009), Scully (2016), du Toit and Neves (2009), and Seekings and Nattrass (2005).
21. Mbali Gumede, interviewed by Bridget Kenny, Daveyton, June 12, 1999; Lerato Kgasago, interviewed by Bridget Kenny, Daveyton, August 2, 1999; Ayanda Nkosi, interviewed by Bridget Kenny, Daveyton, August 8, 1999; Nontando Gumbi, interviewed by Bridget Kenny, Daveyton, January 25, 2000.
22. Lerato Kgasago, interview.
23. Sara Dlamini, interviewed by Bridget Kenny, Soweto, June 19, 1999.
24. While no school fees are charged in South Africa for many government schools, there are multiple supplementary but required expenses such as

school uniforms. In addition there is a range of schools with fee structures that demand higher contributions from parents (see Hunter 2015).
25. Palesa Bogasu, interviewed by Bridget Kenny, July 30, 1999.
26. Deregulation of residential segregation occurred in 1986 and with it increased backyard informal dwellings as well as informal settlements (Malinga 2000; Mashabela 1990; Unterhalter 1987).
27. Thabo Phasha, interview. His father had passed away, but his sisters and their children lived in the house.
28. Khenzani Nkuna, interviewed by Bridget Kenny, Daveyton, June 12, 1999, and May 14, 2000. Inkatha is an opposition political party. Its political ethos is based on an ethnic identity of Zulu traditionalism. For the history of its violent conflict with the ANC, particularly on the East Rand in the early 1990s, see Bonner and Ndima (1999), Sapire (1992), Segal (1992), and Sitas (1996).
29. Many of their parents' generation had been forcibly removed to Daveyton from areas closer to the centre of Benoni (see Bonner 1990b).
30. Until 1994, African women could not own property in urban areas in their own name, and could only obtain access to housing as dependents of their husbands. Many single casual workers whom I interviewed had been in this situation (e.g., Phindi Masango, interviewed by Bridget Kenny, Daveyton, July 29, 1999; Khosi Nkosi, interviewed by Bridget Kenny, Daveyton, August 1, 1999; Zama Ntuli, interview; Nontando Gumbi, interview).
31. Daniel Madonsela, interviewed by Bridget Kenny, Ekurhuleni, May 13, 1999; Sara Dlamini, interview; Mandla Moyo, interviewed by Bridget Kenny, Daveyton, June 21, 1999, August 17, 24 and 31, 2000, September 7 and 14, 2000; Mondli Ngayi, interviewed by Bridget Kenny, Daveyton, August 21, 1999, and March 28, 2000.
32. Jabu Mbambisa, interviewed by Bridget Kenny, Daveyton, June 20, 1999, and August 31, 2000; Busi Sithole, interviewed by Bridget Kenny, Daveyton, August 16, 1999. This phenomenon has been at the heart of the social movements in South Africa which emerged in the early 2000s (Naidoo 2007; Naidoo and Veriava 2009; Dawson and Beinart 2010; Von Schnitzler 2016).
33. See, for example, Jabu Mbambisa, interview; Sarah Mahlangu, interviewed by Bridget Kenny, Ekurhuleni, July 27, 1999.
34. Jabu Mbambisa, interview.
35. Vuyo Nokabu, interview.
36. Thabang Maloka, interviewed by Bridget Kenny, Daveyton, August 13, 1999; Mary Nkosi, interviewed by Bridget Kenny, Daveyton, August 26 and December 3, 1999, and September 7, 2000; Buhle Bhengu, interviewed by Bridget Kenny, Daveyton, August 27, 1999; Vuyiswa Xaba, interviewed by Bridget Kenny, Daveyton, August 27, 1999.

37. Mary Nkosi, interview.
38. Mary Nkosi, interview.
39. The Reconstruction and Development Programme provided for small housing subsidies to people earning an income below a set threshold (Bond 2000).
40. Zanele Mathebula, interviewed by Bridget Kenny, Ekurhuleni, May 27, 1999.
41. Household composition in South Africa has shifted with changing wage and non-wage provisioning strategies available to members (Beittel 1992). See, more generally, Smith and Wallerstein (1992) who show how household forms change with periods of economic expansion and contraction, partially related to the relative proportion of income (see also Nelson and Smith 1999).
42. Household members did not necessarily share resources equitably. For a critique of an automatically altruistic "family," see Collier and Yanagisako (1987), and Collier et al. (1997).
43. Kethiwe Dlomo, interviewed by Bridget Kenny, Daveyton, August 1, 1999.
44. Cheryl Isaacs, interview.
45. Ayanda Nkosi, interview.
46. Zodwa Zondi, interviewed by Bridget Kenny, Daveyton, May 7, 2000.
47. Wage income, even any wage income, carries a relatively significant import to households in comparison to households relying only on non-wage income. An increase in household income is correlated with increases in the share of the wage contribution (Finn 2015, 6).
48. Deborah James details how wage work enables the granting of credit. For instance, debts to retailers, particularly clothing and furniture retailers and banks, account for a large proportion of debt, as do debts to informal moneylenders (James 2015, 168; see also Bond 2013). Thus, being linked into wage labour often enables these circuits.
49. See Morrell et al. (2012) for an overview of masculinity studies in South Africa.
50. Certain South African cultural traditions include the initiation of young men, during which they are circumcised and taught gender-specific knowledge and skills (Vuyo Nokabu, interview).
51. Vuyo Nokabu, interview.
52. For a wider literature on these connections, see also Bourgois (1995) and Townsend (2000).
53. Jabu Mbambisa, interview.
54. Jabu Mbambisa, interview.
55. Jabu Mbambisa, interview.

56. See Salo (2003) for the importance of the changing meanings of "motherhood" to women's power in different historical moments, including under increasing unemployment, in other contexts in South Africa.
57. For a broader literature, see Clark (1999) and Freeman (2000).
58. Zanele Mathebula, interview.
59. Thandile Ziyane, interviewed by Bridget Kenny, Daveyton, February 22, 2000.
60. Although see Hunter (2015, 1298) for how fathers' assistance with schooling may also alter these relationships.
61. The choice she, and many others, made to remain the sole supporter of her child could be linked to findings that suggest that fathers' contributions to maintenance costs toward children often came with demands of access to the mother (Khunou 2012).
62. Busi Sithole, interview.
63. Kethiwe Dlomo, interview.
64. Kethiwe Dlomo, interview.

CHAPTER 8

Consuming Politics: Wal-Mart, the New Terrain of Belonging and the Endurance of Abasebenzi

The chief executive officer (CEO) of Wal-Mart International wrote the following words about saving South Africans money in an opinion piece in a business newspaper in 2011 as the South African government was gearing up to review its majority share acquisition of Johannesburg Stock Exchange (JSE)-listed Massmart Holdings:

> We desire to have stores in Africa because we're convinced that Wal-Mart's core mission – to save people money so they can live better – is a compelling fit with Africa's growing economic vitality. Nowhere is that vitality more apparent than in SA ... We plan to open new stores in SA and the region, in communities where consumers have been traditionally underserved. (McMillon 2011)

He specifically promised to contribute to the country by offering the (black) working class, the "traditionally underserved," access to consumer markets. He invoked, then, the kinds of households that we met in Chap. 7 engaged in a praxis of providing, by allying with them to save them money. He concluded his pitch with the rousing words: "Wal-Mart looks forward to earning our credentials as a responsible and productive citizen of South Africa." And so, he signified the retailer's commitment to the nation.

The Wal-Mart CEO's framing brings us to the last conjuncture in our story, where a new terrain of belonging is projected, focused on

© The Author(s) 2018
B. Kenny, *Retail Worker Politics, Race and Consumption in South Africa*, Rethinking International Development series, https://doi.org/10.1007/978-3-319-69551-8_8

participation in the market as consumers, now black consumers formerly not well serviced. This articulation shifts the space of retail as nation from the 1950s affective realms of racial affirmation where white women's labour reassured a white public of its place (Chap. 2). Now retailing is important as a distribution channel, supplying commodities to new populations and ensuring profits for its shareholders while investment from domestic and global retailers brings a promise of salvation to South Africa's ailing economy.

This chapter examines Massmart/Wal-Mart as an example of the latest moment in retail worker politics. As a company, Massmart is divided into four divisions under which a range of branded subsidiaries trade in South Africa and across Africa.[1] None of these subsidiaries are branded as Wal-Mart. While Wal-Mart has chosen to introduce its branded stores in places such as China, Mexico, and Argentina, it has not rebranded the stores it acquired from Massmart (Kenny 2014; Muñoz et al. 2018; Chan 2011).[2] The brand Game most resembles Wal-Mart stores in the United States, and Makro operates similarly to Sam's Club, with a nominal buyers' club membership. Thus, Massmart subsidiaries look similar to Wal-Mart stores.

Massmart has sought to expand its market share in food retailing specifically: it acquired independent food retailers and consolidated stores into a new brand, Cambridge Food, examined in this chapter, and it is enlarging the food department in its Game stores.[3] It has also acquired a number of smaller chains of wholesalers, which operate in rural areas, small towns, and townships. In 2013, Massmart ranked as the fifth largest food retail firm in South Africa (Macquarie 2013, 46). Massmart has a diversified market strategy given the range of brands it owns, but certainly a core pillar is low-income consumers and big box retailing and wholesaling.

While Cambridge Food presents a particular segment of the retail market, and conditions in other retailers may offer alternate readings, the practices and relations described in this chapter speak to trends that this book has tracked over many decades. For the service workers working in these places, in new ways precarious labour relations reproduce both the chain of signifiers tying blackness to bulk labour supply and the attachment to an idea of "employee" defined in relationship to the law and through store-level relations. In this conjuncture workers' subjectivities articulate through multiply determined affective routes in retail sites, where belonging in nation now means access to the market. The labour of service constituting such concrete places becomes devalued in the process and so alters these arenas as sites of relationality. This chapter outlines these newest iterations and concludes the book by posing questions around what these articulations bode for retail worker politics and the endurance of the political subject abasebenzi in South Africa.

The Market as Nation

Today the retail sector in South Africa is acknowledged as a major economic contributor. Since the days of Hyperama in the early 2000s (see Chap. 5), retail trading space has increased dramatically, particularly with mall developments, and retailers have expanded to rural areas and townships, altering physical landscapes and local economies. Between 2002 and 2010, the square metres of retail space per capita in the country expanded threefold (Gauteng Province 2012, 5).[4] By 2015, wholesale, retailing, catering, and accommodation made up 15% of the gross domestic product (GDP), the third highest contributor after finance and business, and government services, and ahead of manufacturing and mining (IDC 2016, 5). The sector accounted for over 19% of employment in 2015 (IDC 2016, 9). The state, too, has looked to retailers more pointedly as a key node of development, in particular to get food to the citizenry and to open supply chains to local producers.

Retail expansion in South Africa is integrated into trends in global retailing. Starting in the 1990s and increasing in the 2000s, retail capital – led specifically by food and general merchandisers – expanded outward from domestic markets into global investments, including entry into developing economies (Coe and Wrigley 2007, 342; Wrigley 2000; Reardon and Berdegué 2002; Weatherspoon and Reardon 2003; Humphrey 2007; Bianchi and Arnold 2004; Wrigley et al. 2005; Dawson 2007). Wal-Mart was an important player in these moves. The share of Wal-Mart's foreign revenue increased from 4% in 1995 to greater than 20% by 2005 (Durand and Wrigley 2009, 3), and by 2011 that had increased to 28.4% (Luce 2013, 4). Wal-Mart continues to be the world's leading retailer by revenue (Luce 2013, 4; Deloitte 2017), and it remains the largest private employer in the world.

Wal-Mart's entry into South Africa was part of these expansionary efforts. Yet South African retailers have been part of the same moves. Thus, all major South African retailers have increased the percentage of their turnover from business outside of South Africa over the past

10–15 years primarily in sub-Saharan Africa but also beyond the continent (Macquarie 2013; Weatherspoon and Reardon 2003; Miller 2008). Five of the largest South African retailers came within the top 250 global retailers in 2015 (Deloitte 2017, 17–22).[5] South African retailers account for a larger share of global revenue than Brazilian, Russian, Chilean, or Mexican firms among the top 250. Of developing economies making this list, only Chinese and South Korean companies contributed a greater share.[6] Indeed, Massmart had already established subsidiaries in 11 other African countries by the time that Wal-Mart approached it.[7] Thus, South African corporations are global players in their own right in transnational retail investment, and these firms define local dynamics, as we have seen in this book.

South African markets are relatively formalized and formal channels have deepened steadily since the early 2000s. South Africa's formal mass grocery retail sector is the largest in Africa in terms of value, worth some US$29 billion (BMI 2013). In 2003, the share of the formal food retailing market, in contrast to informal retailing through hawkers, spaza shops, and other informal traders, was already 55% (Weatherspoon and Reardon 2003, 1). In 2012, formal channels had increased to account for 62.3% of the food market, which is higher than in many other developing countries (BMI 2013; see also Dávila 2016; Quayson 2014; Dholakia et al. 2012; Tilly 2006).[8] Within the formal food market in South Africa, furthermore, there is high corporate concentration (Weatherspoon and Reardon 2003), which, as we have seen, has increased over the period traced in this book.[9]

Finally, given the historical depth of "modern" retailing systems in South Africa (see Chap. 5), when Wal-Mart entered, retailers were already practising many of the methods which are described as "Walmartization" (Lichtenstein 2006, 2009; Fishman 2007; Brunn 2006), which taken together have made such corporate retailers increasingly important distribution channels. Walmartization is characterized by the introduction of several interlinked "innovations" in the retail sector, all standard practice in South Africa.

Big box retailing combines wholesale and retail hybrids to enable economies of scale, practised by Massmart before its acquisition by Wal-Mart (Planting 2010, 34; and see Brunn 2006) (Photo 8.1). Centralized distribution systems allow retailers to focus on supply chain management to externalize the costs and risks of stock control. Shoprite was an early leader and other major retailers followed suit, building new distribution centres over the past decade (Thomas 2011; and see Bonacich and Hardie 2006). Tiered relationships with suppliers allow retailers to set

Photo 8.1 In the aisles of a Wal-Mart subsidiary in Johannesburg, 2017 (Image by Simon Gush)

up product "category leaders" and increase competition among suppliers for access to these distribution channels. This increases the power of the large retailers in relation to producers and suppliers, and reinforces economic integration through more highly formalized capital, which can meet standards and requirements, but also thereby reproduces features of apartheid capitalism, such as privileging large producers and commercial farmers (van der Hijden and Vink 2013; Khumalo 2013; Greenberg and Paradza 2013; Mather and Kenny 2005; and see Burch and Goss 1999). Global sourcing of commodities continues apace since deregulation of trade regimes in the 1990s in South Africa, with all retailers sourcing widely (Igumbor et al. 2012; Greenberg 2017; and see Gereffi 1994; Appelbaum and Lichtenstein 2006). Retailers use data and analytics to predict and adapt supply and demand, with new technologies introduced over the past decade to improve bar coding and till point accounting. Thus by the time that Wal-Mart entered South Africa, these practices were already standard and had ensured retailers were integrated economic actors, constituting national distribution through supply chain dynamics.

Since the early 2000s, there have also been changes to ownership structures of South African retail firms with increasing foreign – of which Wal-Mart was a particularly newsworthy example – and institutional ownership, such as pension and investment funds (Greenberg 2017). Retail companies have done well on the JSE. The "economic vitality" about which the Wal-Mart CEO spoke, then, draws its energy from these existing infrastructural resources and relations combined with access to the "untapped" potential markets of South Africa's new consumers and those on the rest of the continent. Retailing expands decisively from the affective arena of the shop to these market relations within the national imaginary in this period.

Corporate retailers anchor the most lavish and largest malls in South Africa (and indeed, in Africa). Proliferation of malls across the country has restructured the geography of South Africa (Murray 2008). Where mall development in Latin America, for example, only began in the 1980s (Dávila 2016, 2), malls in South Africa started earlier with regional centres in suburbs and around highway developments in the 1970s, as discussed in Chap. 5 (Tomlinson and Larsen 2003, 46; Beavon 2004, 249 fig 7.3, 251; Murray 2008).[10] By the 1980s South African malls took off, decentralizing from city centres with shifts in racial geographies, as they followed white consumers into suburbs (Tomlinson and Larsen 2003, 46–47; Beavon 2004, 251–54; Murray 2008). These developments then extended to black residential areas in multiple sizes and formats (Tomlinson and Larsen 2003, 47–49; Kenny 2009; Posel 2010). In 2010 shopping centre space in South Africa totalled over 16 million square metres in 1,400 centres nationwide (Gauteng Province 2012, 14).[11]

Malls attract South Africa's so-called "new" (black) middle class (Southall 2016; Iqani 2016; Posel 2010; Nuttall 2008; de Vries 2008). Yet writing about Latin America, Dávila argues that retail agglomerations like malls in developing economies may have more to do with "large numbers and concentration of new consumers than with their economic well-being and purchasing power" (Dávila 2016, 3). For safety and entertainment, Johannesburg residents of all classes head to their malls. Thus, much of the appeal to shoppers could be said to be the "illusion of accessibility to a middle-class world" (Dávila 2016, 3), an appeal that generates profitability for developers and retailers nonetheless.[12]

In developing economies, these new consumer markets are more tenuous than such bases in previous periods, often much more reliant on consumer credit (Dávila 2016, 4). While consumer sales have bolstered the

South African economy, much of it has been based on growing household debt (James 2015; and see Bond 2013). Mapping global borrowing trends, the 2014 Global Findex database, a World Bank Gallup poll, found that, on average, two in five people around the world took out a loan between 2013 and 2014 (Banning-Lover 2015). In South Africa a reported 86% of adults needed to borrow money in 2014, the number one country for borrowing. South Africans also reported requiring loans for healthcare and education, both public services, as well as to cover costs of basic food (Banning-Lover 2015; and see Demirguc-Kunt et al. 2015). The "credit-debt revolution" of the post-apartheid period also signals how borrowing now puts into motion future-looking expectations of lifeways and mobilities (James 2015) (see Chap. 7).

The semiotics of consumption in the past decade in South Africa has shaped discussions of race and (in)equality (Posel 2010; Iqani 2016; Iqani and Kenny 2015). Belonging and contested futures have been mobilized through the language and symbolism of consumption (Mupotsa 2015). What is being consumed and how it is displayed have been matters of intense public debate, marking distinction and status by class and race, and relying on tropes of foreign and local (van Staden 2015). Debate about what signifies South African success via global luxury consumer products has been counterposed to a discourse of equality of access to consume (Kistner 2015; Iqani 2016; Nuttall 2008) (Photo 8.2).

For working-class black South Africans, being able to shop in malls closer to where they live or to wander shiny aisles for greater food selection is seen as a genuine improvement to lives since apartheid. Thus, newer format stores such as Massmart-owned Cambridge Food, discussed below, offer these symbols of market inclusion to working-class commuters at convenient interchanges. Massmart opened its Cambridge Food stores in central business districts and townships, particularly focusing on taxi ranks and other public transit routes (Photo 8.3). As we saw in the CEO's promise to South Africa quoted above, Wal-Mart seeks to compete with other retailers to tap this new market by offering people access.

Furthermore, the state has supported consumer spending among the poor through the expansion of social grants using smart cards redeemable at retailers (Vally 2017; Jika and Saba 2017).[13] Grant recipients can use their cards or cash their grants at supermarket tills, and many do so precisely because retail shops are accessible.[14] Retailers have actively participated, indeed reaping large rewards as grant claimants often make purchases at the same time. Between October and December 2016, for

Photo 8.2 A Game store in Johannesburg with a mural of the South African flag, 2017 (Image by Simon Gush)

instance, Shoprite benefitted with a reported R2.14 billion spent directly through payments with grant smart cards. Massmart-owned companies took in over R109 million, with Cambridge Food making up R47 million of that (Jika and Saba 2017; and see Vally 2017, 87–88).[15] Retail workers at Cambridge Food branches in greater Johannesburg were used to the ebb and flow of foot traffic around grant dispersal times. A cashier explained, "When it's time for grants … that's a very busy time in the

Photo 8.3 A Cambridge Food store in a busy street, 2017 (Image by William Matlala)

month because people just got money and they are buying. So we do stay extra hours."[16]

The state has also supported a range of supplier development initiatives in order to bring "emerging" (black) farmers and producers into retailers' supply chains (Greenberg and Paradza 2013). Indeed, this type of initiative was one of the conditions which the state Competition Tribunal put on its approval of Wal-Mart's acquisition of Massmart after unions and the departments of Economic Development, Trade and Industry, and Agriculture, Forestry and Fisheries presented concerns over the potential effects of Wal-Mart's global supply chain on local industry (Kenny 2014). Thus, the state's developmentalist agenda has come to see retailers as conduits to the distribution of commodities, particularly to expand access to affordable and quality food to low-income citizens, and as a way to drive industrial strategy through facilitating access to retailer shelves for local producers (Greenberg 2010; Kenny 2014). Wal-Mart's entry, in fact, focused state attention onto retailers as drivers of economic "opportunity," offering a new model of nation in the market for consumers and producers alike.[17]

Still, this model of nation and belonging in the market wears thin if examined closer. Retail workers at Cambridge Food explained that low-income customers shopped there indeed because of cost: "The really poor people go for Cambridge because of the price, nothing less nothing more. It is because of the low price."[18] Yet they explained that customer service was not attentive in their stores, partly because the company frequently hired new staff. Some argued that managers treated customers badly because of racism: "because our store manager is a white man or maybe, I don't know, maybe they feel that customers don't know their rights ... because they are in [a township]."[19] Another cashier said, "The customers are always complaining because of the bad service and so forth. Sometime things are expired. There is generally very bad treatment of customers. Even our store manager [who is black] does not respect customers."[20] And products were frequently mismarked or expired: "They are just crooks and they don't care about customers here."[21]

Many workers reported that the stores were unclean and the food was often rotten: "You try to pretend because you want to polish this scene, but it is dirty."[22] Like Ingrid du Toit's description of how white women shop assistants in the 1950s proudly scrubbed, polished, and shined their counters (Chap. 2), this service worker cared to offer customers a fine service in a beautiful environment, but any effort was undermined by the reality behind the façade on offer today. They themselves would not buy the food from their own shops, the workers explained: "Even some of the food from the kitchen is rotten and smells but they still put it out to be sold to customers." Or as another cashier put it: "That food is a laxative."[23]

The image of inclusion in the market as consumers – brought by Wal-Mart during its public relations effort to win approval for its acquisition of Massmart and supported by state developmentalist directions – may work for middle-class consumers, although excessive debt also raises questions. The idea of the retail store as pinnacle of modernity takes a cynical turn here, as an indicator of upward mobility but through some cruel mimicry where capital now sees working-class and poor people as a "new" market segment. This marks a "reverse Fordism" where economies now require cheap commodities distributed to the poor – Wal-Mart's hallmark "everyday low prices" – precisely because jobs and incomes are so precarious (Collins 2009). Instead, retailers are reaping enormous profits and consolidating their economic power while poor customer service and low product quality reproduce apartheid service relations. The site of retail remains a place of potent affect and relationality, remapping city streets and promising access to malls and markets. As the South African economy inheres in "consumer confidence," retailing tracks multiple dimensions of scale and scope as global and local relations articulate through capital circulation, physical infrastructure, developmental coordination, and national imaginaries of access and equality. This current conjuncture reiterates a contradiction that we have seen in earlier moments: the market as nation and democratic space is constituted paradoxically in and through its de-nationalization through global practices and capital flows (see Hart 2013, 8–9).

The next sections examine workers' experiences within these stores and explore what happens with retail worker politics and the political subject abasebenzi in this moment.

Labour Broking and Bulk Labour Supply

Based on employment data for the greater Johannesburg area, Crankshaw and Borel-Saladin (2014) show that between 1970 and 2010 the region's labour market shifted away from manufacturing and toward service jobs. Yet, they argue that this change in sectoral structure does not explain growing inequality as increases in skilled and semi-skilled service jobs during this period exceeded growth in unskilled manual jobs in both service and in manufacturing (Crankshaw and Borel-Saladin 2014, 1860). (Instead, they attribute growing inequality in the region to the gap between those employed and those unemployed.) They count retail service and sales jobs among those semi-skilled occupations that have risen and therefore contributed to the "professionalization" of the local labour market (Crankshaw and Borel-Saladin 2014, 1857–61).[24] By contrast, by taking a qualitative look at the long history of retail work in this labour market, this book has demonstrated the continued decline in the skill of those retail service jobs over time, such that for many workers "lucky" to get service work today, the occupational classification between white-collar and manual ("unskilled") labour may itself be blurring.

In the branches surveyed in 2013, permanent employees of Cambridge Food, who had worked for the previous company bought by Massmart, recalled that the biggest change with Massmart's ownership was that contract workers replaced most staff in stores. One shop steward said, "So some stores [branches] have no permanent staff while others have few."[25] Cambridge Food used labour brokers to supply the cashiers, bag packers, and merchandisers, and to staff speciality food departments like the bakery and butchery. Some of the supervisors and administrators were also contract workers.[26] In many of the branches, direct employees of the retailer, then, accounted for only a handful of workers.[27] A shop steward said, "I mean, it's fine, we acknowledge that Cambridge came in and helped a lot of South Africans get jobs and stuff. However, you will never be happy working for Cambridge because we are not treated the same, not paid the same, and don't work the same hours."[28]

Those hired by labour brokers, like the cashiers, worked long hours – serving during those unsocial hours that casual workers had filled in the early 2000s, only now for even longer hours as store trading times had lengthened.[29] As we saw with Ninah Ndlovu in Chap. 1, contract workers often had to work still later hours with no notice, extending past the end of shifts: "You'll work until they say go home."[30] And, women served more often in those jobs that demanded staying late. Thus, control of time directly affected women workers more. A shop steward explained,

> You have children, etc., to take care of. They are supposed to let us know in advance so you can tell them if you are able to or not. But if you dare complain, they just fire you because it's allowed in the contract.[31]

In this manner women confirmed findings from other contexts that the unpredictability of working hours significantly increased stress (Henly and Lambert 2014). To solve their need for flexible staffing, the retailer relied on contract labour to fill these shifts.

In addition to long working hours, contract workers were paid lower than permanent workers. Most contract workers interviewed earned less than R3,000 per month, while direct employees of the retailer earned between R3,000 and R5,000 per month (Kenny 2018), a relatively low wage regardless for full-time employment. Unlike with casual workers in the early 2000s (Chaps. 5 and 6), the issue for contract workers in 2013 was not working too few hours, but that workers felt that they were not being paid adequately for the long hours they worked. Their pay could vary by several hundred rand from month to month because of fluctuations in working hours. The company relied on sophisticated biometric clocking technology and smart cards to track working hours and deferred to the abstract accuracy of its records. Yet workers complained that these systems were also often inaccurate: "How do we know if we have been cheated? … We are being scammed in actual fact!"[32]

Other workers described how labour brokers would not approve corrections that workers had entered on hard copy registers when they had worked longer hours, instead threatening to discipline them.[33] Wal-Mart has been charged with wage theft in other contexts (Milkman et al. 2010; Ruan 2012; Rosen 2005). While workers acknowledged the company's "right" to deploy them when stores were busy,[34] for contract workers the burden of underpayment of wages was heavy given the sobering threat of easy replacement.

By 2013, workers still reported receiving little training and having no opportunities for promotion, as Karabo Khwele, a cashier, captured when she described her first day on the job: "They just explained to us verbally that this is what this button does, and 'I know you will do it correctly because you ladies, you are too clever.' That's it." Eyes twinkling, Ninah added, "And of course we are brilliant you see. Without training."[35] Karabo said their work was dictated by the technology: "We just work a knob. Do this! Don't do this! Do this in two minutes. After a second, do this. We look like we are not right in the mind."[36] Permanent workers, in turn, complained that the company did not promote from within but rather hired from outside. Similar to the early 2000s, they were sensitive to the fact that they had to train the new recruits who would become their supervisors.[37] And, like earlier, a symbolic shorthand for this lack of meaningful participation was the unqualified white person who was simply given a better job, bypassing permanent workers regardless of their qualifications and experience: "'Hello, did this person go to school?' 'No, that's John.' He's white."[38]

These stores now serviced working-class black commuters, near taxi ranks and in busy city streets, but unlike white women decades earlier who reaped a reward from their service labour by assisting white customers, black service workers found little joy in that part of the job. As front-line workers, the cashiers described the relationship with customers as a locus of discipline (as it was for casual cashiers in the 2000s, see Chap. 5).[39] Yet now it was often black managers who remonstrated with workers to an audience of black customers. Service workers admitted that the stress of the job sometimes distracted them: "Sometimes I am so angry that it makes me want to cry … It really hurts. I will help you, but I won't be doing a good job because I'm angry. You see."[40]

The affect of these jobs was palpable in this cashier's frustration, and yet with the skill of service less essential, till workers could be easily replaced, especially through labour brokers: "[Management] will just call somebody else because they have a lot of cashiers and when you come back then in the morning they will tell you that your contract is finished."[41]

Workers became ever more an interchangeable labour supply. Like with casual workers before, contract workers complained about having to wear black and white street clothes, which they had to supply at their own cost; the clothing made them unidentifiable in the shop, as Ninah said: "At least let them give us … a jersey to show that we wear a uniform. You can come there and say [pointing] 'That lady'. [Now] you can't even describe that lady. Who is that lady?"[42]

Cashiers were also required to do work that they regarded as outside their job descriptions, such as fetching trolleys and cleaning shelves and refrigerators:

> Can I just ask you how are you going to feel? You are at work and you tell yourself you are at the till, and they say "Go push the trolleys!" … And they're not asking you, they're demanding … They say "From here to here, I want this space with the sweets to have no expiry date, to have no dust!" … Did you come to work to be a cashier or do you come to work to do the sweets? We were not hired to do the sweets, you see.[43]

These contract service workers resented having to do the work of merchandisers and packers (see Chaps. 5 and 6). The occupational division between service and manual jobs that operated in the 1960s to bolster the status of service work (see Chap. 3) was less sustainable. Workers' interchangeability now extended into multi-tasking across departments.

This sense of being generic labourers – nameless and unknown – pervaded contract workers' narratives. Their position outside the direct employment relation denied them access to engage store managers. They were told what to do. Contract workers had to rely on someone in a permanent position to intervene on their behalf.[44] Like casual workers in the 2000s (Chap. 6), one difference between contract and permanent workers now (unlike with contract merchandisers earlier) was marked by authority to represent themselves to retail managers. When they tried they were often thwarted:

> And say you need something, maybe a day off. [The manager] will say to you that he does not know you. How can someone say that? I mean I work under him, of course he knows me … So I asked myself why [the manager] doesn't know our names. Why doesn't he teach himself? Clearly this person

doesn't care about us. Tomorrow they can say I'm dead, will he even know who they are talking about?[45]

Displaced from the normative employment relation with retail managers and hired as bulk labour supply, contract workers had limited ability to affect this relationship. They endured in this gap within the labour relation. While jobs in service, sales, and clerical work offer employment to black residents of greater Johannesburg, they have also become deskilled in important ways from when their white working-class women colleagues occupied these jobs in the 1950s and 1960s in the same city streets. In 2013, labour brokers supplied most of the labour force to the Cambridge Food branches surveyed. This new iteration of bulk labour supply reproduced the affect of linked signifiers servant/native/labourer that we have traced throughout this book: outsider, unskilled, input, mass. These retail arenas partly explain, then, the reproduction of inequalities in the reinscription of emotive racialized labour relations.

In these spaces of consumption, where access for working-class (black) consumers was to be democratized, those who laboured to sell the commodities had again been displaced from the rights of the liberal subject of labour law and that recognition as "employee," with substantive meaning attached, as we see in more detail below. Yet once again these workers affirmed their collective subjectivity in precisely the relationality of these "social sites" (Hall 1985, 99).

THE LAW AND POLITICAL SUBJECT ABASEBENZI

In 2013, South African labour law defined the temporary employment service as the employer of the contract workers (see Chap. 4). The employer was responsible for meeting basic conditions of employment around wages, working time, break times, uniforms, and with respect to meeting labour rights, such as free association and fair procedure. Yet workers experienced little compliance from the agencies. This relationship was encapsulated for these employees in the issue of their employment contracts. Workers knew that they were legally entitled to a copy of their employment contract, and yet they reported that labour brokers did not allow them to read or keep a copy of their contracts. One worker said, "They just made us sign and we don't even know what is written in that contract."[46] Another contract cashier confirmed, "I did not see [my contract]. They were saying, 'Sign page four. Sign page nine. Sign. Hurry up!'"⁴⁷

The foundation of the definition of "employee," the ability to conclude a "free" contract, thereby defining the liberal subject of law, the logic from which black workers once were excluded (Chap. 4), now reproduced contract workers' precariousness. When a group of contract workers charged a labour broker with unfair dismissal at the Commission for Conciliation, Mediation and Arbitration (CCMA), a dispute resolution body established in terms of the Labour Relations Act of 1995, the employer

> pulled out [the] contracts that [the workers had] signed. It has a start date, [and] there is an end date on the page signed. But, the end date [was] not written before the contract [was] signed. So whenever they decide to fire you they just put in a date. Your signature was there a long time ago but they just slotted in the end date after.⁴⁸

Armed with the signed employment contracts, employers allegedly dismissed workers with immediate effect by filling in end dates of the contracts after the fact. The contract workers could not rely on the labour contract to claim their rights, precisely because of how the short-term contract could be manipulated.

What do changes since the early 2000s as exhibited in this Massmart/Wal-Mart subsidiary mean for retail worker politics? While conditions of work seem even more fragmented and degraded than in the 1990s, with labour broking enabling an extreme version of low wage, low status labour even for service work, workers continued to understand their experiences collectively. In 2013, these experiences provoked anger and constant contestation as groups of workers took up specific complaints. Because labour broking made dismissal so likely, workers often contested issues in groups to protect themselves. The stores continued to be a terrain of fraught relationships where battles with (black) supervisors or managers were understood as being defined by distant white bosses. Thus workers said, "these supervisors" were "selling us out, just taking commands from the *mhlungu* [white person/boss]."⁴⁹ These sites reinforced a collective subjectivity based on race and class, such as when workers (above) spoke of being "scammed" by employers. Workers came to feel their common experience was precisely in enduring such persistent wearing away (see Povinelli 2011).

Many of the women contract cashiers affirmed their lack of power, but also explained that they continued to contest conditions, even under such threatening circumstances. Workers discussed their problems together:

"You see, we support each other because we have seen how we are treated over there. So if ever this lady is being cheated ... must you disown her? No! ... We discuss it. The whole store [the workers], we discuss it because we can see that at [the labour broker] there is a problem."[50]

The South African Commercial, Catering and Allied Workers Union (SACCAWU) had few members in these stores because there were so few permanent employees; and yet branch shop stewards argued that they represented all workers, including contract workers and members of other unions who did not have shop stewards: "I don't stand for workers as a member of SACCAWU but I represent each worker without differentiating or favouritism."[51] Like in Chap. 6, shop stewards defined their roles as brokering specific in-store grievances. But, unlike the early 2000s, when shop stewards only assisted non-member casual workers but not labour broker employees, they now intervened for them too as labour broker employees formed the majority of workers in the shops: "I have to step up always because I am representing the workers, not SACCAWU."[52] Such new possibilities affirmed the affective potency of the collective subject, abasebenzi.

Finally, another round of labour law changes further reinforced workers' attachment to the never-quite-realized status of the standard bearer of labour rights. From 2009 the Congress of South African Trade Unions (COSATU) challenged the law around temporary employment services. After years of negotiation by the federation, in which SACCAWU participated at the National Economic Development and Labour Council (NEDLAC), a statutory body that brings together government, labour, and business, in 2015 labour law was revised in favour of workers.[53] The amendments put significant restrictions on the use of temporary employment services.[54] Unless the work is genuinely temporary,[55] after three months all temporary employment agency employees are deemed to be working for the client firm (although this ultimate judgment of sole employer involved legal dispute which lasted several years).[56] This legal amendment has affirmed the significance of the category direct "employee". The key change is that, after three months, contract workers now become employees of the client firm (i.e., the retailer), which thus becomes liable with respect to labour rights and conditions. The significance of the status of employer can be seen in court challenges over the interpretation of the law (see op cit. n56), such that only in June 2017 did a Labour Appeal Court judgment rule for sole employer status.

It is still relatively early to assess the range of retailer responses to the amendments of the act, especially in the context of changing legal terrain. There remains room for manipulation. For instance, a fixed-term contract of limited duration is legal. And, while abuse such as that sketched by contract workers above is illegal, it may continue to operate tacitly. Alternatively, retailers will adapt employment categories to continue to facilitate staffing in flexible times and at minimum pay. Cambridge Food has reportedly embarked on a process of insourcing jobs that were previously staffed by labour brokers. This process is still ongoing, yet SACCAWU reports that it involves ending existing contracts and re-advertising positions as flexitime contracts with a maximum of 27 hours per week. Only a small number of full-time, permanent positions would remain in stores at supervisory level. The union anticipates that the flexitime posts may be designated for "general workers," allowing the company to deploy workers across departments as needed to perform a range of tasks. SACCAWU demands that provincial negotiations around these processes be centralized to better standardize the process across the country.[57] The restructuring could mean that contract workers in these stores, if rehired, could earn less per month because of shorter hours and could be converted to general workers, precisely about what cashiers above complained. This conjuncture is still in flux.

In this last moment of legal reform, even as labour broking has been limited and potentially these workers installed in a relationship of employment with the retailer, nevertheless, the core category of "employee" with its affective association with a norm of full-time, standard hours and occupational integrity becomes reproduced as political object, through the ever-diminishing horizon of realizing it. The forms of difference both external and internal to the category of "employee" continue to reproduce the affective attachment to the norm of "employee" (see Berlant 2011) and the labour relation as a site of political terrain.

I offer one final example of workers' action from a different subsidiary of Massmart, which refracts the vibrant lines that have traversed this long history towards new angles. At a Makro branch in greater Johannesburg, a retail manager was sexually harassing contract cashiers, offering the women longer hours or even permanent employment if they would have sex with him. One cashier refused and complained to SACCAWU. The shop steward followed due process and lodged a grievance during which other women contract workers came forward to confess that they had in fact slept with the manager (without seeing any of his promises fulfilled). The union and workers demanded that the manager be removed, but the manager remained in the store while the case proceeded. The women workers, including permanent retail employees, then protested saying, according to a SACCAWU official, "'We are mothers. If our daughters were treated this way, you would expect us to use any means necessary to fight. If you are not listening to us, then we have no choice.'"[58] Sixty-nine women "workers eventually took the law into their own hands and lifted [physically] the manager out of the store," the unionist reported. Most of the women were dismissed for this action, although the union was successful in getting the majority reinstated with the remaining dismissals pending in the Labour Court. The manager was transferred from that branch to another province. The workers "were told they were troublemakers." A shop steward summarized: "The relationship is in trouble"[59]. The gendering of precariousness for all workers suggests that struggles may become, indeed, more militant even as this relationship remits less and less. The workers are fed up, and they are mobilizing precisely because of how articulations of race, class, and gender subjugation are reproduced in these retail spaces.

Workers united collectively, as they did in the bib protest in the 2000s (see Chap. 6), when internal company procedure obscured their grievances. Sexual abuse has constituted relations in retailing since its start. Here, even as women workers balance precarious jobs against the work of providing, they continue to refuse such interpellations. The labour relation endures as a site of political struggle because of the long history of affective attachment to a relational order positing the possibility of mutual, adult, decision-making relyant on a collective subject. Abasebenzi retake these sites as their terrain, and so persist in disrupting the significations binding blackness to bulk labour, as objectified input, yet in an ever-more troubled relationship, as markets reflect nation and belonging flatters consumers.

* * *

Conclusion: Enduring Retail Worker Politics

This book contributes to showing how the formation and mobilization of abasebenzi as a collective political subject has been multiply determined, involving articulations and condensations at particular historical conjunctures (Hall 1985). I have traced this history through a story of retail worker politics in greater Johannesburg over nearly a century. These imbrications have been made through changing conceptions of nation, belonging, work and consumption, and the role of the law to structure workplace and social relations. Through these processes, retail worker politics has endured; women and men continue to contest their conditions in some of the few remaining jobs available and to do so collectively at the site of the workplace. But, this book has shown that such labour politics cannot be reduced to trade union strategy or worker interest. These service workers reproduce optimism for forms of relationality (Berlant 2011) proffered by abasebenzi as a political subject.

The history of retail worker politics affirms that the political subject abasebenzi is constitutive of shop floors, retail spaces, class, race, and gender relations, law, and the polity. Workers have refashioned attachments to its affect and to the site of retailing in their everyday lives and in national imaginaries of belonging. These articulations have reproduced the semiotics of abasebenzi as connoting a collective category of personhood, as bringing others into being. It has variously activated adult, participative, collective, public, skilled, and generative subjectivities. In different conjunctures it has operated through and against legal categories, redrawing the law and social boundaries between workers, even as the standard-bearer of rights has been reproduced in the full-time, direct employee, itself linked to children, families, and futures.

This book has tracked the changes in retail service jobs since white women's employment in the first half of the twentieth century. In the 1960s, self-service eroded the built-in skill of white women's feminine and "familiar" labour and product knowledge. In the 1970s, the expansion of retailing arenas to huge, modern entertainment "hypermarkets," marked by self-service and task fragmentation, deskilled service jobs at the same time as black workers were entering the sector. In the 1990s, casualization split retail jobs into shorter hours and lower paid positions, and "service" was reduced to a perfunctory engagement, epitomized in the slogan "the customer is always right." By 2013, service workers, as shown in the example of Massmart/Wal-Mart, had become contract staff supplied by labour brokers precisely as working-class black consumers became the market. Like casual workers in the earlier period, they served in flexible working hours at the erratic command of supervisors, encountered regular wage underpayment, and were barred from building in-store relationships that would include them in decision-making. Many may still be converted to general workers in shorter shifts and deployed to multi-task across departments in response to labour law reform.

We seem to return, then, to the 1950s when black men worked as "unskilled" distributive workers (Chap. 2), and again to the 1970s when black women shop assistants were expected to do general worker duties in addition to the service work they had been hired to do, or were hired as general workers but in practice worked as shop assistants (Chap. 3), and again to the 1990s when casual workers were hired en masse such that they did not feel that they were even seen to be "workers" (Chap. 5). Each reiteration happened within a different conjuncture of relations and meanings, but in some ways each reproduced the long history of the chain of signifiers, servant/native/labourer (Chap. 4), linking presumed unskilled bulk labour supply to blackness, binding race and (un)belonging yet again into the labour relation.

The long battle to be "treated the same," dating as we have seen in Chaps. 2 and 3 from divisions between black and white women workers on the shop floor, continued under new conditions. This process of "boundary drawing" (Silver 2003, 20–25) has indeed been definitive of this labour market, promulgated by the state through law, by capital through the use of various forms of part-time, flexible labour and labour broking, and by workers themselves through the ways that they have articulated their subjectivities. Within the long history of retail worker politics in South Africa, each new division reproduced not only the impulse by those in more marginal categories to contest their poor employment conditions (Silver 2003, 25) but also – as a central thesis of this book – the site of the labour relation as political terrain and therefore the political subject "workers," as specifically articulated "subjects-in-struggle" in particular moments (Hall 1985, 112).

Thus, the ruptural power of abasebenzi as constituted in the 1970s enacted the very subject position from which black workers were denied in law, the category "employee" (Chap. 3). In the 1990s, abasebenzi drew on various meanings as adult, skilled, race-class subjects ultimately to articulate differentiated dispositions, dividing workers by employment categories. These contestations reaffirmed the norm of the full-time, standard-shift employee, simultaneously a masculine subjectivity even as common precariousness was feminized and marginalized as definitive of "casual" workers (Chaps. 5, 6 and 7). In this latest conjuncture, workers are turned into a nameless supply of labour delivered by labour brokers and yet return to the labour relation as a political terrain, defined through its normative power and its historical constitution in direct employment. In the always-deferred prospect of (equal) participation in retail workplaces, workers reaffirmed attachments to these political relations (see Kenny 2016).

Denning (2010, 80) argues that we need to "decentre wage labour" in analyses of experiences of capitalism particularly in the global South. He writes, "The fetishism of the wage may well be the source of capitalist ideologies of freedom and equality, but the employment contract is not the founding moment. For capitalism begins not with the offer of work, but with the imperative to earn a living." Indeed, the impulse to not "sit at home and do nothing" refigures the meaning of work for these precarious retail workers (Chap. 7), many of whom are women and work to build futures for and through their children. Yet the employment contract is also a site marking political relationality, a moment of interpellation into a political world in which the so-called acting, autonomous subject gains its authority, which has a concrete history in post-colonial South Africa, where labour remains a category of both subjugation and of desired equality.

For South African retail workers who continue to fight to constitute the polity, the labour relation in retailing remains an enervated "social site" (Hall 1985, 99) in which relations resignify blackness through unskilled, "general labour" as service becomes less central. Indeed, as retailers seek to open new consumer markets, through the co-constitution of global and local economies, they dovetail with state developmentalist concerns that seek to offer participation in the (national) market as political inclusion. Yet without the labour of service, these stores become distribution points, shelves from which consumers may take what they can pay for. Retail jobs are expected to disappear, to be replaced with technology like "cashier-less tills" that completely obviates the role of the service worker.[60] Hence the very future of these workplaces is precarious.

Still, the effort to expel affect from these spaces shows how it re-forms around older significations where quality and service constituted modernity for a white public served by white women. And in so doing, it reconfirms belonging in access and gracious service in the new "publics" of shops and malls. The labour relation, too, reproduces these meanings as it reconfigures workers like Ruth Ngobeni and Ninah Ndlovu as ever more available to stay late and risk safety in order to ring up the last customer or to reconcile biometric clocking.

Abasebenzi is a political subject which both limits and opens possibilities. It is a category that has come to distinguish some workers from other workers, explained by law and the liberal democratic subject, by concrete workplace struggles around what constitutes an "adult," and by notions of providing and the antinomies of dependency. And, it is a category that continues to express a constitutive relation, not an identity, in ways that have reproduced its affective appeal for all workers. Second, the reproduction of the chain of signification linking blackness to labour both has reinscribed retail workplaces as sites of subjugation and ensured that they continue to be places of contestation. As symbol of post-apartheid work, retail workers bring into being a world of public engagement directed through commodities that underpins the national economy and that shores up neoliberal rationality. For Ruth, Ninah, and their colleagues, collective political subjectivity is also always an attachment to worlds that keep open the ambiguity of claims of political relationality, particularly in the case of the workers described in this book who are neither quite the consumers of a bright new age nor the fully incorporated rights-bearing subjects of a new democracy.

Notes

1. The divisions are Masscash, Massdiscounters, Masswarehouse, and Massbuild. Branded subsidiaries falling under these include a mass general dealer (Game), an electronics retailer (Dion Wired), DIY and building material suppliers (Builders Warehouse, Builders Trade Depot, Builders Express and Builders Superstore), mass wholesalers (Makro and The Fruitspot), food retailers (Cambridge Food and Rhino Cash & Carry), and a cluster of smaller wholesalers (Trident, Powersave Liquorland, Saverite, Shield, Jumbo Cash and Carry, and CBW).
2. This is possibly due to existing South African brand recognition from consumers as well as critical public mobilization by the labour movement when the state Competition Tribunal sat to consider approving the merger (Kenny 2014).
3. Pick n Pay, a major South African food retailer, claimed that Game's expansion of its food sections in stores located in malls violated mall lease exclusivity clauses, which limit competition among anchor chains. It sought an interdict against Game on the basis that its increased percentage of food brought it into direct competition with Pick n Pay's stores in these malls. Other retailers joined its suit. The issue of mall exclusivity and anti-competitive practices is being investigated by the Grocery Retail Sector Inquiry under the Economic Development Department. The review was carried out in 2016 and 2017 and is still underway.
4. In 2002 there were 5.72 million square metres of retail space in South Africa. By 2010 the retail space had increased to 18.42 million square metres (Gauteng Province 2012, 5).
5. The five largest South African retailers in 2005 were, in the order of size of revenue: Steinhoff International Holdings N.V. (no. 72), Shoprite Holdings Limited (no. 110), The SPAR Group Limited (no. 155), Pick n Pay Stores Limited (no. 171), and Woolworths Holdings Limited (no. 197) (Deloitte 2017, 17–22).
6. I based my calculations on the table "Global Powers of Retailing Top 250, FY2015" in Deloitte (2017, 17–22). South African firms made up 0.89% of revenue among the top 250; China including Hong Kong made up

3.7%, and South Korea made up 1.29%. Brazil had only one firm in the list contributing 0.13%; Chilean firms contributed 0.70%; Mexican firms 0.75%; and Russian firms 0.87%.
7. Massmart Holdings now trades in 13 countries in Africa, including Botswana, Ghana, Kenya, Lesotho, Malawi, Mozambique, Namibia, Nigeria, South Africa, Swaziland, Tanzania, Uganda, and Zambia.
8. Indian retailing remains defined by small stores and a powerful national trader lobby (Dholakia et al. 2012); in 2011, "modern stores" accounted for only 10% of total retail. By contrast, in China the figure was 65% (Dholakia et al. 2012, 252), a share similar to South Africa. In Africa as a whole, formal retailing accounts for only 8% of the sector (Shevel 2017).
9. For example, in food retailing by the early 2000s four large corporations – Shoprite, Pick n Pay, Spar, and Woolworths – accounted for over 90% of supermarket sales (Weatherspoon and Reardon 2003, 4). See Greenberg (2017) for a portrait of the complexity of corporate power in the food system in South Africa.
10. Johannesburg's Eastgate Mall, for a time the largest mall in Africa, was built in 1979 (Tomlinson and Larsen 2003, 44).
11. While the smallest province, Gauteng was home to 45% of the country's shopping centres in 2010 (Gauteng Province 2012, 5), and a greater percentage of its employment comes from the sector at 22.8% of employment in the province in 2012 (Gauteng Province 2012, 33). It is even higher (at 27% in 2011) for young people (Gauteng Province 2012, 32).
12. Retail capital is integrally linked to property developments (Murray 2008). Over the past decade, retail property portfolios (RIETS) listing clusters of malls have grown rapidly and consistently made high returns for investors.
13. The distribution of social grants via this technology was at the heart of long-standing allegations of corruption against companies that had won the grant-distribution tenders (see Jika and Saba 2017).
14. This service was not necessarily as "efficient" as the grant distributers and the South African Social Security Agency touted the arrangement, as claimants often have to wait in queues for long times (Vally 2017, 87).
15. These figures are based only on card swipes and do not take into account money withdrawn from automated teller machines and later spent at retailers (Saba 2017).
16. Focus group interview with contract workers by Bongani Xezwi, Soweto, May 19, 2013.
17. The Economic Development Department's investigation into the Grocery Retail Sector Inquiry (ongoing) is framed in terms of the recognition of the retail sector's role in structuring relations of distribution in the economy.

18. Focus group interview with contract workers by Bongani Xezwi, Soweto, May 13, 2013.
19. Focus group interview with contract workers by Bongani Xezwi, Soweto, May 13, 2013.
20. Focus group interview with contract workers by Bongani Xezwi, Soweto, May 19, 2013.
21. Focus group interview with contract workers by Bongani Xezwi, Soweto, May 19, 2013.
22. Focus group interview with contract workers by Bongani Xezwi, Soweto, May 13, 2013.
23. Focus group interview with contract workers by Bongani Xezwi, Soweto, May 19, 2013.
24. Crankshaw and Borel-Saladin (2014, 1857 Table 1) define their categories by occupational category and income brackets, which puts service and sales occupations within a scale for average annual salary higher than semi-skilled machine operators and far higher than unskilled workers. My issue is not that this statistical category does not mark "better" jobs than unskilled ones, but that the content of the semi-skilled, white-collar job is becoming deskilled in ways that call into question the use of the occupational category (with markers of status from a former time) as a measure of stability ("professionalization").
25. Focus group interview with shop stewards by Bongani Xezwi, Johannesburg, September 29, 2013.
26. 74.3% of workers in the survey were employed by temporary employment agencies, 14.7% were employed directly by Cambridge Food, and 11% directly by suppliers (Kenny 2018).
27. One shop steward reported that only 4 of 125 workers at her branch were permanent workers. Focus group interview with shop stewards by Bongani Xezwi, Johannesburg, September 29, 2013.
28. Focus group interview with shop stewards by Bongani Xezwi, Johannesburg, September 29, 2013.
29. Focus group interview with contract workers by Bongani Xezwi, Soweto, May 19, 2013.
30. Focus group interview with contract workers by Bongani Xezwi, Soweto, May 19, 2013.
31. Focus group interview with shop stewards by Bongani Xezwi, Johannesburg, September 29, 2013.
32. Focus group interview with contract workers by Bongani Xezwi, Soweto, May 19, 2013.
33. Focus group interview with contract workers by Bongani Xezwi, Johannesburg, August 7, 2013.

34. Focus group interview with contract workers by Bongani Xezwi, Soweto, May 19, 2013.
35. Focus group interview with contract workers by Bongani Xezwi, Soweto, May 19, 2013.
36. Focus group interview with contract workers by Bongani Xezwi, Soweto, May 19, 2013.
37. Focus group interview with contract workers by Bongani Xezwi, Soweto, May 13, 2013.
38. Focus group interview with contract workers by Bongani Xezwi, Soweto, May 13, 2013.
39. Focus group interview with contract workers by Bongani Xezwi, Johannesburg, August 7, 2013.
40. Focus group interview with contract workers by Bongani Xezwi, Soweto, May 19, 2013.
41. Focus group interview with contract workers by Bongani Xezwi, Soweto, May 13, 2013.
42. Focus group interview with contract workers by Bongani Xezwi, Soweto, May 19, 2013.
43. Focus group interview with contract workers by Bongani Xezwi, Soweto, May 19, 2013. Shop stewards said they tried to intervene in this issue, but they were told their stores did not have the budget to hire other people and cashiers had to do the additional work. Focus group interview with shop stewards by Bongani Xezwi, Johannesburg, September 29, 2013.
44. Focus group interview with contract workers by Bongani Xezwi, Soweto, May 19, 2013.
45. Focus group interview with contract workers by Bongani Xezwi, Soweto, May 19, 2013.
46. Focus group interview with contract workers by Bongani Xezwi, Soweto, May 19, 2013.
47. Focus group interview with contract workers by Bongani Xezwi, Johannesburg, August 7, 2013.
48. Focus group interview with shop stewards by Bongani Xezwi, Johannesburg, September 29, 2013.
49. Focus group interview with contract workers by Bongani Xezwi, Soweto, May 19, 2013.
50. Focus group interview with contract workers by Bongani Xezwi, Soweto, May 19, 2013.
51. Focus group interview with shop stewards by Bongani Xezwi, Johannesburg, September 29, 2013.
52. Focus group interview with contract workers by Bongani Xezwi, Soweto, May 13, 2013. SACCAWU has recognition agreements with each of the

four Massmart divisions. Between each division and in different brands conditions can differ and coverage is complex.
53. The relevant sections are 198 A-D of the Labour Relations Act, as amended by the Labour Relations Amendment Act, 2014.
54. These restrictions apply in relation to workers such as contract retail workers who earn less than the threshold of R205,443 per year.
55. The amendment defines temporary work as less than three months in duration; filling in for a temporarily absent employee; or if thus defined in a collective agreement, a sectoral determination or a bargaining council agreement that is entered into with union consent.
56. The amendments came into force in January 2015. The CCMA ruled on the matter of whether the client firm becomes the *sole* employer after three months arguing that it did. This decision was taken on appeal to the Labour Court, where it was set aside. Instead, the Labour Court judgment found that both the client and the temporary employment service are employers. While this meant that labour brokers continued in their relationship with employees, it did ensure that employees could seek to exercise their rights under the LRA with respect to the client firm, in other words hold the client firm liable for ensuring protections (see the Labour Court of South Africa, Johannesburg Judgment, *Assign Services (Pty) Ltd.* vs. *CCMA, NUMSA and Krost Shelving & Racking (Pty) Ltd.* JR1230/15, September 8, 2015). However, in 2017 NUMSA challenged this interpretation of section 198A(3)(b)(i) of the Labour Court judgment in the Labour Appeal Court. On July 10, 2017, the Labour Appeal Court set aside the Labour Court judgment, ruling against an interpretation of dual employers, instead affirming that the client firm alone became the sole employer after three months. See the Labour Appeal Court of South Africa, *NUMSA* vs. *Assign Services and Others.* JA 96/15, July 10, 2017.
57. Focus group interview with SACCAWU shop steward and union officials by Bridget Kenny, Johannesburg, February 16, 2017.
58. Darlington Ndlovu, SACCAWU Chair of the Massmart company council, interviewed by Bridget Kenny by telephone, June 20, 2017.
59. Focus group interview with SACCAWU shop steward and union officials by Bridget Kenny, Johannesburg, February 16, 2017.
60. In 2016, cashier-less till points were being piloted by Pick n Pay in Cape Town.

REFERENCES

ARCHIVES

Congress of South African Trade Unions (COSATU) Papers. 1984–1997 (AH2373). Historical Papers Research Archive, University of the Witwatersrand.

Jeremy Baskin Papers. 1982–1988 (AH2920). Historical Papers Research Archive, University of the Witwatersrand.

Karis-Gerhart Collection of South African Political Materials. 1964–1990 (A2675). Historical Papers Research Archive, University of the Witwatersrand.

National Accounts: Public Companies. (SAB, SES, F1900). National Archives of South Africa (NASA).

National Union of Distributive Workers (Head Office) Records. 1933–1980 (AH1494). Historical Papers Research Archive, University of the Witwatersrand.

National Union of Distributive Workers (Natal Branch) Records. 1937–1978 (AH1202). Historical Papers Research Archive, University of the Witwatersrand.

National Union of Distributive Workers (Witwatersrand Branch) Records. 1939–1984 (AH1601). Historical Papers Research Archive, University of the Witwatersrand.

Original SAHA Collection (AL2457). South African Historical Archive (SAHA).

Government Documents

South Africa. 1952. Bureau of Census and Statistics. "First Census of Distribution and Service Establishments, 1946–47, Report No. 70, Retail Establishments, Summary".

———. 1955a. Commission of Inquiry into the Regulation of Monopolistic Conditions Act. Report of the Commission of Inquiry into the Regulation of Monopolistic Conditions Act, 1955. Report RP63/75.

———. 1955b. Department of Labour. "Annual Report, 1953, UG 20/1955."

———. 1958a. Board of Trade and Industries. "Report 437 (M): Monopolistic Conditions in the Grocery Trade".

———. 1958b. Department of Commerce and Industries. Regulation of Monopolistic Conditions Act, 1955, as Amended. *Government Gazette* No. 1839, December 5.

———. 1960. Bureau of Census and Statistics. "Census of Distribution and Service Establishments, 1952: Part I, Retail Detailers, Report 36, Summary".

———. 1967. Bureau of Statistics. "Census of Wholesale and Retail Distributive Trade, 1960–61: Part 2, Retailers, Report 35, Summary".

———. 1970. House of Assembly. *Debates*, fifth session, third parliament, 30 January to 27 February, Vol 28.

———. 1973. Department of Statistics. "Census of Wholesale and Retail Trade, 1966–67, Part 2, Retailers, Report 04–41–16, Summary".

———. 1981. Department of Statistics. "Census of Wholesale and Retail Trade, 1977, Retailers, Report 04–41–36".

———. 1998. Central Statistical Services. "Labour Statistics, Employment and Salaries and Wages; Wholesale, Retail and Motor Trade and Hotels." Statistical Release P0244.

Union of South Africa, Basutoland, Bechuanaland Protectorate, and Swaziland. 1947. Union Office of Census and Statistics, Labour and Industrial Conditions. *Official Year Book of the Union of South Africa and of Basutoland, Bechuanaland Protectorate, and Swaziland, No. 23–1946*.

Secondary Literature

Abelson, Elaine S. 1989. *When Ladies Go A-Thieving: Middle Class Shoplifters in the Victorian Department Store*. New York: Oxford University Press.

Acker, Joan. 1990. Hierarchies, Jobs, Bodies: A Theory of Gendered Organizations. *Gender and Society* 4 (2): 139–158.

Ackerman, Raymond. 2001. *Hearing Grasshoppers Jump: The Story of Raymond Ackerman*. Cape Town: David Philip.

Adler, Glenn, and Eddie Webster. 1995. Challenging Transition Theory: The Labor Movement, Radical Reform, and Transition to Democracy in South Africa. *Politics and Society* 23 (1): 75–106.

———, eds. 2000. *Trade Unions and Democratization in South Africa, 1985–1997*. Basingstoke: Palgrave Macmillan.

Agarwala, Rina. 2013. *Informal Labor, Formal Politics, and Dignified Discontent in India*. New York: Cambridge University Press.

Ahmed, Sara. 2006. *Queer Phenomenology: Orientations, Objects, Others*. Durham: Duke University Press.

Albertyn, J.R., A.D. Luckhoff, T.F. Cronje, and M.E. Rothman. 1932. Part V: Sociological Report. In *Report of the Carnegie Commission of Investigation on the Poor White Question in South Africa*. Stellenbosch: Carnegie Corporation.

Alexander, Peter. 2000. *Workers, War and the Origins of Apartheid: Labour and Politics in South Africa, 1939–48*. Oxford: Ohio University Press.

Ally, Shireen. 2009. *From Servants to Workers: South African Domestic Workers and the Democratic State*. Ithaca/London: Cornell University Press.

———. 2013. 'Ooh, eh eh ... Just One Small Cap Is Enough!' Servants, Detergents and Their Prosthetic Significance. *African Studies* 72 (3): 321–352.

Althusser, Louis. 1971. Ideology and Ideological State Apparatuses (Notes towards an Investigation). Chap. 1 In *Essays on Ideology*, 1–60. London: Verso.

Anderson, David M. 2004. Kenya, 1895–1939: Registration and Rough Justice. In *Masters, Servants, and Magistrates in Britain and the Empire, 1562–1955*, ed. Douglas Hay and Paul Craven, 498–528. Chapel Hill: University of North Carolina Press.

Appadurai, Arjun. 1986. *The Social Life of Things: Commodities in Cultural Perspective*. Cambridge: Cambridge University Press.

Appelbaum, Richard, and Nelson Lichtenstein. 2006. A New World of Retail Supremacy: Supply Chains and Workers' Chains in the Age of Wal-Mart. *International Labor and Working-Class History* 70: 106–125.

Appolis, Patricia. 1998. Workers as Fathers. *Agenda* 14 (37): 78–81.

Arendt, Hannah. 1958. *The Human Condition*. Chicago: University of Chicago Press.

———. 2005. *The Promise of Politics*, ed. and with an introduction by Jerome Kohn. New York: Schocken Books.

Askenazy, Philippe, Jean-Baptiste Berry, Françoise Carré, Sophie Prunier-Poulmaire, and Chris Tilly. 2012. Working in Large Food Retailers in France and the USA: The Key Role of Institutions. *Work, Employment and Society* 26 (4): 588–605.

Austin, Ralph A. 1993. The Moral Economy of Witchcraft: An Essay in Comparative History. In *Modernity and Its Malcontents: Ritual and Power in Postcolonial Africa*, ed. Jean Comaroff and John Comaroff, 89–110. Chicago: Chicago University Press.

Bailey, Janis, Robin A. Price, Amanda Pyman, and Jane Parker. 2015. Union Power in Retail: Contrasting Cases in Australia and New Zealand. *New Zealand Journal of Employment Relations* 40 (1): 1–18.

Bank, Leslie J. 2011. *Home Spaces, Street Styles: Contemporary Power and Identity in a South Africa City*. Johannesburg: Wits University Press.

Bank Muñoz, Carolina, Bridget Kenny, and Antonio Stecher, eds. 2018. *Walmart in the Global South: Workplace Culture, Labor Politics, and Supply Chains*. Austin: University of Texas Press.

Bannerji, Himani. 2000. *The Dark Side of the Nation: Essays on Multiculturalism, Nationalism and Gender*. Toronto: Canadian Scholars Press.

Banning-Lover, Rachel. 2015. The Bank, the Boss, Your Parents: Global Borrowing Trends Mapped. *The Guardian*, May 28. https://www.theguardian.com/global-development-professionals-network/2015/may/28/the-bank-the-boss-your-parents-global-borrowing-trends-mapped

Barchiesi, Franco. 2011. *Precarious Liberation: Workers, the State, and Contested Social Citizenship in Postapartheid South Africa*. Albany: State University of New York Press.

———. 2016a. Work in the Constitution of the Human: Twentieth-Century South African Entanglements of Welfare, Blackness, and Political Economy. *South Atlantic Quarterly* 115 (1): 149–174.

———. 2016b. The Violence of Work: Revisiting South Africa's 'Labour Question' Through Precarity and Anti-blackness. *Journal of Southern African Studies* 42 (5): 875–891.

Baskin, Jeremy. 1991. *Striking Back: A History of COSATU*. Johannesburg: Ravan Press.

Baum, Céline, and Cédric Durand. 2012. Financialization, Globalization and the Making of Profits by Leading Retailers. *Socio-Economic Review* 10 (2): 241–266.

Bauman, Zygmunt. 1998. *Work, Consumerism and the New Poor*. Buckingham: Open University Press.

Beall, Jo, Owen Crankshaw, and Susan Parnell. 2002. *Uniting a Divided City: Governance and Social Exclusion in Johannesburg*. London: Earthscan Publications, Ltd.

Beavon, Keith. 2004. *Johannesburg: The Making and Shaping of the City*. Pretoria: UNISA Press.

Beittel, Mark. 1992. The Witwatersrand: Black Households, White Households. In *Creating and Transforming Households: The Constraints of the World-Economy*, ed. Joan Smith and Immanuel Wallerstein, 197–230. Cambridge: Cambridge University Press.

Benjamin, Jessica. 1988. *The Bonds of Love: Psychoanalysis, Feminism and the Problem of Domination*. New York: Pantheon Books.

Benjamin, Walter. 2002. *The Arcades Project*. Trans. Howard Eiland, and Kevin McLaughlin. Cambridge, MA: Harvard University Press.

Benjamin, Paul. 2013. *Law and Practice of Private Employment Agency Work in South Africa*. Sector Working Paper No. 292. Geneva: International Labour Office. http://www.ilo.org/sector/Resources/publications/WCMS_231442/lang-en/index.htm

———. 2014. The Persistence of Unfree Labour: The Rise of Temporary Employment Agencies in South Africa and Namibia. In *Temporary Work, Agencies and Unfree Labour: Insecurity in the New World of Work*, ed. Judy Fudge and Kendra Strauss, 118–142. New York: Routledge.

Benson, Susan Porter. 1986. *Counter Cultures: Saleswomen, Managers, and Customers in American Department Stores 1890–1940*. Urbana: University of Illinois Press.

Benya, Asanda. 2015. The Invisible Hands: Women in Marikana. *Review of African Political Economy* 42 (146): 545–560.

Berger, Iris. 1992. *Threads of Solidarity: Women in South African Industry 1900–1980*. Bloomington: Indiana University Press.

Berlant, Lauren. 2011. *Cruel Optimism*. Durham: Duke University Press.

Bernhardt, Annette. 1999. *The Future of Low-Wage Jobs: Case Studies in the Retail Industry*. IEE Working Paper No. 10, March 1999. https://pdfs.semanticscholar.org/6a3f/c0ff9c4d274eb2f41d1386d7dacff6385923.pdf

Beukes, Rochelle, Ada Jansen, Mariana Moses, and Yu. Derek. 2016. Exploring the Eligibility Criteria of the Child Support Grant and its Impact on Poverty. *Social Indicators Research*: 1–19. https://doi.org/10.1007/s11205-016-1433-z.

Bezuidenhout, Andries, and Khayaat Fakier. 2006. Maria's Burden: Contract Cleaning and the Crisis of Social Reproduction in Post-apartheid South Africa. *Antipode* 38 (3): 462–485.

Bhengu, Sitembiso. 2010. Workplace Regimes, Identity and Everyday Life of African Working Men in Post-Apartheid South Africa: The Case Study of Dunlop. In *Society in Focus – Change, Challenge and Resistance: Reflections from South Africa and Beyond*, ed. Lindy Heinecken and Heidi Prozesky, 198–214. Newcastle upon Tyne: Cambridge Scholars Publishing.

Bhorat, Haroon, Aalia Cassim, and Derek Yu. 2016. *Temporary Employment Services: Assessing the Industry's Economic Contribution*. Pretoria: Labour Market Intelligence Partnership.

Bianchi, Constanza, and Stephen J. Arnold. 2004. An Institutional Perspective on Retail Internationalization Success: Home Depot in Chile. *International Review of Retail, Distribution, and Consumer Research* 14 (2): 149–169.

BMI (Business Monitor International). 2013. *South Africa Food and Drink Report*. London: Business Monitor International.

Boehmer, Elke. 1992. Stories of Women and Mothers: Gender and Nationalism in the Early Fiction of Flora Nwapa. In *Motherlands: Black Women's Writing from Africa, the Caribbean and South Asia*, ed. Susheila Nasta, 3–23. New Brunswick: Rutgers University Press.

Bonacich, Edna, and Khaleelah Hardie. 2006. Wal-Mart and the Logistics Revolution. In *Wal-Mart: The Face of Twenty-First-Century Capitalism*, ed. Nelson Lichtenstein, 163–188. New York: The New Press.

Bond, Patrick. 2000. *Cities of Gold, Townships of Coal: Essays on South Africa's New Urban Crisis*. Trenton: Africa World Press.

———. 2013. Debt, Uneven Development and Capitalist Crisis in South Africa: From Moody's Macroeconomic Monitoring to Marikana Microfinance Mashonisas. *Third World Quarterly* 34 (4): 569–592.

Bonner, Philip. 1990a. Desirable or Undesirable Basotho Women? Liquor, Prostitution and the Migration of Basotho Women to the Rand, 1920–1945. In *Women and Gender in Southern Africa to 1945*, ed. Cherryl Walker, 221–250. Cape Town: David Philip.

———. 1990b. The Politics of Black Squatter Movements on the Rand, 1944–1952. *Radical History Review* 47 (7): 89–116.

———. 1995. African Urbanisation on the Rand Between the 1930s and 1960s: Its Social Character and Political Consequences. *Journal of Southern African Studies* 21 (1): 115–129.

Bonner, Philip, and Vusi Ndima. 1999. *The Roots of Violence on the East Rand, 1980–1990*. Paper presented at University of the Witwatersrand Institute for Advanced Social Research, Johannesburg, October 18.

Bonnin, Debby, and Karen Hurt. 1987. The O.K. Strike: A Battle on Many Fronts. *Agenda: Empowering Women for Gender Equity* 1: 31–44.

Bourgois, Philippe. 1995. *In Search of Respect: Selling Crack in El Barrio*. Cambridge: Cambridge University Press.

Bowlby, Rachel. 2001. *Carried Away: The Invention of Modern Shopping*. New York: Columbia University Press.

Bowles, Paul, and Fiona MacPhail. 2008. Introduction to the Special Issue on Pathways from Casual Work to Economic Security: Canadian and International Perspectives. *Social Indicators Research* 88 (1): 1–13.

Bozkurt, Ödül, and Irena Grugulis. 2011. Why Retail Work Demands a Closer Look. In *Retail Work*, ed. Irena Grugulis and Ödül Bozkurt, 1–24. London: Palgrave Macmillan.

Bozzoli, Belinda with Mmantho Nkotsoe. 1991. *Women of Phokeng: Consciousness, Life Strategy, and Migrancy in South Africa, 1900–1983*. Johannesburg: Ravan Press.

Bramble, Tom, and Franco Barchiesi, eds. 2003. *Rethinking the Labour Movement in the "New South Africa"*. New York: Ashgate.

Breckenridge, Keith. 1998. The Allure of Violence: Men, Race and Masculinity on the South African Goldmines, 1900–1950. *Journal of Southern African Studies* 24 (4): 669–693.

Breman, Jan. 2010. *Outcast Labour in Asia: Circulation and Informalization of the Workforce at the Bottom of the Economy*. New Delhi: Oxford University Press.

Breman, Jan, and Marcel van der Linden. 2014. Informalizing the Economy: The Return of the Social Question at a Global Level. *Development and Change* 45: 920–940.

Brink, Elsabé. 1986. *The Afrikaner Women of the Garment Worker's Union, 1918–1938.* Master's thesis, University of Witwatersrand.

———. 1987. Maar 'n klomp "factory" meide': The Role of the Female Garment Workers in the Clothing Industry, Afrikaner Family and Community on the Witwatersrand During the 1920s. In *Class, Community and Conflict: South African Perspectives,* ed. Belinda Bozzoli, 177–208. Johannesburg: Ravan Press.

———. 1990. Man-Made Women: Gender, Class and the Ideology of the *Volksmoeder.* In *Women and Gender in Southern Africa to 1945,* ed. Cherryl Walker, 273–292. Cape Town: David Philip.

Broadbridge, Adelina. 1999. A Profile of Female Retail Managers: Some Insights. *Services Industries Journal* 19 (3): 135–161.

———. 2002. Retail Managers: Their Work Stressors and Coping Strategies. *Journal of Retailing and Consumer Services* 9 (3): 173–183.

Brown, Wendy. 1995. *States of Injury: Power and Freedom in Late Modernity.* Princeton: Princeton University Press.

Brunn, Stanley D., ed. 2006. *Wal-Mart World: The World's Biggest Corporation in the Global Economy.* New York: Routledge.

Bryant, Alfred T. 1905. *A Zulu-English dictionary with notes on pronunciation, a revised orthography and derivations and cognate words from many languages; including also a vocabulary of Hlonipa words, tribal-names, etc., a synopsis of Zulu grammar and a concise history of the Zulu people from the most ancient times.* Pinetown: The Mariannhill Mission Press.

Buhlungu, Sakhela. 2006. Rebels Without a Cause of Their Own? The Contradictory Location of White Officials in Black Unions in South Africa, 1973–94. *Current Sociology* 54 (3): 427–451.

———. 2010. *A Paradox of Victory: COSATU and the Democratic Transformation in South Africa.* Scottsville: University of KwaZulu-Natal Press.

Bulan, Heather Ferguson, Rebecca J. Erickson, and Amy S. Wharton. 1997. Doing for Others on the Job: The Affective Requirements of Service Work, Gender, and Emotional Well-Being. *Social Problems* 44 (2): 235–256.

Burawoy, Michael. 1985. *Politics of Production: Factory Regimes Under Capitalism and Socialism.* London: Verso.

Burch, David, and Jasper Goss. 1999. Global Sourcing and Retail Chains: Shifting Relationships of Production in Australian Agri-Foods. *Rural Sociology* 64 (2): 334–350.

Burke, Timothy. 1996. *Lifebuoy Men, Lux Women: Commodification, Consumption, and Cleanliness in Modern Zimbabwe.* Durham: Duke University Press.

Butler, Judith. 1997. *The Psychic Life of Power: Theories of Subjection.* Stanford: Stanford University Press.

———. 2004. *Precarious Life: The Powers of Mourning and Violence.* London: Verso Books.

Campbell, Iain, and Peter Brosnan. 1999. Labour Market Deregulation in Australia: The Slow Combustion Approach to Workplace Change. *International Review of Applied Economics* 13 (3): 353–394.

Campbell, Iain, and John Burgess. 2001a. A New Estimate of Casual Employment? *Australian Bulletin of Labour* 27 (2): 85–108.

———. 2001b. Casual Employment in Australia and Temporary Employment in Europe: Developing a Cross-National Comparison. *Work, Employment and Society* 15 (1): 171–184.

Carré, Françoise, Chris Tilly, and Diana Denham. 2010a. Explaining Variation in the Quality of U.S. Retail Jobs. Paper prepared for the annual meeting of the Labor and Employment Relations Association, Denver, CO, January 6–9. http://www.russellsage.org/research/reports/retail-jobs-in-the-us

Carré, Françoise, Chris Tilly, Maarten van Klaveren, and Dorothea Voss-Dahm. 2010b. Retail Jobs in Comparative Perspective. In *Low-Wage Work in the Wealthy World,* ed. Jérôme Gautié and John Schmitt, 211–268. New York: Russell Sage Foundation.

Chan, Anita, ed. 2011. *Walmart in China.* Ithaca: ILR Press.

Chanock, Martin. 2004a. *The Making of South African Legal Culture 1902–1936: Fear, Favour and Prejudice.* Cambridge: Cambridge University Press.

———. 2004b. South Africa, 1841–1924: Race, Contract, and Coercion. In *Masters, Servants, and Magistrates in Britain and the Empire, 1562–1955,* ed. Douglas Hay and Paul Craven, 338–364. Chapel Hill: University of North Carolina Press.

Chipkin, Clive. 1993. *Johannesburg Style: Architecture and Society, 1880s–1960s.* Cape Town: David Philip.

Christopherson, Susan. 1996. The Production of Consumption: Retail Restructuring and Labor Demand in the USA. In *Retailing, Consumption and Capital: Towards the New Retail Geography,* ed. Neil Wrigley and Michelle Lowe, 159–177. Harlow: Longman.

Chun, Jennifer J. 2009. *Organizing at the Margins: The Symbolic Politics of Labor in South Korea and the United States.* Ithaca: ILR Press.

Clark, Gracia. 1999. Mothering, Work, and Gender in Urban Asante Ideology and Practice. *American Anthropologist* 101 (4): 717–729.

Clarke, Marlea. 2000. Checking Out and Cashing Up: The Rise of Precarious Employment in the Retail Sector. Paper presented at the Trade and Industry Policy Secretariat 2000 Annual Forum, Muldersdrift, September 18–20.

———. 2004. Challenging Segmentation in South Africa's Labour Market: 'Regulated Flexibility' or Flexible Regulation? In *Challenging the Market: The Struggle to Regulate Work and Income*, ed. Jim Stanford and Leah F. Vosko, 97–118. Montreal: McGill-Queen's University Press.

Clarke, Marlea, Shane Godfrey, and Jan Theron. 2003. South African Labour Legislation: Protection for Casual Workers. Unpublished ms. Women on Farms Project, Stellenbosch University.

Clowes, Lindsey. 1994. *Making It Work: Aspects of Marriage, Motherhood and Money-Earning Among White South African Women 1960–1990*. MA thesis, University of Cape Town.

Cobble, Dorothy Sue. 1991. *Dishing It Out: Waitresses and Their Unions in the Twentieth Century*. Chicago: University of Illinois Press.

———. 2004. *The Other Women's Movement: Workplace Justice and Social Rights in Modern America*. Princeton: Princeton University Press.

Cobble, Dorothy Sue, and Leah F. Vosko. 2000. Historical Perspectives on Representing Nonstandard Workers. In *Nonstandard Work: The Nature and Challenges of Changing Employment Arrangements*, ed. Françoise Carré, Marianne A. Ferber, Lonnie Golden, and Stephen A. Herzenberg, 291–312. Ithaca: Cornell University Press.

Cock, Jacklyn. 1980. *Maids and Madams: Domestic Workers Under Apartheid*. Johannesburg: Ravan Press.

Cockburn, Cynthia. 1983. *Brothers: Male Dominance and Technological Change*. London: Pluto Press.

Coe, Neil M., and Neil Wrigley. 2007. Host Economy Impacts of Transnational Retail: The Research Agenda. *Journal of Economic Geography* 7 (4): 341–371.

Cohen, Lizbeth. 2003. *A Consumers' Republic: The Politics of Mass Consumption in Postwar America*. New York: Vintage Books.

Collier, Jane F., and Sylvia J. Yanagisako, eds. 1987. *Gender and Kinship: Essays Toward a Unified Analysis*. Stanford: Stanford University Press.

Collier, Jane, Michelle Z. Rosaldo, and Sylvia Yanagisako. 1997. Is There a Family? New Anthropological Views. In *The Gender/Sexuality Reader: Culture, History, Political Economy*, ed. Roger N. Lancaster and Micaela di Leonardo, 71–81. New York/London: Routledge.

Collins, Jane L. 2003. *Threads: Gender, Labor, and Power in the Global Apparel Industry*. Chicago: University of Chicago Press.

———. 2009. The Age of Wal-Mart. In *The Insecure American: How We Got Here and What We Should Do About It*, ed. Hugh Gusterson and Catherine L. Besteman, 97–112. Berkeley: University of California Press.

Comaroff, Jean. 1985. *Body of Power, Spirit of Resistance: The Culture and History of a South African People*. Chicago/London: University of Chicago Press.

Comaroff, John L. 1987. Sui Generis: Feminism, Kinship Theory, and Structural 'Domains'. In *Gender and Kinship: Essays Toward a Unified Analysis*, ed. Jane F. Collier and Sylvia J. Yanagisako, 53–85. Stanford: Stanford University Press.

Comaroff, Jean. 1996. The Empire's Old Clothes: Fashioning the Colonial Subject. In *Cross-Cultural Consumption: Global Markets, Local Realities*, ed. David Howes, 19–38. London: Routledge.

Comaroff, Jean, and John L. Comaroff. 1987. The Madman and the Migrant: Work and Labor in the Historical Consciousness of a South African People. *American Anthropologist* 14 (2): 191–209.

Comaroff, John L., and Jean Comaroff. 1992. *Ethnography and the Historical Imagination*. Boulder: Westview Press.

Comaroff, Jean, and John L. Comaroff. 1999. Occult Economies and the Violence of Abstraction: Notes from the South African Postcolony. *American Ethnologist* 26 (2): 279–303.

Comaroff, John L., and Jean Comaroff. 2001. On Personhood: An Anthropological Perspective from Africa. *Social Identities* 7 (2): 267–283.

Comaroff, Jean, and John L. Comaroff. 2003. Reflections on Liberalism, Policulturalism, and ID-ology: Citizenship and Difference in South Africa. *Social Identities* 9 (4): 445–473.

———, eds. 2006. *Law and Disorder in the Postcolony*. Chicago: University of Chicago Press.

Comaroff, John L., and Simon Roberts. 1981. *Rules and Processes: The Cultural Logic of Dispute in an African Context*. Chicago: University of Chicago Press.

Cook, Gillian. 1975. *Spatial Dynamics of Business Growth in the Witwatersrand*. Chicago: Department of Geography, University of Chicago.

Cooper, Frederick, ed. 1983. *Struggle for the City: Migrant Labor, Capital, and the State in Urban Africa*. Beverly Hills: Sage.

———. 1996. *Decolonization and African Society: The Labor Question in French and British Africa*. Cambridge: Cambridge University Press.

Coulter, Kendra. 2014. *Revolutionizing Retail: Workers, Political Action, and Social Change*. New York: Palgrave Macmillan.

Crankshaw, Owen. 1997. *Race, Class and the Changing Division of Labour Under Apartheid*. London: Routledge.

Crankshaw, Owen, and Jacqueline Borel-Saladin. 2014. Does Deindustrialisation Cause Social Polarisation in Global Cities? *Environment and Planning A* 46 (8): 1852–1872.

Crompton, Rosemary, and Gunn E. Birkelund. 2000. Employment and Caring in British and Norwegian Banking: An Exploration through Individual Careers. *Work, Employment and Society* 14 (2): 331–352.

Crompton, Rosemary, and Gareth Jones. 1984. *White-Collar Proletariat: Deskilling and Gender in Clerical Work*. Philadelphia: Temple University Press.

Davies, Rob. 1978. The Class Character of South Africa's Industrial Conciliation Legislation. In *Essays in South African Labour History*, ed. Eddie Webster, 69–81. Johannesburg: Ravan Press.

Davies, Robert H. 1979. *Capital, State and White Labour in South Africa, 1900–1960: An Historical Materialist Analysis of Class Formation and Class Relations*. Brighton: Harvester Press.
Dávila, Arlene M. 2016. *El Mall: The Spatial and Class Politics of Shopping Malls in Latin America*. Berkeley: University of California Press.
Davis, Oliver. 2010. *Jacques Rancière*. Cambridge: Polity Press.
Dawson, John A. 2007. Scoping and Conceptualising Retailer Internationalisation. *Journal of Economic Geography* 7 (4): 373–397.
Dawson, Marcelle C., and William Beinart, eds. 2010. *Popular Politics and Resistance Movements in South Africa*. Johannesburg: Wits University Press.
De Villiers, Ingrid. 1999. An Analysis of Labour Disputes in the Retail Industry, 1 July 1997–31 August 1998. Unpublished ms. Commission for Conciliation, Mediation and Arbitration.
de Vries, Fred. 2008. Megamalls, Generic City. In *Johannesburg: The Elusive Metropolis*, ed. Sarah Nuttall and Achille Mbembe, 297–306. Johannesburg: Wits University Press.
"Deadlock in OK Bazaars strike." 1987. *The Sowetan*, January 6.
Deloitte. 2017. *Global Powers of Retailing 2017: The Art and Science of Customers*. London: Deloitte Touche Tohmatsu.
Demirguc-Kunt, Asli, Leora Klapper, Dorothe Singer, and Peter van Oudheusden. 2015. *The Global Findex Database 2014: Measuring Financial Inclusion Around the World*. Policy Research Working Paper WPS 7255. Washington, DC: World Bank Group.
Denning, Michael. 2010. Wageless Life. *New Left Review* 66 (Nov/Dec): 79–97.
Desai, Rehad. 1997. *Race, Gender and Class in the National Union of Distributive Workers, 1937–53*. Master's thesis, University of the Witwatersrand.
Desai, Ashwin. 2002. *We Are the Poors: Community Struggles in Post-apartheid South Africa*. New York: Monthly Review Press.
Dholakia, Nikhilesh, Ruby Roy Dholakia, and Atish Chattopadhyay. 2012. India's Emerging Retail Systems: Coexistence of Tradition and Modernity. *Journal of Macromarketing* 32 (3): 252–265.
Dlamini, S. Nombuso. 2005. *Youth and Identity Politics in South Africa, 1990–94*. Toronto: University of Toronto Press.
Doel, Christine. 1996. The Changing Place of Retailer-Supplier Relations in British Retailing. In *Retailing, Consumption and Capital: Towards the New Retail Geography*, ed. Neil Wrigley and Michelle Lowe, 68–89. Harlow: Longman.
Douglas, Mary. 1966. *Purity and Danger: An Analysis of the Concepts of Pollution and Taboo*. London: Routledge.
Du Plessis, Irma. 2010. Afrikaner Nationalism, Print Culture and the 'Capacity To Aspire': The Imaginative Powers of Popular Fiction for Young Readers. *African Identities* 8 (1): 3–20.

———. 2011. Nation, Family, Intimacy: The Domain of the Domestic in the Social Imaginary. *South African Review of Sociology* 42 (2): 45–65.
Du Toit, Marijke. 2003. The Domesticity of Afrikaner Nationalism: Volksmoeders and the ACVV, 1904–1929. *Journal of Southern African Studies* 29 (1): 155–176.
Du Toit, Andries, and David Neves. 2009. *Informal Social Protection in Post-Apartheid Migrant Networks: Vulnerability, Social Networks and Reciprocal Exchange in the Eastern and Western Cape, South Africa*. Working Paper 2. Programme for Land and Agrarian Studies (PLAAS), University of the Western Cape. http://www.plaas.org.za/plaas-publication/wp-2
Duncan, David. 1995. *The Mills of God: The State and African Labour in South Africa, 1918–1948*. Johannesburg: Witwatersrand University Press.
Dupree, Paulette. 1969. Inquiry into 'Mixed Serving in Shops'. *Sunday Express*, October 5.
Durand, Cédric, and Neil Wrigley. 2009. Institutional and Economic Determinants of Transnational Retailer Expansion and Performance: A Comparative Analysis of Wal-Mart and Carrefour. *Environment and Planning A* 41 (7): 1534–1555.
Eales, Kathy. 1989. Patriarchs, Passes and Privilege: Johannesburg's African Middle Classes and the Question of Night Passes for African Women, 1920–1931. In *Holding Their Ground: Class, Locality and Culture in 19th and 20th Century South Africa*, ed. Philip Bonner, Isabel Hofmeyr, Deborah James, and Tom Lodge, 105–140. Johannesburg: Ravan Press.
Enstad, Nan. 1999. *Ladies of Labor, Girls of Adventure: Working Women, Popular Culture, and Labor Politics at the Turn of the Century*. New York: Columbia University Press.
Erickson, Rebecca J., and Amy S. Wharton. 1997. Inauthenticity and Depression: Assessing the Consequences of Interactive Service Work. *Work and Occupations* 24 (2): 188–213.
Erlmann, Veit. 1998. How Beautiful Is Small? Music, Globalization and the Aesthetics of the Local. *Yearbook for Traditional Music* 30: 12–21.
Evans, Ivan. 1997. *Bureaucracy and Race: Native Administration in South Africa*. Berkeley: University of California Press.
Fakier, Khayaat, and Jacklyn Cock. 2009. A Gendered Analysis of the Crisis of Social Reproduction in Contemporary South Africa. *International Feminist Journal of Politics* 11 (3): 353–371.
Fanon, Franz. 1967. *Black Skin, White Masks*. New York: Grove Press.
Featherstone, Mike. 1991. *Consumer Culture and Postmodernism*. London: Sage.
Felstead, Alan, and Nick Jewson, eds. 1999. *Global Trends in Flexible Labour*. London: Macmillan.
Ferguson, James. 2015. *Give a Man a Fish: Reflections on the New Politics of Distribution*. Durham: Duke University Press.

Finn, Arden. 2015. *A National Minimum Wage in the Context of the South African Labour Market*. Working Paper Series No. 1. Johannesburg: National Minimum Wage Research Initiative, University of the Witwatersrand.

Fishman, Charles. 2007. *The Walmart Effect: How an Out-of-Town Superstore Became a Superpower*. London: Penguin.

Folbre, Nancy R. 1994. *Who Pays for the Kids? Gender and the Structure of Constraint*. London: Routledge.

Forrest, Kally. 2005. *Asijiki: A History of the South African Commercial Catering and Allied Workers Union (SACCAWU)*. Johannesburg: STE Publishers.

Frank, Dana. 2001. Girl Strikers Occupy Chain Store, Win Big: The Detroit Woolworth's Strike of 1937. In *Three Strikes: Miners, Musicians, Salesgirls, and the Fighting Spirit of Labor's Last Century*, ed. Howard Zinn, Dana Frank, and Robin D.G. Kelley, 57–118. Boston: Beacon Press.

Fraser, Nancy. 1997. *Justice Interruptus: Critical Reflections on the "Postsocialist" Condition*. New York: Routledge.

Fraser, Nancy, and Axel Honneth. 2003. *Redistribution or Recognition? A Political-Philosophical Exchange*. Trans. Joel Golb, James Ingram, and Christiane Wilke. London: Verso Books.

Freathy, Paul, and Leigh Sparks. 1996. Understanding Retail Employment Relations. In *Retailing, Consumption and Capital: Towards the New Retail Geography*, ed. Neil Wrigley and Michelle Lowe, 178–195. Harlow: Longman.

Freeman, Carla. 2000. *High Tech and High Heels in the Global Economy: Women, Work, and Pink-Collar Identities in the Caribbean*. Durham/London: Duke University Press.

Frenkel, Stephen J., Marek Korczynski, Karen A. Shire, and May Tam. 1999. *On the Front Line: Organization of Work in the Information Economy*. Ithaca: ILR Press.

Friedberg, Anne. 1993. *Window Shopping: Cinema and the Postmodern*. Berkeley: University of California Press.

Fudge, Judy, and Leah F. Vosko. 2001. Gender, Segmentation and the Standard Employment Relationship in Canadian Labour Law, Legislation and Policy. *Economic and Industrial Democracy* 22 (2): 271–310.

Fuller, Linda, and Vicki Smith. 1991. Consumers' Reports: Management by Customers in a Changing Economy. *Work, Employment and Society* 5 (1): 1–16.

Gaitskell, Deborah. 1990. Devout Domesticity? A Century of African Women's Christianity in South Africa. In *Women and Gender in Southern Africa to 1945*, ed. Cherryl Walker, 251–272. Cape Town: David Philip.

Gauteng Province. 2012. *Quarterly Bulletin, April – June 2012: The Retail Industry on the Rise in South Africa*. Johannesburg: Economic Analysis Unit, Gauteng Province.

Gelb, Stephen. 1991. South Africa's Economic Crisis: An Overview. In *South Africa's Economic Crisis*, ed. Stephen Gelb, 1–32. Cape Town: David Philip.

Gereffi, Gary. 1994. The Organization of Buyer-Driven Global Commodity Chains: How U.S. Retailers Shape Overseas Production Networks. In *Commodity Chains and Global Capitalism*, ed. Gary Gereffi and Miguel Korzeniewicz, 95–122. Westport: Praeger.
Gibbs, Andrew, Yandisa Sikweyiya, and Rachel Jewkes. 2014. 'Men Value their Dignity': Securing Respect and Identity Construction in Urban Informal Settlements in South Africa. *Global Health Action* 7 (1): 115–124.
Gill, Fraser. 1957. *The Story of Stuttafords: Commemorating the First Centenary of Stuttaford & Company Limited*. Cape Town: Cape Times.
Glaser, Clive. 2000. *Bo-Tsotsi: The Youth Gangs of Soweto, 1935–1976*. Portsmouth: Heinemann.
Greenberg, Stephen. 2010. *Contesting the Food System in South Africa: Issues and Opportunities*. Research Report 42. Cape Town: Institute for Poverty, Land and Agrarian Studies.
———. 2017. Corporate Power in the Agro-food System and the Consumer Food Environment in South Africa. *Journal of Peasant Studies* 44 (2): 467–496.
Greenberg, Stephen, and Gaynor Paradza. 2013. Smallholders and the 'Walmart Effect' in South Africa. In *Smallholders and Agro-food Value Chains in South Africa: Emerging Practices, Emerging Challenges*, ed. Stephen Greenberg, 54–65. Bellville: Institute for Poverty, Land and Agrarian Studies.
Grosskopf, J.F.W. 1932. Part I: Economic Report. In *Report of the Carnegie Commission of Investigation on the Poor White Question in South Africa*. Stellenbosch: Carnegie Corporation.
Grugulis, Irena, and Ödül Bozkurt, eds. 2011. *Retail Work*. London: Palgrave Macmillan.
Grugulis, Irena, Ödül Bozkurt, and Jeremy Clegg. 2011. 'No Place to Hide'? The Realities of Leadership in UK Supermarkets. In *Retail Work*, ed. Irena Grugulis and Ödül Bozkurt, 193–212. Basingstoke: Palgrave Macmillan.
Grundlingh, Albert. 2008. 'Are We Afrikaners Getting Too Rich?' Cornucopia and Change in Afrikanerdom in the 1960s. *Journal of Historical Sociology* 21 (2&3): 143–165.
Gunner, Elizabeth. 1986. A Dying Tradition? African Oral Literature in a Contemporary Context. *Social Dynamics* 12 (2): 31–38.
Gutek, Barbara A. 1996. Service Workers: Human Resources or Labor Costs? *The Annals of the American Academy of Political and Social Sciences* 544 (March): 68–82.
Gutek, Barbara A., Bennett Cherry, Anita D. Bhappu, Sherry Schneider, and Loren Woolf. 2000. Features of Service Relationships and Encounters. *Work and Occupations* 27 (3): 319–352.
Guyer, Jane I. 1993. Wealth in People and Self-Realization in Equatorial Africa. *Man (n.s.)* 28 (2): 243–265.

———. 1995. Wealth in People, Wealth in Things – Introduction. *Journal of African History* 36 (1): 83–90.
———. 2004. *Marginal Gains: Monetary Transactions in Atlantic Africa*. Chicago: University of Chicago Press.
Habermas, Jürgen. 1994. Struggles for Recognition in the Democratic Constitutional State. In *Multiculturalism: Examining the Politics of Recognition*, ed. Charles Taylor and Amy Gutmann, 107–148. Princeton: Princeton University Press.
Hall, Stuart. 1980. Race, Articulation and Societies Structured in Dominance. In *Sociological Theories: Race and Colonialism*, ed. Mary O'Callaghan, 305–345. Paris: UNESCO.
———. 1985. Signification, Representation, Ideology: Althusser and the Post-Structuralist Debates. *Critical Studies in Mass Communication* 2 (2): 91–114.
———. 1986. The Problem of Ideology – Marxism Without Guarantees. *Journal of Communication Inquiry* 10 (2): 28–44.
———. 2000. Who Needs 'Identity'? In *Identity: A Reader*, ed. Paul du Gay, Jessica Evans, and Peter Redman, 15–30. London: Sage Publications.
———. 2003. Marx's Notes on Method: A 'Reading' of the '1857 Introduction'. *Cultural Studies* 17 (2): 113–149.
Hansen, Karen Tranberg. 1997. *Keeping House in Lusaka*. New York: Columbia University Press.
Hanser, Amy. 2008. *Service Encounters: Class, Gender, and the Market for Social Distinction in Urban China*. Stanford: Stanford University Press.
Hardt, Michael. 1999. Affective Labor. *boundary 2* 26 (2): 89–100.
Harries, David [Baruch Hirson]. 1981. Daniel Koza: A Working Class Leader. *Africa Perspective* 19: 2–38.
Hart, Gillian. 2002. *Disabling Globalization: Places of Power in Post-Apartheid South Africa*. Pietermaritzburg: University of Natal Press.
———. 2008. The Provocations of Neoliberalism: Contesting the Nation and Liberation After Apartheid. *Antipode* 40 (4): 678–705.
———. 2013. *Rethinking the South African Crisis: Nationalism, Populism, Hegemony*. Athens/London: The University of Georgia Press.
———. 2016. Relational Comparison Revisited: Marxist Postcolonial Geographies in Practice. *Progress in Human Geography*: 1–24. https://doi.org/10.1177/0309132516681388.
Hassim, Shireen. 2006. *Women's Organizations and Democracy in South Africa: Contesting Authority*. Scottsville: University of KwaZulu-Natal Press.
Hay, Douglas, and Paul Craven, eds. 2004. *Masters, Servants, and Magistrates in Britain and the Empire, 1562–1955*. Chapel Hill: University of North Carolina Press.
Hellmann, Ellen. 1935. Native Life in a Johannesburg Slum Yard. *Africa* 8 (1): 34–62.

———. 1953. *Sellgoods: A Sociological Survey of an African Commercial Labour Force*. Johannesburg: South African Institute of Race Relations.

Hemson, David. 1995. Asinamali! Then and Now. *Alternation* 2 (1): 117–146.

Henly, Julia R., and Susan J. Lambert. 2014. Unpredictable Work Timing in Retail Jobs: Implications for Employee Work-Life Conflict. *ILR Review* 67 (3): 986–1016.

Herd, Norman. 1974. *Counter Attack: The Story of the South African Shopworkers*. Cape Town: National Union of Distributive Workers.

Hindson, Doug. 1987. *Pass Controls and the Urban African Proletariat in South Africa*. Johannesburg: Ravan Press.

Hirson, Baruch. 1979. *Year of Fire, Year of Ash. The Soweto Revolt: Roots of a Revolution?* London: Zed Books.

———. 1990. *Yours for the Union: Class and Community Struggles in South Africa*. Johannesburg: Witwatersrand University Press.

Hochschild, Arlie R. 1983. *The Managed Heart: Commercialization of Human Feeling*. Berkeley: University of California Press.

Hofmeyr, Isabel. 1987. Building a Nation from Words: Afrikaans Language, Literature and Ethnic Identity, 1902–1924. In *The Politics of Race, Class and Nationalism in Twentieth Century South Africa*, ed. Shula Marks and Stanley Trapido, 95–123. London: Longman.

Honneth, Axel. 1996. *The Struggle for Recognition: The Moral Grammar of Social Conflicts*. Trans. Joel Anderson. Cambridge, MA: MIT Press.

Horvitch, Sonita. 1970. *Concentration in the Retail Trade in South Africa: Causes and Effects*. B Comm with honours thesis, University of the Witwatersrand.

Hughes, Alexandra. 1996. Forging New Cultures of Food Retailer-Manufacturer Relations? In *Retailing, Consumption and Capital: Towards the New Retail Geography*, ed. Neil Wrigley and Michelle Lowe, 90–115. Harlow: Longman.

Humphrey, Kim. 1998. *Shelf Life: Supermarkets and the Changing Cultures of Consumption*. Cambridge: Cambridge University Press.

Humphrey, John. 2007. The Supermarket Revolution in Developing Countries: Tidal Wave or Tough Competitive Struggle? *Journal of Economic Geography* 7 (4): 433–450.

Hunter, Monica. 1936. *Reaction to Conquest: Effects of Contact with Europeans on the Pondo of South Africa*. London: Oxford University Press.

Hunter, Mark. 2010. *Love in the Time of AIDS: Inequality, Gender, and Rights in South Africa*. Bloomington: Indiana University Press.

———. 2014. The Bond of Education: Gender, the Value of Children, and the Making of Umlazi Township in 1960s South Africa. *Journal of African History* 55 (3): 467–490.

———. 2015. The Intimate Politics of the Education Market: High-Stakes Schooling and the Making of Kinship in Umlazi Township, South Africa. *Journal of Southern African Studies* 41 (6): 1279–1300.

Hunter, Mark, and Dorrit Posel. 2012. Here to Work: The Socioeconomic Characteristics of Informal Dwellers in Post-Apartheid South Africa. *Environment and Urbanization* 24 (1): 285–304.

Hyslop, Jonathan. 1995. White Working-Class Women and the Invention of Apartheid: 'Purified' Afrikaner Nationalist Agitation for Legislation against 'Mixed' Marriages, 1934–9. *Journal of African History* 36 (1): 57–81.

———. 1999. *The Classroom Struggle: Policy and Resistance in South Africa, 1940–1990.* Pietermaritzburg: University of Natal Press.

———. 2000. Why Did Apartheid's Supporters Capitulate? 'Whiteness', Class and Consumption in Urban South Africa, 1985–1995. *Society in Transition* 31 (1): 36–44.

———. 2005. Shopping During a Revolution: Entrepreneurs, Retailers and 'White' Identity in the Democratic Transition. *Historia* 50 (1): 173–190.

IDC (Industrial Development Corporation of South Africa). 2016. *Economic Trends: Key Trends in the South African Economy.* Sandton: Department of Research and Information, IDC.

Igumbor, Ehimario U., David Sanders, Thandi R. Puoane, Lungiswa Tsolekile, Cassandra Schwarz, Christopher Purdy, Rina Swart, Solange Durão, and Corinna Hawkes. 2012. 'Big Food', the Consumer Food Environment, Health, and the Policy Response in South Africa. *PLoS Medicine* 9 (7): e1001253. https://doi.org/10.1371/journal.pmed.1001253.

Ikeler, Peter. 2011. Organizing Retail: Ideas for Labor's Ongoing Challenge. *The Journal of Labor and Society* 14 (3): 367–392.

———. 2016a. *Hard Sell: Work and Resistance in Retail Chains.* Ithaca: ILR Press.

———. 2016b. Deskilling Emotional Labour: Evidence from Department Store Retail. *Work, Employment and Society* 30 (6): 966–983.

International Labour Office (ILO). 2015a. *Global Wage Report 2014/2015: Wages and Income Inequality.* Geneva: International Labour Office.

International Labour Office (ILO). 2015b. *World Employment Social Outlook: Trends 2015.* Geneva: International Labour Office.

Iqani, Mehita. 2016. *Consumption, Media and the Global South: Aspiration Contested.* Scottsville: University of KwaZulu-Natal Press.

Iqani, Mehita, and Bridget Kenny, eds. 2015. *Consumption, Media and Culture in South Africa: Perspectives on Freedom and the Public.* London: Routledge.

Izzard, Wendy. 1985. Migrants and Mothers: Case-Studies from Botswana. *Journal of Southern African Studies* 11 (2): 258–280.

James, Deborah. 1999. Bagagešu (Those of My Home): Women Migrants, Ethnicity, and Performance in South Africa. *American Ethnologist* 26 (1): 69–89.

———. 2015. *Money from Nothing: Indebtedness and Aspiration in South Africa*. Stanford: Stanford University Press.

Jika, Thanduxolo, and Athandiwe Saba. 2017. Sassa's Spending Splurge. *Sunday Times*, February 12, p. 4.

Johnson, Val Marie. 2007. 'The Rest Can Go to the Devil': Macy's Workers Negotiate Gender, Sex, and Class in the Progressive Era. *Journal of Women's History* 19 (1): 32–57.

Joyce, Peter, ed. 1981. *South Africa's Yesterdays*. Cape Town: Reader's Digest Association.

Kalleberg, Arne. 2013. *Good Jobs, Bad Jobs: The Rise of Polarized and Precarious Employment Systems in the United States, 1970s to 2000s*. New York: Russell Sage Foundation.

Kalyvas, Andreas. 1999. Critical Theory at the Crossroads: Comments on Axel Honneth's Theory of Recognition. *European Journal of Social Theory* 2 (1): 99–108.

Kaplan, Mendel. 1986. *Jewish Roots in the South African Economy*. Cape Town: C. Struik.

Kaye, Alison. 1994. 'No Skill Beyond Manual Dexterity Involved': Gender and the Construction of Skill in the East London Clothing Industry. In *Women, Work, and Place*, ed. Audrey Kobayashi, 112–129. Montréal: McGill-Queen's University Press.

Kelley, Robin D.G. 1996. *Race Rebels: Culture, Politics, and the Black Working Class*. New York: The Free Press.

Kennedy, Duncan. 1979. The Structure of Blackstone's Commentaries. *Buffalo Law Review* 28: 205–382.

———. 1985. The Role of Law in Economic Thought: Essays on the Fetishism of Commodities. *American University Law Review* 34 (4): 939–1001.

Kenny, Bridget. 2001. 'We Are Nursing These Jobs': The Impact of Labor Market Flexibility on South African Retail Workers. In *Is There an Alternative? South African Workers Confronting Globalisation*, ed. Neil Newman, John Pape, and Helga Jansen, 90–107. Cape Town: International Labor Resource and Information Group.

———. 2007. Claiming Workplace Citizenship: 'Worker' Legacies, Collective Identities and Divided Loyalties of South African Contingent Retail Workers. *Qualitative Sociology* 30 (4): 481–500.

———. 2008. Servicing Modernity: White Women Shop Workers on the Rand and Changing Gendered Respectabilities, 1940s–1970s. *African Studies* 67 (3): 365–396.

———. 2009. Consumption or Collectivity? Malls and Working Class Life on the East Rand. In *Sun Tropes: Sun City and (Post-)Apartheid Culture in South Africa*, ed. Marietta Kesting and Aljoscha Weskott, 249–262. Bonn: Berlin August Verlag.

———. 2011. Reconstructing the Political?: Mall Committees and South African Precarious Retail Workers. *Labour, Capital and Society* 44 (1): 44–69.

———. 2014. Citizen Wal-Mart? South African Food Retailing and Selling Development. In *New South African Review 4*, ed. Gilbert M. Khadiagala, Prishani Naidoo, Devan Pillay, and Roger Southall, 56–74. Johannesburg: Wits University Press.

———. 2015. Retail, the Service Worker and the Polity: Attaching Labour and Consumption. *Critical Arts* 29 (2): 199–217.

———. 2016. Affect and the State: Precarious Workers, the Law, and the Promise of Friendship. In *Ties that Bind: Race and the Politics of Friendship in South Africa*, ed. Shannon Walsh and Jon Soske, 166–191. Johannesburg: Wits University Press.

———. 2018. Walmart and Labor Conditions in South Africa: Local Retailing, Contract Labor, and Union Challenges. In *Walmart in the Global South: Workplace Culture, Labor Politics, and Supply Chains*, ed. Carolina Bank Muñoz, Bridget Kenny, and Antonio Stecher, 64–86. Austin: University of Texas Press.

Kenny, Bridget, and Andries Bezuidenhout. 1999. Contracting, Complexity and Control: An Overview of the Changing Nature of Subcontracting in the South African Mining Industry. *Journal of the South African Institute of Mining and Metallurgy* 99 (4): 185–191.

Kenny, Bridget, and Edward Webster. 1998. Eroding the Core: Flexibility and the Re-segmentation of the South African Labour Market. *Critical Sociology* 24 (3): 216–243.

Kessler-Harris, Alice. 1982. *Out to Work: A History of Wage-Earning Women in the United States*. New York: Oxford University Press.

———. 2007. *Gendering Labor History*. Urbana/Chicago: University of Illinois Press.

Khumalo, Lusito D. 2013. Big Business for Small Farmers: The Case of Venda Avocado Growers. In *Smallholders and Agro-food Value Chains in South Africa: Emerging Practices, Emerging Challenges*, ed. Stephen Greenberg, 29–37. Cape Town: Institute for Poverty, Land and Agrarian Studies.

Khunou, Grace. 2012. Money and Gender Relations in the South African Maintenance System. *South African Review of Sociology* 43 (1): 4–22.

Kistner, Ulrike. 2015. Trading in Freedom: Rethinking Conspicuous Consumption in Post-Apartheid Political Economy. *Critical Arts* 29 (2): 240–259.

Klein, Marcia. 2000. Better Management Leads to Fine Results for Shoprite. *Business Day* 30: 20.

Klug, Heinz. 2005. Transnational Human Rights: Exploring the Persistence and Globalization of Human Rights. *Annual Review of Law and Social Science* 1 (1): 85–103.

Knights, David, and Glenn Morgan. 1990. Management Control in Sales Forces: A Case Study from the Labour Process of Life Insurance. *Work, Employment and Society* 4 (3): 369–389.

Kocka, Jurgen. 1980. *White Collar Workers in America 1890–1940: A Social-Political History in International Perspective*. Trans. Maura Kealey. London: Sage.

Korczynski, Marek, Karen Shire, Stephen Frenkel, and May Tam. 2000. Service Work in Consumer Capitalism: Customers, Control and Contradictions. *Work, Employment and Society* 14 (4): 669–687.

Krikler, Jeremy. 2005. *The Rand Revolt: The 1922 Insurrection and Racial Killing in South Africa*. Johannesburg: Jonathan Ball.

Kruger, Lou-Marie. 1991. *Gender, Community and Identity: Women and Afrikaner Nationalism in the Volksmoeder Discourse of Die Boerevrou, 1919–1931*. Master's thesis, University of Cape Town.

Lambrecht, B., E. Meisel, and J. Rushburne. 1967. *A Survey of the Retail Trade in South Africa*. Cape Town: Stasinfrom.

Laurenson, Helen B. 2005. *Going Up, Going Down: The Rise and Fall of the Department Store*. Auckland: Auckland University Press.

Le Roux, Rochelle. 2010. The Evolution of the Contract of Employment in South Africa. *Industrial Law Journal* 39 (2): 139–165.

Leach, William. 1993. *Land of Desire: Merchants, Power, and the Rise of a New American Culture*. New York: Vintage Books.

Lee, Ching Kwan. 2007. *Against the Law: Labor Protests in China's Rustbelt and Sunbelt*. Berkeley: University of California Press.

Legassick, Martin. 1974. Legislation, Ideology and Economy in Post-1948 South Africa. *Journal of Southern African Studies* 1 (1): 5–35.

———. 1977. Gold, Agriculture, and Secondary Industry in South Africa, 1885–1970: From Periphery to Sub-metropole as a Forced Labour System. In *The Roots of Rural Poverty in Central and Southern Africa*, ed. Robin Palmer and Neil Parsons, 175–200. London: Heinemann.

Leidner, Robin. 1993. *Fast Food, Fast Talk: Service Work and the Routinization of Everyday Life*. Berkeley: University of California Press.

Lerner, Paul. 2015. *The Consuming Temple: Jews, Department Stores, and the Consumer Revolution in Germany, 1880–1940*. Ithaca: Cornell University Press.

Lever, Jeff. 1978. Capital and Labour in South Africa: The Passage of the Industrial Conciliation Act, 1924. In *Essays in South African Labour History*, ed. Eddie Webster, 82–110. Johannesburg: Ravan Press.

Levinson, Marc. 2011. *The Great A&P and the Struggle for Small Business in America*. New York: Hill and Wang.

Lewis, Jon. 1984. *Industrialisation and Trade Union Organisation in South Africa, 1924–55: The Rise and Fall of the South African Trades and Labour Council*. Cambridge: Cambridge University Press.

Lewis, Peter. 2001. Deregulation and Working Hours in the Retail Sector. In *Working Time: Towards a 40-hour Week in South Africa*, ed. Glenn Adler, 11–54. Johannesburg: Naledi.

Lichtenstein, Alex. 2005. Making Apartheid Work: African Trade Unions and the 1953 Native Labour (Settlement of Disputes) Act in South Africa. *Journal of African History* 46 (2): 293–314.

Lichtenstein, Nelson. 2006. *Wal-Mart: The Face of Twenty-first-Century Capitalism*. New York: The New Press.

———. 2009. *The Retail Revolution: How Wal-Mart Created a Brave New World of Business*. New York: Metropolitan Books.

Lindell, Ilda, ed. 2010. *Africa's Informal Workers: Collective Agency, Alliances and Transnational Organizing in Urban Africa*. London: Zed Books.

Lucas, George H., Robert P. Bush, and Larry G. Gresham. 1994. *Retailing*. Boston: Houghton Mifflin.

Luce, Stephanie. 2013. *Global Retail Report*. UNI Global Union. http://blogs.uniglobalunion.org/commerce/wp-content/uploads/sites/7/2013/10/Global-Retail-Report-EN.pdf

Lund, Francie. 2002. Social Security and the Changing Labour Market: Access for Non-standard and Informal Workers in South Africa. *Social Dynamics* 28 (2): 177–206.

Lynch, S., R. Price, A. Pyman, and J. Bailey. 2011. Representing and Organizing Retail Workers: A Comparative Study of the UK and Australia. In *Retail Work*, ed. Irena Grugulis and Ödül Bozkurt, 277–296. Basingstoke: Palgrave Macmillan.

Mabena, Gugulethu. 2017. *Loxion Management: Social Networks and Precarious Economies, a Case Study of Tembisa*. Master's report, University of the Witwatersrand.

Mabin, H.S. 1955. Some Notes on the Commercial Sector of the South African Economy. *South African Journal of Economics* 23 (4): 315–324.

Mabin, Alan. 1991. The Dynamics of Urbanization Since 1960. In *Apartheid City in Transition*, ed. Mark Swilling, Richard Humphries, and Khehla Shubane, 33–47. Cape Town: Oxford University Press.

———. 1992. Comprehensive Segregation: The Origins of the Group Areas Act and Its Planning Apparatuses. *Journal of Southern African Studies* 18 (2): 405–429.

———. 2005. Suburbanisation, Segregation, and Government of Territorial Transformations. *Transformation: Critical Perspectives on Southern Africa* 57: 41–63.

Mabin, Alan, and Dan Smit. 1997. Reconstructing South Africa's Cities? The Making of Urban Planning 1900–2000. *Planning Perspectives* 12 (2): 193–223.
Macdonald, Cameron L., and Carmen Sirianni, eds. 1996. *Working in the Service Society*. Philadelphia: Temple University Press.
Macquarie First South. 2013. *South African Food Retailers*. Report Published by Macquarie First South Securities, Johannesburg.
Madondo, Louis M.M.S. 2001. *Some Aspects of Word-Formation in isiZulu: With Specific Reference to Morphological and Lexical Processes*. PhD thesis, University of Zululand.
Magubane, Zine. 2004. *Bringing the Empire Home: Race, Class, and Gender in Britain and Colonial South Africa*. Chicago: University of Chicago Press.
Malherbe, E.G. 1932. *The Poor White Problem in South Africa: Report of the Carnegie Commission*. III. Educational Report: Education and the Poor White. Stellenbosch: Pro-Ecclesia-Drukkery.
Malinga, Simangaliso S. 2000. *The Development of Informal Settlements in South Africa, with Particular Reference to Informal Settlements around Daveyton on the East Rand, 1970–1999*. PhD thesis, Rand Afrikaans University.
Mamdani, Mahmood. 1996. *Citizen and Subject: Contemporary Africa and the Legacy of Late Colonialism*. Princeton: Princeton University Press.
Marais, Hein. 1998. *South Africa: Limits to Change?* Cape Town: University of Cape Town Press.
Maré, Gerard. 2014. *Declassified*. Johannesburg: Jacana Press.
Maree, Johann, ed. 1987. *The Independent Trade Unions, 1974–1984: Ten Years of the "South African Labour Bulletin"*. Johannesburg: Ravan Press.
Markell, Patchen. 2003. *Bound by Recognition*. Princeton: Princeton University Press.
Marks, Shula. 1994. *Divided Sisterhood: Race, Class and Gender in the South African Nursing Profession*. Johannesburg: University of the Witwatersrand Press.
Martin, William G. 1992. Lesotho: The Creation of the Households. In *Creating and Transforming Households: The Constraints of the World-Economy*, ed. Joan Smith and Immanuel Wallerstein, 231–250. Cambridge: Cambridge University Press.
Martins, J.H. 1988. *Urban Black Attitudes to Shops and Shopping, 1987*. Research Report, 153. Pretoria: Bureau of Market Research, University of South Africa.
Marx, Karl. 1976. *Capital: A Critique of Political Economy; Volume 1. Introduced by Ernest Mandel*. Harmondsworth: Penguin Books.
Mashabela, Harry. 1990. *Mekhukhu: Urban African Cities of the Future*. Johannesburg: South African Institute of Race Relations.
Mashinini, Emma. 1991. *Strikes Have Followed Me All My Life: A South African Autobiography*. New York: Routledge.

Masondo, Themba. 2008. Are Unions Being Casual About Casuals? *South African Labour Bulletin* 32 (1): 12–13.
Massey, Doreen. 1994. *Space, Place, and Gender.* Minneapolis: University of Minnesota Press.
Mather, Charles, and Bridget Kenny. 2005. The Difficulties of 'Emerging' Markets: Cross-Continental Investment in the South African Dairy Sector. In *Cross-Continental Food Chains*, ed. Niels Fold and Bill Pritchard, 179–190. London: Routledge.
May, Julian, ed. 1998. *Poverty and Inequality in South Africa: Report prepared for the Office of the Executive Deputy President and the Inter-Ministerial Committee for Poverty and Inequality.* Durban: Praxis Publishing.
Mbembe, Achille. 2008. Aesthetics of Superfluity. In *Johannesburg: The Elusive Metropolis*, ed. Sarah Nuttall and Achille Mbembe, 37–67. Johannesburg: University of the Witwatersrand Press.
McAllister, P.A. 1980. Work, Homestead and the Shades: The Ritual Interpretation of Labour Migration Among the Gcaleka. In *Black Villagers in an Industrial Society: Anthropological Perspectives on Labour Migration in South Africa*, ed. Philip Mayer, 205–252. Cape Town: Oxford University Press.
McBride, Theresa M. 1978. A Woman's World: Department Stores and the Evolution of Women's Employment, 1870–1920. *French Historical Studies* 10 (4): 664–683.
McClintock, Anne. 1993. Family Feuds: Gender, Nationalism and the Family. *Feminist Review* 44: 61–80.
———. 1995. *Imperial Leather: Race, Gender and Sexuality in the Colonial Contest.* London: Routledge.
McIntyre, Michael, and Heidi J. Nast. 2011. Bio(necro)polis: Marx, Surplus Populations, and the Spatial Dialectics of Reproduction and 'Race'. *Antipode* 43 (5): 1465–1488.
McIvor, David W. 2015. Pressing the Subject: Critical Theory and the Death Drive. *Constellations* 22 (3): 405–419.
McMillon, Doug. 2011. Why Is Wal-Mart knocking on SA's Door? *Business Day* January 26, 2011, p. 9.
McNay, Lois. 2008. *Against Recognition.* Cambridge: Polity.
Milanesio, Natalia. 2013. *Workers Go Shopping in Argentina: The Rise of Popular Consumer Culture.* Albuquerque: University of New Mexico Press.
Milkman, Ruth, Ana Luz Gonzalez, and Victor Narro. 2010. *Wage Theft and Workplace Violations in Los Angeles: The Failure of Employment and Labor Law for Low-Wage Workers.* Los Angeles: Institute for Research on Labor and Employment, University of California.
Miller, Darlene. 2008. 'Retail Renaissance' or Company Rhetoric? The Failed Partnership of a South African Corporation and Local Suppliers in Zambia. *Labour, Capital and Society* 41 (1): 34–55.

Mills, C. Wright. 1956. *White Collar: The American Middle Classes.* New York: Oxford University Press.
Miraftab, Faranak. 2004. Neoliberalism and Casualization of Public Sector Services: The Case of Waste Collection Services in Cape Town, South Africa. *International Journal of Urban and Regional Research* 28 (4): 874–892.
Moodie, T. Dunbar with Vivienne Ndatshe. 1994. *Going for Gold: Men, Mines, and Migration.* Johannesburg: Witwatersrand University Press.
Mooney, Katie. 2006. *"Die eendstert euwel" and Societal Responses to White Youth Subcultural Identities on the Witwatersrand, 1930–1964.* PhD thesis, University of the Witwatersrand.
Moreton, Bethany. 2009. *To Serve God and Wal-Mart: The Making of Christian Free Enterprise.* Cambridge: Harvard University Press.
Morrell, Robert. 1998. Of Boys and Men: Masculinity and Gender in Southern African Studies. *Journal of Southern African Studies* 24 (4): 605–630.
———, ed. 2001. *Changing Men in Southern Africa.* Scottsville: University of Natal Press.
Morrell, Robert, Rachel Jewkes, and Graham Lindegger. 2012. Hegemonic Masculinity/Masculinities in South Africa: Culture, Power, and Gender Politics. *Men and Masculinities* 15 (1): 11–30.
Mosoetsa, Sarah. 2011. *Eating from One Pot: The Dynamics of Survival in Poor South African Households.* Johannesburg: Wits University Press.
Mrozowicki, Adam, Triin Roosalu, and Tatiana Bajuk Senčar. 2013. Precarious Work in the Retail Sector in Estonia, Poland and Slovenia: Trade Union Responses in a Time of Economic Crisis. *Transfer: European Review of Labour and Research* 19 (2): 267–278.
Mupotsa, Danai. 2015. The Promise of Happiness: Desire, Attachment and Freedom in Post/Apartheid South Africa. *Critical Arts* 29 (2): 183–198.
Murray, Colin. 1987. Class, Gender and the Household: The Developmental Cycle in Southern Africa. *Development and Change* 18 (2): 235–249.
Murray, Martin J. 2008. *Taming the Disorderly City: The Spatial Landscape of Johannesburg After Apartheid.* Cape Town: University of Cape Town Press.
Naidoo, Prishani. 2007. Struggles Around the Commodification of Daily Life in South Africa. *Review of African Political Economy* 34 (111): 57–66.
Naidoo, Prishani, and Ahmed Veriava. 2005. Re-membering Movements: Trade Unions and New Social Movements in Neoliberal South Africa. In *From Local Processes to Global Forces.* Centre for Civil Society Research Reports, vol. 1, 27–62. Durban: University of KwaZulu-Natal.
———. 2009. From Local to Global (and Back Again?): Anti-commodification Struggles of the Soweto Electricity Crisis Committee. In *Electric Capitalism: Recolonising Africa on the Power Grid*, ed. David A. McDonald, 321–337. London: Earthscan.
Nash, June C. 1979. *We Eat the Mines and the Mines Eat Us: Dependency and Exploitation in Bolivian Tin Mines.* New York: Colombia University Press.

Ndala, Nathaniel. 2000. *The Erosion of Solidarity: A Case Study of a Union Branch in the Retail Sector on the East Rand, 1988–2000*. Master's thesis, University of the Witwatersrand.

Nelson, Margaret K., and Joan Smith. 1999. *Working Hard and Making Do: Surviving in Small Town America*. Berkeley: University of California Press.

Neves, David, and Andries du Toit. 2012. Money and Sociality in South Africa's Informal Economy. *Africa* 82 (1): 131–149.

———. 2013. Rural Livelihoods in South Africa: Complexity, Vulnerability and Differentiation. *Journal of Agrarian Change* 13 (1): 93–115.

Nieftagodien, Noor. 2017. South Africa's New Left Movements: Challenges and Hopes. In *Southern Resistance in Critical Perspective: The Politics of Protest in South Africa's Contentious Democracy*, ed. Marcel Paret, Carin Runciman, and Luke Sinwell, 171–187. London/New York: Routledge.

Nuttall, Sarah. 2008. Stylizing the self. In *Johannesburg: The Elusive Metropolis*, ed. Sarah Nuttall and Achille Mbembe, 91–118. Johannesburg: University of the Witwatersrand Press.

O'Meara, Dan. 1983. *Volkskapitalisme: Class, Capital and Ideology in the Development of Afrikaner Nationalism, 1934–1948*. Johannesburg: Ravan Press.

Opler, Daniel J. 2007. *For All White-Collar Workers: The Possibilities of Radicalism in New York City's Department Store Unions, 1934–1953*. Columbus: The Ohio State University Press.

Otis, Eileen. 2012. *Markets and Bodies: Women, Service Work, and the Making of Inequality in China*. Stanford: Stanford University Press.

Owens, Rosemary J. 1993. Women, 'Atypical' Work Relationships and the Law. *Melbourne University Law Review* 19 (2): 399–430.

———. 2001. The 'Long-term or Permanent Casual' – An Oxymoron or 'A Well Enough Understood Australianism' in the Law. *Australian Bulletin of Labour* 27 (2): 118–136.

Peck, Jamie. 1996. *Work Place: The Social Regulation of Labor Markets*. New York: Guilford Press.

Perrons, Diane. 2000. Flexible Working and Equal Opportunities in the United Kingdom: A Case Study from Retail. *Environment and Planning A* 32 (10): 1719–1734.

Pettinger, Lynne. 2004. Brand Culture and Branded Workers: Service Work and Aesthetic Labour in Fashion Retail. *Consumption, Markets & Culture* 7 (2): 165–184.

———. 2015. *Work, Consumption and Capitalism*. London: Palgrave.

Phadi, Mosa, and Owen Manda. 2013. The Language of Class: Confusion, Complexity and Difficult Words. In *Class in Soweto*, ed. Peter Alexander, Claire Ceruti, Keke Motseke, Mosa Phadi, and Kim Wale, 190–209. Scottsville: University of KwaZulu-Natal Press.

Pitkin, Hanna F. 1998. *The Attack of the Blob: Hannah Arendt's Concept of the Social*. Chicago: University of Chicago Press.
Planting, Sasha. 2010. Into the Trolley. *Financial Mail*, July 23, pp. 32–35.
Pollak, Hansi P. 1932. *Women in Witwatersrand Industries: An Economic and Sociological Study*. Master's thesis, University of Witwatersrand.
Portelli, Alessandro. 1997. *The Battle of Valle Giulia: The Art of Dialogue in Oral History*. Madison: University of Wisconsin Press.
Posel, Deborah. 1991. *The Making of Apartheid 1948–1961: Conflict and Compromise*. Oxford: Oxford University Press.
———. 2010. Races to Consume: Revisiting South Africa's History of Race, Consumption and the Struggle for Freedom. *Ethnic and Racial Studies* 33 (2): 157–175.
Povinelli, Elizabeth A. 2002. *The Cunning of Recognition: Indigenous Alterities and the Making of Australian Multiculturalism*. Durham: Duke University Press.
———. 2011. *Economies of Abandonment: Social Belonging and Endurance in Late Liberalism*. Durham: Duke University Press.
Preston-Whyte, Eleanor. 1993. Women Who Are Not Married: Fertility, "Illegitimacy," and the Nature of Households and Domestic Groups Among Single African Women in Durban. *South African Journal of Sociology* 24 (3): 63–71.
Price, Robin. 2016. Controlling Routine Front Line Service Workers: An Australian Retail Supermarket Case. *Work, Employment and Society* 30 (6): 915–931.
Qotole, Msokoli. 2000. Workplace Reorganisation: Implications of 'Just-in-Time' Work Methods for Workers and Unions. Paper presented at International Labour Resource and Information Group workshop on Restructuring and Work Re-organisation Challenges, Johannesburg, March 9.
Quayson, Ato. 2014. *Oxford Street, Accra: City Life and the Itineraries of Transnationalism*. Durham: Duke University Press.
Rachleff, Peter. 2001. The Current Crisis of the South African Labour Movement. *Labour/Le Travail* 47: 151–169.
Ramphele, Mamphela, and Emile Boonzaier. 1988. The Position of African Women: Race and Gender in South Africa. In *South African Keywords: The Uses and Abuses of Political Concepts*, ed. Emile Boonzaier and John Sharp, 153–166. Cape Town: David Philip.
Rancière, Jacques. 2010. *Dissensus: On Politics and Aesthetics*. Ed. and trans. Steven Corcoran. London: Continuum.
Randall, Amy E. 2008. *The Soviet Dream World of Retail Trade and Consumption in the 1930s*. Basingstoke: Palgrave Macmillan.

Rathbone, Richard. 2004. West Africa, 1874–1948: Employment Legislation in a Nonsettler Peasant Economy. In *Masters, Servants, and Magistrates in Britain and the Empire, 1562–1955*, ed. Douglas Hay and Paul Craven, 481–497. Chapel Hill: University of North Carolina Press.

Reardon, Thomas, and Julio A. Berdegué. 2002. The Rapid Rise of Supermarkets in Latin America: Challenges and Opportunities for Development. *Development Policy Review* 20 (4): 371–388.

Rees, Robyn. 1997. Irregular Labour in the Manufacturing, Retail and Construction Sectors: A Review of Conditions and Policy. Paper presented to Department of Labor/Community Agency for Social Enquiry/National Labor, Economic and Development Institute/Sociology of Work Programme workshop on Regulating New-Employment Forms, Johannesburg, July 15.

Richter, Linda M., and Robert Morrell, eds. 2006. *Baba: Men and Fatherhood in South Africa*. Cape Town: HSRC Press.

Robins, Steven L. 2008. *From Revolution to Rights in South Africa: Social Movements, NGOs and Popular Politics After Apartheid*. London: James Currey.

Roseberry, William. 1989. *Anthropologies and Histories: Essays in Culture, History, and Political Economy*. New Brunswick: Rutgers University Press.

Rosen, Ellen I. 2005. Life Inside America's Largest Dysfunctional Family: Working for Wal-Mart. *New Labor Forum* 14 (1): 31–39.

Ruan, Nantiya. 2012. What's Left to Remedy Wage Theft? How Arbitration Mandates that Bar Class Actions Impact Low-Wage Workers. *Michigan State Law Review* 2012 (4): 1103–1147.

Saba, Athandiwe. 2017. Inset: Big Business Gets the Biggest Share of Grants. *Sunday Times*, February 12, p. 4.

Salo, Elaine. 2003. Negotiating Gender and Personhood in the New South Africa: Adolescent Women and Gangsters in Manenberg Township on the Cape Flats. *European Journal of Cultural Studies* 6 (3): 345–365.

Salzinger, Leslie. 2003. *Genders in Production: Making Workers in Mexico's Global Factories*. Berkeley: University of California Press.

Samson, Melanie. 2003. *Dumping on Women: Gender and Privatisation of Waste Management*. Cape Town: Municipal Services Project.

Sanders, Lise S. 2006. *Consuming Fantasies: Labor, Leisure, and the London Shopgirl, 1880–1920*. Columbus: Ohio State University Press.

Sapire, Hilary. 1992. Politics and Protest in Shack Settlements of the Pretoria-Witwatersrand-Vereeniging Region, South Africa, 1980–1990. *Journal of Southern African Studies* 18 (3): 670–697.

Satgar, Vishwas, and Roger Southall, eds. 2015. *COSATU in Crisis: The Fragmentation of an African Trade Union Federation*. Sandton: KMM Review Publishing and Friedrich Ebert Stiftung.

Schoenberger, Erica. 1997. *The Cultural Crisis of the Firm*. Oxford: Blackwell.
Scott, Joan Wallach. 1988. *Gender and the Politics of History*. New York/Oxford: Columbia University Press.
———. 1991. The Evidence of Experience. *Critical Inquiry* 17 (4): 773–797.
Scully, Ben. 2016. From the Shop Floor to the Kitchen Table: The Shifting Centre of Precarious Workers' Politics in South Africa. *Review of African Political Economy* 43 (148): 295–311.
Seekings, Jeremy, and Nicoli Nattrass. 2005. *Class, Race and Inequality in South Africa*. Pietermaritzburg: University of KwaZulu-Natal Press.
———. 2015. *Policy, Politics and Poverty in South Africa*. Basingstoke: Palgrave Macmillan.
Segal, Lauren. 1992. The Human Face of Violence: Hostel Dwellers Speak. *Journal of Southern African Studies* 18 (1): 190–231.
Seidman, Gay W. 1994. *Manufacturing Militance: Workers' Movements in Brazil and South Africa, 1970–1985*. Berkeley: University of California Press.
Selwyn, Ben. 2012. *Workers, State and Development in Brazil: Powers of Labour, Chains of Value*. Manchester: Manchester University Press.
Sharp, John S., and Andrew D. Spiegel. 1985. Vulnerability to Impoverishment in South African Rural Areas: The Erosion of Kinship and Neighbourhood as Social Resources. *Africa* 55 (2): 133–152.
Shaw, Gareth, Andrew Alexander, John Benson, and Deborah Hodson. 2000. The Evolving Culture of Retailer Regulation and the Failure of the 'Balfour Bill' in Interwar Britain. *Environment and Planning A* 32 (11): 1977–1989.
Sherman, Rachel. 2007. *Class Acts: Service and Inequality in Luxury Hotels*. Berkeley: University of California Press.
Shevel, Adele. 2017. How being Sceptical Paid Off for Massmart. *Financial Mail*, January 12, p. 43.
"Shoprite strike to go ahead". 2003. *Mail & Guardian*, October 22. http://mg.co.za/article/2003-10-22-shoprite-strike-to-go-ahead. Accessed 23 Jan 2017.
Silver, Beverly J. 2003. *Forces of Labor: Workers' Movements and Globalization since 1870*. Cambridge: Cambridge University Press.
Simmel, Georg. 2004. *The Philosophy of Money*. Trans. Tom Bottomore and David Frisby, ed. D. Frisby, 3rd ed. London: Routledge.
Sitas, Ari. 1983. *African Workers Responses on the East Rand to Changes in the Metal Industry, 1960–1980*. PhD thesis, University of the Witwatersrand.
———. 1996. The New Tribalism: Hostels and Violence. *Journal of Southern African Studies* 22 (2): 235–248.
Skeggs, Beverley. 1997. *Formations of Class and Gender: Becoming Respectable*. London: Sage.

Smith, Derek. 1967. Shopworkers Warned: Absentees May Affect Higher Wage Demand. *Rand Daily Mail*, July 6.

Smith, Vicki. 1996. Employee Involvement, Involved Employees: Participative Work Arrangements in a White-Collar Service Occupation. *Social Problems* 43 (2): 166–179.

Smith, Andrew, and Fiona Elliott. 2012. The Demands and Challenges of Being a Retail Store Manager: 'Handcuffed to the Front Doors'. *Work, Employment and Society* 26 (4): 676–684.

Smith, Joan, and Immanuel M. Wallerstein, eds. 1992. *Creating and Transforming Households: The Constraints of the World Economy*. Cambridge: Cambridge University Press.

Soper, Kate. 2004. Rethinking the 'Good Life': The Consumer as Citizen. *Capitalism Nature Socialism* 15 (3): 111–116.

———. 2007. Re-thinking the 'Good Life': The Citizenship Dimension of Consumer Disaffection with Consumerism. *Journal of Consumer Culture* 7 (2): 205–229.

South African Commercial Catering and Allied Workers Union. 1993. *SACCAWU Activities as Reported by Head Office Units and Regions*. Johannesburg: South African Commercial, Catering and Allied Workers Union.

Southall, Roger. 2016. *The New Black Middle Class in South Africa*. Johannesburg: Jacana.

Standing, Guy. 1999. *Global Labour Flexibility: Seeking Distributive Justice*. Basingstoke: Macmillan.

———. 2008. Economic Insecurity and Global Casualisation: Threat or Promise? *Social Indicators Research* 88 (1): 15–30.

———. 2011. *The Precariat: The New Dangerous Class*. London: Bloomsbury.

———. 2014. *A Precariat Charter: From Denizens to Citizens*. London: Bloomsbury.

Standing, Guy, John Sender, and John Weeks. 1996. *Restructuring the Labour Market: The South African Challenge*. Geneva: ILO.

Stanford, Jim, and Leah F. Vosko. 2004. *Challenging the Market: The Struggle to Regulate Work and Income*. Montreal: McGill-Queen's University Press.

Stanley, Liz. 2013. *Imperialism, Labour and the New Woman: Olive Schreiner's Social Theory*. London/New York: Routledge.

Statistics South Africa. 2015. *Employment, Unemployment, Skills and Economic Growth: An Exploration of Household Survey Evidence on Skills Development and Unemployment Between 1994 and 2014.* http://www.statssa.gov.za/presentation/Stats%20SA%20presentation%20on%20skills%20and%20unemployment_16%20September.pdf

———. 2017. *Statistical Release, P0211: Quarterly Labour Force Survey, Quarter 1: 2017.* Pretoria: Statistics South Africa.

Steedman, Carolyn Kay. 1987. *Landscape for a Good Woman: A Story of Two Lives*. New Brunswick: Rutgers University Press.

Stewart, Kathleen. 1996. *A Space on the Side of the Road: Cultural Poetics in an "Other" America.* Princeton: Princeton University Press.

Swaisland, Cecillie. 1993. *Servants and Gentlewomen to the Golden Land: The Emigration of Single Women from Britain to Southern Africa, 1820–1939.* Oxford: Berg.

Swanson, Maynard W. 1977. The Sanitation Syndrome: Bubonic Plague and Urban Native Policy in the Cape Colony, 1900–1909. *Journal of African History* 18 (3): 387–410.

Swilling, Mark, Richard Humphries, and Khehla Shubane, eds. 1991. *Apartheid City in Transition.* Cape Town: Oxford University Press.

Tannock, Stuart. 2001. *Youth at Work: The Unionized Fast-Food and Grocery Workplace.* Philadelphia: Temple University Press.

Taussig, Michael T. 1980. *The Devil and Commodity Fetishism in South America.* Chapel Hill: University of North Carolina Press.

Taylor, Charles. 1994. The Politics of Recognition. In *Multiculturalism: Examining the Politics of Recognition,* ed. and introduced by Amy Gutmann, 25–74. Princeton: Princeton University Press.

Theron, Jan. 2005. Employment Is Not What It Used to Be: The Nature and Impact of the Restructuring of Work in South Africa. In *Beyond the Apartheid Workplace: Studies in Transition,* ed. Eddie Webster and Karl von Holdt, 293–316. Scottsville: University of KwaZulu-Natal Press.

Theron, Jan, with Shane Godfrey, and Peter Lewis. 2005. *The Rise of Labour Broking and Its Policy Implications.* Cape Town: Institute of Development and Labour Law, University of Cape Town.

Thomas, Stafford. 2011. Shoprite Competition Closes In. *Financial Mail,* February 25.

Thompson, Edward P. 1967. Time, Work-Discipline, and Industrial Capitalism. *Past & Present* 38: 56–97.

———. 1971. The Moral Economy of the English Crowd in the Eighteenth Century. *Past & Present* 50: 76–136.

Tilly, C. 2006. Wal-Mart in Mexico: The Limits of Growth. In *Wal-Mart: The Face of Twenty-First-Century Capitalism,* ed. Nelson Lichenstein, 189–212. New York: The New Press.

Tilly, Chris, and José L.A. Galván. 2006. Lousy Jobs, Invisible Unions: The Mexican Retail Sector in the Age of Globalization. *International Labor and Working-Class History* 70: 61–85.

Tolich, Martin B. 1993. Alienating and Liberating Emotions at Work: Supermarket Clerks' Performance of Customer Service. *Journal of Contemporary Ethnography* 22 (3): 361–381.

Tomlins, Christopher L. 1993. *Law, Labor, and Ideology in the Early American Republic.* Cambridge: Cambridge University Press.

Tomlinson, Richard, and Pauline Larsen. 2003. The Race, Class and Space of Shopping. In *Emerging Johannesburg: Perspectives on the Postapartheid City*, ed. Richard Tomlinson, Robert A. Beauregard, Lindsay Bremner, and Xolela Mangcu, 43–55. London/New York: Routledge.

Townsend, Nicholas W. 2000. Male Fertility as a Lifetime of Relationships: Contextualizing Men's Biological Reproduction in Botswana. In *Fertility and the Male Life-Cycle in the Era of Fertility Decline*, ed. Caroline Bledsoe, Susana Lerner, and Jane I. Guyer, 343–364. Oxford: Oxford University Press.

Trade Union Research Project. 1992. Casualisation in the Retail Trade. Paper presented at South African Commercial, Catering and Allied Workers Union Bargaining Conference, April 10.

Tshoaedi, Malehoko. 2012. Women in the Forefront of Workplace Struggles in South Africa: From Invisibility to Mobilization. *Labour, Capital and Society* 45 (2): 58–83.

"Union Threatens to Intensify Shoprite Strike". 2003. *Mail & Guardian*, October 24. http://mg.co.za/article/2003-10-24-union-threatens-to-intensify-shoprite-strike. Accessed 23 Jan 2017.

Unterhalter, Elaine. 1987. *Forced Removal: The Division, Segregation and Control of the People of South Africa*. London: International Defence and Aid Fund.

Vally, Natasha T. 2016. Insecurity in South African Social Security: An Examination of Social Grant Deductions, Cancellations, and Waiting. *Journal of Southern African Studies* 42 (5): 965–982.

———. 2017. *South African Social Assistance and the 2012 Privatised National Payment System: An Examination of Insecurities and Technopolitics in Social Grant Administration and Payment*. PhD thesis, University of the Witwatersrand.

Vally, Salim. n.d. *Job Flexibility*. Unpublished MS. South African Commercial, Catering and Allied Workers Union.

Valodia, Imraan. 2001. Economic Policy and Women's Informal Work in South Africa. *Development and Change* 32 (5): 871–892.

Van der Hijden, T., and N. Vink. 2013. Good for Whom? Supermarkets and Small Farmers in South Africa – A Critical Review of Current Approaches to Increasing Access to Modern Markets. *Agrekon* 52 (1): 68–86.

Van der Walt, Sunette. 1982. *Work Motives of Women in the Retail Business*. Pretoria: Human Sciences Research Council.

Van Staden, Cobus. 2015. Chewing on Japan: Consumption, Diplomacy and Kenny Kunene's Nyotaimori Scandal. *Critical Arts* 29 (2): 107–125.

Veriava, Ahmed. 2013. *The South African Diagram: The Governmental Machine and the Struggles of the Poor*. PhD thesis, University of the Witwatersrand.

Vincent, Louise. 2000. Bread and Honour: White Working Class Women and Afrikaner Nationalism in the 1930s. *Journal of Southern African Studies* 26 (1): 61–78.

Von Holdt, Karl. 2003. *Transition from Below: Forging Trade Unionism and Workplace Change in South Africa*. Pietermaritzburg: University of Natal Press.
Von Schnitzler, Antina. 2008. Citizenship Prepaid: Water, Calculability, and Techno-Politics in South Africa. *Journal of Southern African Studies* 34 (4): 899–917.
———. 2016. *Democracy's Infrastructure: Techno-Politics and Citizenship After Apartheid*. Princeton: Princeton University Press.
Vosko, Leah F. 2000. *Temporary Work: The Gendered Rise of a Precarious Employment Relationship*. Toronto: University of Toronto Press.
Vosko, Leah F., Martha MacDonald, and Iain Campbell, eds. 2009. *Gender and the Contours of Precarious Employment*. London: Routledge.
Waetjen, Thembisa. 2004. *Workers and Warriors: Masculinity and the Struggle for Nation in South Africa*. Urbana: University of Illinois Press.
Walker, Cherryl, ed. 1990. *Women and Gender in Southern Africa to 1945*. Cape Town: David Philip.
———. 1995. Conceptualising Motherhood in Twentieth Century South Africa. *Journal of Southern African Studies* 21 (3): 417–437.
Walker, Liz. 2001. 'Conservative Pioneers': The Formation of the South African Society of Medical Women. *Social History of Medicine* 14 (3): 483–505.
Weatherspoon, Dave D., and Thomas Reardon. 2003. The Rise of Supermarkets in Africa: Implications for Agrifood Systems and the Rural Poor. *Development Policy Review* 21 (3): 333–355.
Webster, Edward. 1985. *Cast in a Racial Mould: Labour Process and Trade Unionism in the Foundries*. Johannesburg: Ravan Press.
Webster, Eddie, and Karl von Holdt, eds. 2005. *Beyond the Apartheid Workplace*. Scottsville: University of KwaZulu-Natal Press.
Webster, Edward, Robert Lambert, and Andries Bezuidenhout. 2008. *Grounding Globalization: Labour in the Age of Insecurity*. Oxford: Blackwell.
Weeks, Kathi. 2011. *The Problem with Work: Feminism, Marxism, Antiwork Politics, and Postwork Imaginaries*. Durham: Duke University Press.
Wharton, Amy. 1996. Service with a Smile: Understanding the Consequences of Emotional Labor. In *Working in the Service Society*, ed. Cameron L. Macdonald and Carmen Sirianni, 91–112. Philadelphia: Temple University Press.
White, Hylton. 2004. Ritual Haunts: The Timing of Estrangement in a Post-Apartheid Countryside. In *Producing African Futures: Ritual and Reproduction in a Neoliberal Age*, ed. Brad Weiss, 141–166. Leiden: Brill.
———. 2010. Outside the Dwelling of Culture: Estrangement and Difference in Postcolonial Zululand. *Anthropological Quarterly* 83 (3): 497–518.
———. 2012. A Post-Fordist Ethnicity: Insecurity, Authority, and Identity in South Africa. *Anthropological Quarterly* 85 (2): 397–427.
———. 2013a. In the Shadow of Time. *Journal of the Royal Anthropological Institute*, no. 19: 256–257.

———. 2013b. Spirit and Society: In Defence of a Critical Anthropology of Religious Life. *Anthropology Southern Africa* 36 (3&4): 139–145.
Wholesale & Retail Trade Sector Education and Training Authority. 2001. *Wholesale and Retail Trade (W&R) Sector Skills Plan*. Pretoria: Wholesale and Retail Trade Sector Education and Training Authority.
Williams, Raymond. 1973. *The Country and the City*. New York: Oxford University Press.
———. 1977. *Marxism and Literature*. Oxford: Oxford University Press.
Willoughby-Herard, Tiffany. 2015. *Waste of a White Skin: The Carnegie Corporation and the Racial Logic of White Vulnerability*. Berkeley: University of California Press.
Wolpe, Harold. 1972. Capitalism and Cheap Labour-Power in South Africa: From Segregation to Apartheid. *Economy and Society* 1 (4): 425–456.
Wright, Erik Olin. 2000. Working-Class Power, Capitalist-Class Interests, and Class Compromise. *American Journal of Sociology* 105 (4): 957–1002.
Wrigley, Neil. 1996. Sunk Costs and Corporate Restructuring: British Food Retailing and the Property Crisis. In *Retailing, Consumption and Capital: Towards the New Retail Geography*, ed. Neil Wrigley and Michelle Lowe, 116–136. Harlow: Longman.
———. 2000. The Globalization of Retail Capital: Themes for Economic Geography. In *The Oxford Handbook of Economic Geography*, ed. Gordon L. Clark, Meric S. Gertler, Maryann P. Feldmann, and Kate Williams, 292–314. Oxford: Oxford University Press.
Wrigley, Neil, and Michelle Lowe, eds. 1996. *Retailing, Consumption and Capital: Towards the New Retail Geography*. Harlow: Longman.
———. 2002. *Reading Retail: A Geographical Perspective on Retailing and Consumption Spaces*. London/New York: Routledge.
Wrigley, Neil, Neil M. Coe, and Andrew Currah. 2005. Globalizing Retail: Conceptualizing the Distribution-Based Transnational Corporation (TNC). *Progress in Human Geography* 29 (4): 437–457.
Young, Louise. 1999. Marketing the Modern: Department Stores, Consumer Culture, and the New Middle Class in Interwar Japan. *International Labor and Working-Class History* 55: 52–70.
Yudelman, David. 1983. *The Emergence of Modern South Africa: State, Capital, and the Incorporation of Organized Labor on the South African Gold Fields, 1902–1939*. Westport: Greenwood Press.
Yuval-Davis, Nira, and Floya Anthias, eds. 1989. *Woman-Nation-State*. Basingstoke: Macmillan.
Zelizer, Viviana A.R. 1994. *Social Meaning of Money: Pin Money, Paychecks, Poor Relief and Other Currencies*. Princeton: Princeton University Press.
Zhang, Lu. 2015. *Inside China's Automobile Factories: The Politics of Labor and Worker Resistance*. Cambridge: Cambridge University Press.

Ziskind, Minna P. 2003. Labor Conflict in the Suburbs: Organizing Retail in Metropolitan New York, 1954–1958. *International Labor and Working-Class History* 64: 55–73.

Zola, Émile. [1883] 1991. *The Ladies Paradise*. Berkeley: University of California Press.

Zukin, Sharon, and Jennifer Smith Maguire. 2004. Consumers and Consumption. *Annual Review of Sociology* 30: 173–197.

Index[1]

A
Abasebenzi, 144, 145, 158, 229
  divided, 18, 154, 158, 172, 179
  emergence of, 15, 63, 71–73
  meaning of the word, 1, 16, 24n13, 24n15
  as political subject, 3, 6, 12, 15–19, 21, 61–84, 91, 119, 133, 145, 154, 158, 179, 187, 204, 211, 219, 223–228, 230
Absenteeism, 44, 57n63
Ackerman, Raymond, 31, 53n10, 121, 122
Ackermans, 31
Adult status, 91, 158, 160, 187, 204
Advertising, 31, 123, 124
Affective labour, 6, 7, 50
African Commercial and Distributive Workers Union (ACDWU), 55n32, 55n37
African National Congress (ANC), 5, 14, 24n13, 79, 150n95, 158, 193, 195, 206n28
ANC, *see* African National Congress
Anstey's, 29, 30, 42
Arendt, Hannah, 186, 203, 204n2
Argentina, 7, 31, 210
Articulation, 9, 12–15, 27, 36, 40, 42, 51, 52n5, 61–63, 70, 91, 101, 145, 154, 155, 210, 211, 227, 228
Australia, 7, 31, 43, 54n20, 79, 94, 95, 102, 107, 115n24
  casual work, 107, 115n24

B
Bantu Labour Act of 1964, 59n88
Bantu Laws Amendment Act of 1970, 50, 59n89, 87n43
Barchiesi, Franco, 13–14, 204n7

[1] Note: Page numbers followed by 'n' refer to notes.

Bargaining council, 183n77, 235n55
Bargaining power, 4, 5
Basic Conditions of Employment Act of 1997, 109, 117n58, 182n60
Bazaar trading, 31
Benjamin, Walter, 6
Berlant, Lauren, 62
Black
  consumers, 9, 18, 34, 54n18, 61, 68, 83, 146n15, 210, 223, 228
  managers, 129, 221
  men, 36, 40, 45, 55n37, 80, 95, 228
  service workers, 61, 62, 64, 76, 221 (*see also* Black women; Black workers)
Black Consciousness Movement, 76, 77
Black women,
  and discrimination, 46, 64–73
  and full-time work, 100–101, 220
  and respectability, 17, 46, 101
  as service workers, 47–48, 58n69, 100, 128, 226
  and unsocial working hours, 2, 105, 220
  See also Black, as service workers; Black workers; Motherhood; "Praxis of providing"; Skill; Trade unions; Wage(s)
Black workers
  and collective organization, 61–62, 74, 77–78, 88n5
  and discrimination against, 10, 73, 134–144
  See also Commercial Catering and Allied Workers Union of South Africa (CCAWUSA); Employee; Labour law; National Union of Commercial and Allied Workers (NUCAW); "Servant/native/labourer"; South African Commercial, Catering and Allied Workers Union (SACCAWU); Trade unions

Black working class
  access to consumer markets, 83, 209, 221
  See also Housing
Branch managers, 164
Brazil, 212, 232n6
Britain, 31, 53n9, 53n12, 54n20, 79, 94, 124
Bulk labour supply, 11, 12, 19, 94, 140, 154, 177, 210, 219–223, 227, 229
Buyer, 40, 126, 128, 143

C
Cambridge Food, 210, 215
  contract workers, 219, 226
  customer service, 218
  and labour broking, 219
  location, 215–217
  permanent workers, 219
  See also Massmart Holdings
Canada, 94
Cashiers, 1, 2, 44, 45, 65, 66, 69, 83, 103, 111, 125, 126, 134, 136–138, 140, 170, 172, 177, 216, 218–224, 226
Casual employment, 19
  increase in, 17, 107
  legal definitions, 11, 91, 101, 107
  subordinate status, 103, 111, 169
  temporary status, 101, 102
  and young people, 101, 102, 104
  See also Extended trading hours
Casual loading, 102, 115n28
Casual workers, 11, 18, 135, 144, 156, 222
  as adults, 158, 160, 161
  amacasual, 106, 132, 158
  as exploited labour, 168–172
  extra help, 103, 105
  pay and benefits, 101, 107, 176

and permanent workers, 106, 154, 156, 158, 160, 161, 168–172, 176
and promotion, 159, 171, 172
as providers, 161, 196, 201, 203
relations with supervisors, 140
as strike breakers, 106
students, 102, 158
and uniforms, 169, 176
and unions, 101–103, 106, 107, 109, 160, 168, 172, 174, 176
and white casuals, 171, 172
working hours, 102, 104, 105, 171
See also Casual employment; Labour law
CCMA, *see* Commission for Conciliation, Mediation and Arbitration (CCMA)
Chain stores, 8, 31, 74, 83
Chanock, Martin, 108
Checkers, 70, 74, 125
Children as future, 21, 186, 198, 200, 202
Child support grants, 190, 205n19
Chile, 212
China, 9, 54n20, 210, 212, 231n6, 232n8
Class, 17, 52n4, 61, 62, 75, 77, 78, 91, 120, 145, 155, 166, 215, 224
and language differences, 41
See also Black working class; Gender; Race; White working class
Cleaning stores and counters, 45
Clerical jobs, 44, 47, 72
Coloured women, 17, 46–49, 54n26, 55n32, 63–72, 100
Comaroff, Jean, 202, 205n18
Comaroff, John L., 202, 205n18
Commercial Catering and Allied Workers Union of South Africa (CCAWUSA), 77, 83, 100, 103
1986–1987 strike, 61, 79, 82

membership, 62, 80, 85n3, 88n55, 108
and NUDW, 64, 74, 78–80, 84
organization, 71, 74, 78, 79, 87n40
organizing black workers, 62, 71, 74, 77, 78
shop stewards, 79, 83
See also Mashinini, Emma; OK Bazaars; Trade unions
Commission for Conciliation, Mediation and Arbitration (CCMA), 173, 224, 235n56
Competition Tribunal, 217, 231n2
Congress of South African Trade Unions (COSATU), 62, 77, 85n1, 85n3, 88n55, 225
Consumer(s)
credit, 47, 214
culture, 7, 31
"lifestyle," 119, 121, 123
markets, 83, 127, 209, 210, 214, 230
sales, 83, 214
spending, 9, 215
and white "housewife," 8, 124
working-class, 18, 54n16, 215, 221, 223
Consumption
and cosmopolitanism, 30, 31, 47, 50–51
and gender, 6, 7, 17, 19, 51
and nation, 6–9, 51, 119, 144, 204, 227
and race, 6, 15, 19, 47, 215
and shift in patterns, 47, 190
and status, 215
See also Malls
Contract workers, 135, 220
cashiers, 1, 2, 220, 222–224, 226
and casual workers, 91, 120, 135, 156, 158, 167, 168, 183n84, 220

274   INDEX

Contract workers (*cont.*)
  grievances, 142, 226
  and labour brokers, 108, 137, 141, 163–166, 177, 183n84, 219, 223, 224, 228
  merchandisers, amamerchandisers, 141–144, 150n94, 153, 154, 156, 162, 163, 165–167, 175, 176, 178, 188, 193–195, 222
  as outsiders, 135–145, 154, 167, 223
  pay and benefits, 220
  and permanent workers, 1, 156, 158, 162, 166–167, 220, 222
  as providers, 197, 199, 203
  and security, 142, 143, 163
  as skilled men, 162–167
  underpayment of wages, 221
  and unions, 163, 174, 176, 225
  and working hours, 220
  See also Labour law
Countertops, 31, 37
"Culture of threat," 127–131, 144
Customer service, 35, 37, 72, 134, 135, 137–140, 145, 162, 218

D
Daveyton, 185, 191, 193–195, 206n29
Debt, 9, 207n48, 215, 218
Department store, 7, 8, 29–31, 33, 35, 37, 39, 40, 54n18, 64
Deskilling, 223
  and self-service, 127, 138, 228
  and task fragmentation, 43, 228
  and work intensification, 44, 99
  See also Skill
Developing economies, 211, 212, 214
Display, 31, 43, 53n9, 80, 123, 125, 126, 181n40
Distribution, 6, 8, 32, 53n12, 122, 131, 210–213, 217, 230, 232n17
  centre, 212

Distributive worker, 36, 40, 54n26, 55n32, 56n37, 95, 97, 137, 166, 228
Domestic workers, 50, 55n31, 66, 109, 114n10, 148n57

E
Education, 17, 35, 47, 54n22, 63, 75, 77, 79, 132, 171, 191, 200, 201, 215, 221
Eloff Street, 29, 30, 69
Employee, 9–12, 19
  divisions and splits in, 10, 12, 91–112
  and employment contract, 10, 11, 18, 92, 94, 109, 159, 177, 223, 224, 229
  full-time, permanent as standard bearer, 91, 106, 109, 111, 177, 226
  legal definition, 91, 92, 107–109
  and liberal subject, 10, 12, 94, 210, 223, 224
  and trade union rights, 10, 108
  unification of, 11, 108, 109
  See also Casual employment; Contract workers, and labour brokers; Labour law; "Servant/native/labourer"
Endurance, 13, 22, 179, 203, 211
Extended trading hours, 103, 105

F
Ferguson, James, 205n18
Flexible working time, 110, 220, 226
Flexitime contracts, 177, 226
Food retailing, 210, 212, 232n9
France, 53n9, 54n20, 121, 145n3, 145n4

Full-time, 10, 11, 18, 20, 35, 75, 91, 92, 96, 100, 104–106, 110, 171, 177, 188, 191, 195, 220, 226, 228
See also Working time

G

Game, 30, 210, 216, 231n1, 231n3
  See also Massmart Holdings
Garment workers, 35, 52n4, 88n44
GDP, see Gross domestic product
Gender, 61, 70, 91, 120, 124, 145, 154, 155, 161, 178, 187, 198, 203
  and class difference, 41
  and divisions of household labour, 198, 199
  and domesticity, 38, 46, 66, 99, 124
  and femininity, 27, 41, 42, 51, 63, 114n10
  See also Class; Masculinity; Motherhood; "Praxis of providing"; Race; White women
General worker, 11, 12, 17, 18, 21, 44–45, 65, 80, 97, 226, 228
Germany, 7, 54n20
Global
  investment, 18, 210–212
  retail capital, 16, 154, 211
  retailing, 211
  sourcing of commodities, 213, 217
  South, 4, 5, 229
Go-slows, 21, 153–179
Greatermans, 99
Gross domestic product (GDP), 211
Group Areas Act of 1950, 53n12

H

Hall, Stuart, 14, 15, 23n12, 29, 40, 52n5, 62, 84, 133
Hart, Gillian, 15
Hochschild, Arlie, 7

Households, 2, 4, 18, 21, 23n7, 28, 40, 47, 75, 76, 101, 187, 190–192, 195–200, 202, 203, 205n20, 207n41, 207n42, 207n47, 209, 215
Housework, 199
Housing, 192
  disputes among relatives, 194
  informal settlements, 193, 195
  ownership, 193
  RDP houses, 195
  segregation, 75, 206n26
  shortage in urban areas, 193, 194
Hunter, Mark, 198, 200, 208n60
Hyperama, 1, 61, 71, 119, 124
  casual workers, 136, 137, 139, 140, 168, 172
  contract workers, 137, 142, 162, 163
  format, 123
  permanent workers, 132, 155, 172
  shop stewards, 81, 134, 136
  training standards, 128
  See also Hypermarkets
Hypermarkets, 119, 123
  and branding, 124
  and bulk buying, 121, 122
  decentralized organizational model, 121, 126
  economies of scale, 119, 122, 144
  format, 8, 121, 122
  location and size, 121, 122
  marketing, 121–124
  stock control, 125
  See also Hyperama; Pick n Pay; Self-service
"Hypers", see Hypermarkets

I

India, 232n8
Indian women, 17, 46, 48, 49, 54n26, 55n32, 63–71, 74, 140, 173

Industrial
 council, 92, 94, 95, 113n3
 dispute, 92
Industrial Conciliation Act of 1924, 95
Informal settlements, 193, 195, 196, 206n26
Isisebenzi, 16, 24n14

J
Job
 description, 66, 162, 222
 grading, 40, 43, 45, 64, 66
 hierarchies, 40, 45, 66
 reservation, 48, 49, 58n83, 64
Johannesburg
 architecture, 30
 area employment data, 219
 city centre, 30, 31, 215
 Indian and Chinese businesses, 30
 labour market, 219
 modernity, 8, 30
 region, 17, 19, 20, 43, 64, 75, 76, 78, 190, 216
 shopping district, 30, 34
 See also Department store
John Orr's, 29, 32, 34, 40, 41, 65, 67, 70

K
Kennedy, Duncan, 92, 112

L
Labour
 brokers, 17, 18, 21, 108, 110, 111, 141, 163–166, 177, 178, 183n84, 219–221, 223–226, 228, 235n56
 broking, 11, 12, 19, 92, 108–112, 219–224, 226
 market, 3, 4, 8, 9, 17, 22n5, 46–48, 76, 92, 96, 120, 179, 190, 192, 196, 198, 200, 219, 229
 process, 11, 17, 19, 40, 43, 63, 121, 127, 138, 179
 relations, 5, 11, 12, 14–17, 19, 51, 92, 96, 144, 155, 179n3, 210, 223, 226, 229, 230
 rights, 9–11, 17, 18, 20, 39, 91, 93, 111, 162, 223, 225
Labour Appeal Court, 225, 235n56
Labour Court, 227, 235n56
Labour law, 3, 9
 and "civilized labour," 95
 and colonial connections, 93
 and employment contract, 11, 18
 and industrial relations regime, 11, 92
 joint and several liability, 110
 masters and servants laws, 93, 94
 and "pass bearing native," 93
 post-apartheid reform, 11, 109, 110, 177, 179, 225
 and trade union registration, 88n55, 108, 109, 117n57
 See also Casual employment; Employee; Part-time employment; Sectoral determination; "Servant/native/labourer"; Temporary employment service or agency; Trade unions; Wage(s); Wage determination
Labour Relations Act of 1995, 109, 110, 224
Lee, Ching Kwan, 9
Liaison committees, 87n43
Liberalism, 10, 13
Liberal subject, 9, 10, 12, 15, 94, 223, 224

INDEX 277

M
Mall committees, 177
Malls
  and consumption, 214, 215
  corporate retail anchors, 214
  development, Latin America, 214
  Eastgate Mall, 232n10
  and lease exclusivity clauses, 231n3
  and property developers, 232n12
  and property stock portfolios, 232n12
  and suburbanization, 65, 214
Management, 145
  branch managers, 68, 129, 156, 157, 164, 169, 172, 222, 226
  centralization, 130, 131, 140, 148n48, 157
  and disciplinary hearings, 130, 136, 174
  line managers, 69, 100, 129, 131
  and merchandising, 43, 122, 125, 165
  and personnel, 43, 130, 140, 174
  professionalization, 43, 45
  regional managers, 140, 156, 168, 174
  and security, 135, 137, 142, 163, 174
  and surveillance, 135–137 (*see also* Technology)
  training, 43, 126
Manual labour, 12, 45, 72, 92, 166, 167
Market, 6–9, 21, 27, 50, 53n12, 63, 83, 120, 123, 124, 189, 210–219, 230
Masculinity, 142, 178, 187, 198–200, 207n49
Mashinini, Emma, 74, 78, 79, 88n44
  See also Commercial Catering and Allied Workers Union South Africa (CCAWUSA)

Massmart Holdings, 216
  brands, 210, 215, 231n1
  and consumers, 21, 218
  divisions, 210
  and Wal-Mart, 2, 209, 210, 212, 217, 218, 224, 228
  See also Cambridge Food; Game
Maternity rights, 73, 80
McClintock, Anne, 28
Meaning of work, 21, 185–204, 229
Merchandisers, 137
  and customer service, 162
  go-slows, 153, 162, 178
  job descriptions, 162, 222
  and product knowledge, 162, 164, 166, 181n33
  and product representatives, 141, 165
  and stock-keeping, 164, 166
  and store committees, 163
  See also Contract workers, and labour brokers
Merchant, 31, 32, 53n8, 145n4, 166, 181n33
Mexico, 210, 212
Migrant workers, 30, 113n4, 202
Mills, C. Wright, 6, 7
Money, 35, 43, 67, 74, 76, 123, 159, 168–172, 189, 192, 196, 200, 201, 215, 217
"Moral economy," 131–135, 148n58, 149n59, 149n60
Motherhood, 27, 52n4, 98–101, 161, 187, 198, 200, 208n56
Municipal services, 191, 193

N
Nation, 3, 6–9, 15, 16, 21, 27–51, 83, 119–121, 154, 209–219, 227
National belonging, 9, 15, 34, 40, 46, 119, 127, 133, 144, 154, 179, 210, 215, 227

278 INDEX

National Economic Development and Labour Council, 225
Nationalism, 27, 52n2, 55n31
National Party, 29, 39, 47–50, 52n4, 63, 96, 112, 113n7
National Union of Commercial and Allied Workers (NUCAW), 66, 67, 70, 73, 78, 86n19, 117n48
National Union of Distributive Workers (NUDW), 38, 39, 44, 45, 47, 48, 55n32, 64–69, 71, 74, 78, 86n19, 87n43, 95, 100, 102–105, 113n7
   1943 strike, 38, 55n37, 95
   and B branches, 55n32, 86n19
   and black membership, 55n32
   and CCAWUSA, 64, 74, 78
   formation, 38
   and non-standard shifts, 99, 104
   and occupational grading, 39, 80, 98
   Tribunal Agreement, 39, 95
   and wage determinations, 64, 74, 95, 99
   See also Extended trading hours
Native Affairs Department, 93
New Zealand, 31
Non-standard employment, 3, 110

O
Occupational
   categories by gender and race, 47, 172, 173
   divisions, 42, 44, 45, 80, 172, 222
OK Bazaars, 30, 32, 34, 35, 37, 43, 61, 65–68, 71, 79, 121, 125
   1986–1987 strike, 81, 82, 106, 127
   executive training, 43
   and flexitime shifts, 105
   recognition of strike against, 38
   See also Commercial Catering and Allied Workers Union of South Africa (CCAWUSA); Hyperama

Overtime, 39, 69, 99, 105, 110, 131
   See also Working time

P
Packer
   bag, 1, 103, 136, 137, 140, 177, 196, 219
   shelf, 71, 166, 222
Pages, 100
Part-time employment, 98, 99, 107
   and black women, 100
   and domesticity, 99
   legal definitions, 91, 98, 107, 177
   and white women, 100, 103, 111
   See also Labour law; Motherhood; Working time
Permanent workers, 2, 18, 91, 120, 178, 188, 195
   as adults, 158–161
   amapermanents, 106, 154, 158
   and casual workers, 106, 131, 140, 153, 154, 156, 158–161, 168–170, 172, 176, 177, 187
   collective actions, 156, 159
   grievances, 73, 132, 158
   pay and benefits, 132, 220
   as providers, 161, 196, 201, 203
   relations with managers, 157
   and working hours, 156, 220
   See also Labour law; Working time
Personhood, 15, 160, 186, 189, 190, 204, 205n18, 228
Pick n Pay, 65, 74, 121–124, 126, 231n3
Political subject, 3, 10, 12, 15, 18, 20, 61–84, 91, 92, 107, 111, 112, 119, 133, 145, 155, 158, 179, 187, 204, 211, 219, 223–230

Political subjectivity, 6, 13–22, 61, 79, 81, 84, 112, 210, 231
Posel, Deborah, 8
Povinelli, Elizabeth, 13, 202
"Praxis of providing," 21, 187, 190–198, 202, 203, 209
Precarious employment, 2
Promotions, 72, 129, 171, 172, 221

R
Race, 6, 13–17, 19, 22n1, 27, 36, 40, 47, 48, 49, 51, 61–64, 66, 67, 70, 74, 75, 77, 78, 91, 111, 112, 120, 124, 134, 145, 154, 155, 160, 172–178, 215, 221, 224, 229
See also Black; Black women; Black workers; Class; Gender; White; White women; White workers
Racism
and customers, 138, 218
and managers, supervisors, 66
and trade unions, 66
See also Promotions
Rancière, Jacques, 15, 84
Regulation of Monopolistic Conditions Act of 1955, 32, 53n12
Retail capital
Afrikaner, 32, 53n12
corporate concentration, 21, 43, 53n13, 122, 127, 212
corporate expansion, 21, 42
foreign ownership of South African firms, 214
global expansion, 21, 211
Retail sector, 19
employment, 75, 95, 110, 111, 211
and state, 211, 215, 217
See also Gross domestic product (GDP)

Retail stores
expansion, 42
formalization, 212
innovations, 31, 43, 212
marketing, 7
and modernity, 7, 125
and property developments, 43
restructuring, 9, 120, 128, 158
supermarkets, 43, 57n56, 123
trade associations, 32
trading space, 31, 57n56, 145n1, 145n2, 211
See also Chain stores; Distribution; Extended trading hours; Malls; Supply chain management; Technology
Roseberry, William, 133, 149n60
Russia, 7, 54n20, 212

S
Sales House, 34
Sectoral determination, 109–111, 176, 177, 235n55
Security, 111
strip-searches, 69, 172, 173, 174
and workers, 67, 135, 136, 137, 142, 143, 155, 163
See also Management; Shoplifting; Theft
Self-service, 8, 43, 119, 126, 138, 144, 162, 228
Separate development, 48, 59n84, 64
"Servant/native/labourer," 10, 19, 91, 97, 111, 112, 144, 223, 229
Service
work, 6, 7, 17, 23n8, 37, 45, 46, 50, 63–71, 121, 219, 222, 224, 228
workers, 2, 7, 8, 11, 47, 61, 64, 65, 75, 76, 80, 100, 137, 162, 188, 189, 210, 221, 222, 228

Sexual harassment, 46, 69, 227
Shops and Offices Act of 1939, 58n80, 103
  and separate facilities, 46, 58n80, 71
  and trading hours, 103
Shop assistants, 27, 47, 80, 125, 126, 167, 228
Shoplifting, 67, 129
Shoprite, 127, 212, 216
  and casual workers, 131, 168, 172, 176
  and labour brokers, 141, 177
  and OK Bazaars, 128
  and shrinkage, 131
  strike (2003), 172, 176
  See also Retail stores; Supply chain management
Shop stewards, 79, 136, 177
  in-store grievances, 156, 169, 225
  role, 134, 157, 168, 174, 225
  See also Trade unions
Shrinkage, 131, 135, 136
Simmel, Georg, 6–7
Sit-ins, 153, 156, 168, 178
"Sitting," 70, 134, 167, 185–190
  meaning, 21, 186, 189
  See also Unemployment
Skill, 15, 31, 63, 92, 154, 219
  and education
  and gender, 28, 37, 38, 43, 63, 111, 112, 181n33
  occupational, 45, 95
  and product knowledge, 38, 162, 164, 166, 228
  professional, 31, 164
  and race, 21, 63, 91, 111, 112
  and sales, 37, 38, 165–167
  and service, 137, 221
  unskilled, 93–95, 97, 109, 166
    (*see also* Labour law; Manual labour)

See also Deskilling; Johannesburg, labour market; Self-service
"Social site," 3, 14, 120, 223, 230
Social welfare, 190, 197, 232n14
South African Commercial, Catering and Allied Workers Union (SACCAWU), 5, 103, 106, 109, 132, 157, 163, 173, 174, 176, 177, 225, 226
  and casual shop stewards, 177
  and casual workers, 172, 176, 177
  and flexitime agreements, 106, 107
  strike in 2003, 172
  See also Commercial Catering and Allied Workers Union of South Africa (CCAWUSA); Hyperama; Mall committees
South Korea, 212
Steedman, Carolyn, 28
Steyn Commission, 53n12
Strategic leverage, 5
Strikes, 157
  joint actions, 172
  wildcat actions, 21, 153, 157, 174
  See also Commercial Catering and Allied Workers Union of South Africa (CCAWUSA); National Union of Distributive Workers (NUDW); South African Commercial, Catering and Allied Workers Union (SACCAWU)
Stuttafords, 29, 34, 35
Subjectification, 6, 14, 120, 133, 135–145
Subjectivation, 15, 16
"Subjects-in-struggle," 3, 13–22, 62, 84, 229
Supermarkets, *see* Retail stores
Supervisors, 37, 38, 40, 45, 67, 70, 72, 73, 80, 128, 140, 168, 220, 221, 224

INDEX

Supply chain management, 154, 165, 212
Surveillance, 120, 127, 135, 137, 145
  See also Technology

T

Tea rooms, 30, 34, 44
Technology
  bar coding, 135, 181n43, 213
  biometric clocking, 220
  cashier-less till points, 230, 235n60
  closed circuit television (CCTV), 135, 136
  logistics, 120
  point-of-sale, 2, 125, 135, 213, 221
  smart cards, 215, 216, 220
  stock control, 125
Temporary employment service or agency, 1, 11, 110, 111, 117n59, 223, 225, 233n26, 235n56
Temporary labour, 109, 111, 115n24
Theft, 68, 81, 131, 135–137, 188
  See also Shoplifting; Shrinkage
Township, 22n1, 57n57, 67, 69, 76, 167, 180n18, 188–190, 193, 195, 205n9, 210, 211, 215, 218
Trade unions, 5, 55n32, 62, 78, 92, 93, 96, 100, 108, 109, 117n57, 155, 158, 228
  and labour movement, 5, 88n55
  See also Commercial Catering and Allied Workers Union (CCAWUSA); Employee; Labour law; National Union of Distributive Workers (NUDW); Shop stewards; South African Commercial, Catering and Allied Workers Union (SACCAWU); Strikes

U

Umsebenzi, 16, 23n13, 24n14
Unemployment, 4, 23n6, 69, 110, 186–188, 190, 197, 203
Unfair
  dismissal, 61, 74, 75, 110, 163, 224
  labour practices, 110
Uniforms, 65, 169, 176, 178, 222, 223
  and own clothes, 35, 169
United States, 6, 7, 21, 31, 43, 53n9, 53n12, 54n20, 79, 116n34, 120, 122, 146n8, 210
Urbanization, 96, 200

W

Wage(s), 94
  earner, 2, 13, 189, 190, 196, 197
  family wage, 95, 99
  and gender differentials, 95
  and gender differentiation, 96
  and household security, 195
  and pay schedules, 1, 2
  and racial differentiation, 72, 97
  and seniority, 40, 97
  and underpayment, 2, 18, 221
  See also Labour law
Wage Act of 1925, 94
Wage Board, 39, 56n42, 94, 95, 98, 105, 113n6, 113n7
Wage determination, 40, 43, 56n42, 64, 74, 94, 95, 97–100, 102, 107, 115n25, 117n58, 181n53
Wal-Mart, 122, 146n8, 210, 221
  acquisition of Massmart Holdings, 8, 21, 209, 218
  and "everyday low prices," 218
  as global firm, 211, 212
  See also Massmart Holdings; Retail capital
"Walmartization," 212

Warehouse, 36, 73, 80, 97, 141–143, 175
White
 consumers, 8, 27, 30, 72, 123, 124, 127, 138, 214
 managers, 17, 40, 62, 80, 84, 87n42, 129, 140, 160
 men, 10, 28, 29, 36, 40, 95, 96, 126, 138, 142, 218
 public, 17, 19, 28, 47, 50, 64, 104, 210, 230
 service workers, 38, 47, 64, 221
 See also White women; White workers
White, Hylton, 187, 202, 203
White collar work, 40, 47, 58n82
White women, 10, 140
 as part-time workers, 99
 and respectability, 17, 38, 41, 44–46, 98
 as secondary earners, 97, 100
 seniority, 39, 40
 as service workers, 8, 17, 19, 28, 35, 38, 62, 210, 218, 221
 supervisors, 40, 45, 70, 72, 80
 and unsocial working hours, 104, 105
 See also Motherhood; National Union of Distributive Workers (NUDW); Skill; Trade unions; Wage(s)
White workers, 10
 and collective action, 38
 and collective organization, 38
 See also Employee; Labour law; National Union of Distributive Workers (NUDW); Trade unions
White working class, 17, 28
 and consumer markets, 33
 and households, 35, 47, 54n20
Wholesalers, 32, 53n12, 210, 231n1
Wiehahn Commission, 88n43, 88n55, 108, 117n57
Woolworths, 31, 41, 72, 232n9
Working conditions, 2, 4, 39, 61, 65, 94, 99
Working time
 flexitime, 105, 106, 226
 4-hour shift, 168
 full-time, 10, 11, 20, 35, 75, 92, 96, 100, 104, 105, 171, 220, 226
 overtime, 2, 69, 99, 105, 110, 217
 part-time, 10, 17–19, 35, 98–101, 107, 109–111, 117n56, 154, 176, 200, 229
 unsocial hours, 104, 106, 107, 110, 171, 220
 See also Casual employment; Contract workers; Extended trading hours
Workplace culture, 128, 144

Y
Youth, 38, 75, 180n18, 198
 abantwana, 103, 106, 160
 See also Casual employment

The manufacturer's authorised representative in the EU is Springer Nature Customer Service Centre GmbH, Europaplatz 3, 69115 Heidelberg, Germany. If you have any concerns regarding our products, please contact ProductSafety@springernature.com

Printed and bound by CPI Group (UK) Ltd, Croydon, CR0 4YY

23/03/2026

02076738-0007